Defining Art, Creating the Canon

Defining Art, Creating the Canon

Artistic Value in an Era of Doubt

Paul Crowther

CLARENDON PRESS · OXFORD

OXFORD
UNIVERSITY PRESS

Great Clarendon Street, Oxford OX2 6DP

Oxford University Press is a department of the University of Oxford.
It furthers the University's objective of excellence in research, scholarship,
and education by publishing worldwide in

Oxford New York

Auckland Cape Town Dar es Salaam Hong Kong Karachi
Kuala Lumpur Madrid Melbourne Mexico City Nairobi
New Delhi Shanghai Taipei Toronto

With offices in

Argentina Austria Brazil Chile Czech Republic France Greece
Guatemala Hungary Italy Japan Poland Portugal Singapore
South Korea Switzerland Thailand Turkey Ukraine Vietnam

Oxford is a registered trade mark of Oxford University Press
in the UK and in certain other countries

Published in the United States
by Oxford University Press Inc., New York

© Paul Crowther 2007

The moral rights of the authors have been asserted
Database right Oxford University Press (maker)

First published 2007

British Library Cataloguing in Publication Data
Data available

Library of Congress Cataloging in Publication Data
Data available

Typeset by Laserwords Private Limited, Chennai, India
Printed in Great Britain
on acid-free paper by
Biddles Ltd, King's Lynn, Norfolk

ISBN 978-0-19-921068-8

10 9 8 7 6 5 4 3 2 1

Contents

Introduction: Normative Aesthetics and Artistic Value   I

Part I. Culture and Artistic Value   13

1. Cultural Exclusion and the Definition of Art   15
2. Defining Art, Defending the Canon, Contesting Culture   42

Part II. The Aesthetic and the Artistic   65

3. From Beauty to Art: Developing Kant's Aesthetics   67
4. The Scope and Value of the Artistic Image   89

Part III. Distinctive Modes of Imaging   125

5. Twofoldness: Pictorial Art and the Imagination   127
6. Between Language and Perception: Literary Metaphor   145
7. Musical Meaning and Value   163
8. Eternalizing the Moment: Artistic Projections of Time   205
Conclusion: The Status and Future of Art   235
Acknowledgements   247
Bibliography   249
Index   255

Introduction: Normative Aesthetics and Artistic Value

In recent years aesthetic concepts of art and value have had a very rough ride. Their formalist and expressivist varieties have lost much influence through being unable to explain what it is that *enables* aesthetic and/or expressive effects, and also being manifestly at odds with the hugely influential Duchampian tendency in visual art (and its parallels in literature and music).[1]

'Institutional' approaches, in contrast, have accommodated this tendency. They have done so by redefining art per se, on the basis of non-exhibited contextual properties rather than aesthetic ones. This doubt concerning the scope of the aesthetic, however, raises its own immediate problem. For it seems to reduce artistic meaning and value to the expression of context-dependent ideas about art and its cultural settings. But if this is the

---

[1] The most impressive attempt on these lines in recent years is Derek Matravers's elegantly argued *Art and Emotion* (Oxford: Clarendon Press, 2001). Its central problem is that the notion of expressive properties with which it operates is based on feeling. However, it can be argued that the expressive qualities of art far exceed correlation with specific feelings, and that even the medium which Matravers is strongest on, namely music, can only be linked to feeling in a much-qualified way. For more on this issue see Chapter 7 of the present work. A rather more curious case of contemporary expressivism is that offered by Thierry de Duve in his book *Kant After Duchamp* (Cambridge, Mass. and London: MIT Press, 1997). Here de Duve argues that decisions as to whether or not something is art are determined by aesthetic feelings, and that the case of Duchamp fits in with this approach very effectively. There are many problems with this theory, most of which stem from de Duve's rather eccentric use of Kant. A more general one is his idea that judgements concerning what is, or what is not, art, are *always* based on aesthetic feeling. This seems to foreclose, counter-intuitively, on the possibility that one can sometimes *just* make judgements of the kind in question, without, thereby, being aesthetically engaged.

case then there seems to be no compelling way in which artworks might be distinguished from mere exemplars of art theory per se.[2]

The lack of a sense of the distinctively artistic has aided the rise of much broader doubts concerning aesthetic matters. These centre on 'anti-foundationalist' cultural theory involving feminist, post-colonial, and post-structuralist critique.[3] Such theory tends to reject the aesthetic basis of art and its canonic values as white male middle-class social constructs, with no validity outside the west, and a somewhat problematic and oppressive significance within it.

All the points raised so far will be addressed in detail as this book progresses. However, there is enough before us to ask two vital questions. The first is whether there is any real future for an aesthetic approach to the definition of art; and the second is whether art's canonic values can be given *any* justification in philosophical terms.

This book answers 'yes' to both questions. Indeed, it holds that there is a conceptual connection between the answers. To show this, a *normative aesthetics* is outlined in detail. It not only defends aesthetic conceptions of art and canonic value, but also reveals the contradictory and, in some respects, unconsciously racist character of the alternative approaches. Normative aesthetics privileges the intrinsic significance of the art object and the implications of its *made* status—rather than those western consumerist conditions of reception which Institutional definitions of art and anti-foundationalism emphasize. It addresses factors which are the basis of art's value in the deepest sense.

This is a more complex approach than formalism or expressivism. It is based on that which *enables* formal and expressive qualities to be significant. In particular, it conceives art as a mode of *making images* wherein the world is interpreted rather than reflected. It should be emphasized in the very strongest terms that whilst the term 'image' has mainly visual connotations,

---

[2] The most significant representatives of the Institutional approaches remain George Dickie, Arthur Danto, and Jerrold Levinson. Their views will be considered at various points elsewhere in this book.

[3] See e.g. Griselda Pollock's *Differencing the Canon: Feminism and the Writing of Art's Histories* (London: Routledge, 1999), and Victor Burgin's *The End of Art Theory: Criticism and Postmodernity* (London: Macmillan, 1986). It should not, of course, be thought that all anti-foundationalist and cognate approaches are necessarily hostile to art and the aesthetic per se. For a good example of the diversity of feminist ideas on this see H. Heine and C. Korsmeyer (eds.), *Aesthetics in Feminist Perspective* (Bloomington: Indiana University Press, 1993).

it can also be applied to non-visual art forms, as I will show at length in subsequent chapters.

My strategy here involves a revival of the mimetic definition of art, but with the burden of meaning switched from correspondence to the normative significance of *stylistic interpretation*. Kendall Walton's important work has, of course, emphasized the broad importance of mimesis as a contemporary analytic concept per se.[4] However, he is concerned (almost exclusively) with how mimesis functions as an adjunct of make-believe, rather than with the aesthetic significance of the image itself. My approach, in contrast, is concerned centrally with the aesthetic significance of mimesis. On these terms, the making of images for aesthetic appreciation is the basis of art.

Walton's interests also touch upon and diverge from my approach in a further interesting respect. He observes that

The critic must ... go beyond the work before him in order to judge it aesthetically, not only to discover what the correct categories are, but also to be able to perceive it in them. The latter does not require consideration of historical facts, or consideration of facts at all, but it requires directing one's attention nonetheless to things other than the work in question.[5]

In order to aesthetically appreciate art, in other words, one must know that it is an instance of artifice, subject to certain categories of judgement

---

[4] See esp. his *Mimesis as Make-Believe: On the Foundations of the Representational Arts* (Cambridge, Mass. and London: Harvard University Press, 1990). It is worth underlining the great difference of orientation between my approach and Walton's. He suggests that representations 'are things possessing the social function of serving as props in games of make-believe, although they *prompt* imaginings and are sometimes *objects* of them as well' (p. 69). He develops this argument through many accomplished analyses of how pictures and forms of literature are used. However, as far as I can tell, he does not assign any far-reaching cognitive centrality to the imagination. The burden of my own approach, in contrast, falls on showing that imagination does have such centrality, and that the artistic image is given much of its intrinsic significance through its relation to it. This significance converges on how style interprets types or kinds of subject matter in the image—another factor which is not a major part of Walton's project.

[5] Kendall Walton, 'Categories of Art', included in Joseph Margolis (ed.), *Philosophy Looks at the Arts* (Philadelphia: Temple University Press, 1978), 88–114. The major weakness with Walton's approach is that his concept of intention is left much too broad. Clearer sets of distinction need to be made concerning intention as exemplified through a learned code—such as knowing how to paint a picture—and intention in the iconographic sense where the picture is meant to be of 'such and such' a particular person. It could be argued that aesthetic appreciation is impossible without seeing the picture as something made intentionally but that the role of iconographic and kindred empirical intentions is contingent. (I return to the aesthetic significance of this latter point in Chapter 4.) The best survey of major issues concerning the role of the artist's intentions is in Stephen Davies's *Definitions of Art* (Ithaca and London: Cornell University Press, 1991), 158–221. (This includes a useful discussion of Walton.)

but not others. I will follow this approach in broad outline, but with a very different set of emphases from Walton. In particular, I will link artistic image-making to the work's development of the specific medium of which it is an instance. This means that awareness of individuality and originality will be central to the aesthetic appreciation of art.

The definition which I am working towards here is by no means stipulative. It has a compelling character on conceptual, empirical, and critical grounds. In terms of the first of these, for example, I will show in detail how *some* image-making has distinctive characteristics which separate it from other forms of knowledge and artifice. *If we did not already have a name for this practice, we would have to invent one.*

And this links to the empirical point, directly. *We do have a name for the practice—it is art.* In historical terms, the concept art has developed around a distinctive class of mimetic artefacts.

Now, of course, developments in twentieth-century western modernism indicate, superficially, that a mimetic approach is no longer viable. But this conclusion has been drawn much too readily. *The explanatory scope of mimesis has been left undeveloped rather than refuted.*[6] In this work, I will develop its explanatory scope, and criticize the alternatives. I will also give reasons why certain forms of activity which are supposed to have extended the boundaries of art, should only count as art, at best, in a marginal or honorific sense.

Since I take image-making for purposes of aesthetic appreciation to be the conceptual core of art, my approach may appear to be what Stephen Davies would call a *functional* definition of art. However, as I will argue later, images have aesthetic significance even in cultures which have no concept of art, and which do not make images for purposes of aesthetic appreciation. Indeed, as well as enabling the western concept 'art', the image's aesthetic significance is deeply implicated in many complex informative, persuasive,

---

[6] In Chapter 4, I will show the image-character of abstract art, and in Chapter 1, will also indicate ways in which works from the Duchamp tradition might count as art in a peripheral or honorific sense. For very detailed accounts of how the bulk of 20th-cent. Modernist visual art in effect extends the scope of mimesis see John Golding's *Paths to the Absolute: Malevich, Kandinsky, Pollock, Newman, Rothko, and Still* (London: Thames & Hudson, 2004). For an account which extends it even further see my *The Language of Twentieth-Century Art: A Conceptual History* (New Haven and London: Yale University Press, 1997). It is also interesting that Walton anticipates the approach which I will take in Chapter 4, by emphasizing the optical basis of abstract art's representational qualities. He does not, however, develop this. And in particular, he does not test its modus operandi in terms of abstraction's complex historical dimension. See his *Mimesis as Make-Believe* 54–7.

and/or ritual functions which images serve in different times and places throughout world history.

My definition, in other words, focuses on the origins of artistic meaning as well as its specialised pursuit through 'art' as a social practice. For this reason, my definition is better described as *pre-functional* in Davies's terms.[7]

Now the terms 'aesthetic' and 'image' will be considered in great detail as this book progresses. At this point, however, I must introduce the decisive concept of *style* since it is the feature which links aesthetic structure and image, and is at the very core of art's interpretative power. It will be a key concept in each chapter of this book.

It is quite surprising how—in comparison with other concepts—style has not acquired a large volume of philosophical interpretative literature.[8]

---

[7] See Davies, *Definitions of Art*, 23–31. Here are a few more thoughts on Davies's notion of a functional definition. The aesthetic significance of an artefact can exist in an intuitively enjoyed form within a broader network of practical functions. It is only under specific cultural circumstances that it is identified as a distinctive factor and is pursued as 'art'. But if what is conceptualized as 'art' is something which pre-exists it, then one must be very wary of describing the definition as 'functional'. This is because it begins to look as though the real defining factor is not the aesthetic image per se, but rather one's making it the basis of a practice. The upshot is that functional definitions then work as lead-ins to what Davies calls 'procedural' definitions where social institutions and conventions 'have a tendency to take on a life of their own, as it were, and in this way drift apart from the function they were intended to serve' (ibid. 31). Once the definition of art is interpreted procedurally, then the artwork amounts to little more than what can be made of it by the changing tastes of western art's managerial classes. As we shall see later, this is the outcome of the Institutional definitions.

[8] A classic study is Meyer Schapiro's 'Style' included in his collection *Theory and Philosophy of Art: Style, Artist, and Society* (New York: George Braziller, Inc., 1994), 51–102. His analysis of style's historical understanding, and its function as a term for collective activity is admirable. However, his account lacks a philosophically incisive account of style applied to the individual creator. Richard Wollheim's treatment of the topic does have this emphasis. It focuses on style as an originating and guiding factor in the artist's *process* of creation. (See e.g. his discussion in *The Mind and its Depths* (Cambridge, Mass. and London: Harvard University Press, 1993), esp. 176–80). The scope and limitations of Wollheim's approach are brilliantly discussed in Carolyn Wilde's 'Style and Value in the Art of Painting', included in Rob van Gerwen (ed.), *Richard Wollheim on the Art of Painting* (Cambridge: Cambridge University Press, 2001), 121–34. Wilde's discussion is important in its own right as well as for her critical discussion of Wollheim. In particular, she offers an account of style in painting which gives careful attention to the significance of the medium. This gives her approach some affinity to mine, in so far as I emphasize style as it is exemplified in the finished work. Interestingly, this emphasis diverges somewhat from the approach taken in the most impressive sustained treatment of the topic in recent years, namely Jonathan Gilmore's *The Life of a Style* (Ithaca and London: Cornell University Press, 2000). Gilmore's book specifically addresses the visual arts and is mainly orientated towards style in its collective sense. He also provides a very useful outline of its individual application (see esp. pp. 80–104). Again, however, his emphasis is on style as a factor which guides the creative process rather than on its embodiment *in* the finished work. The fourfold analysis which I propose in contrast, gravitates around what is given in the finished work, understood in relation to the comparative history of the medium. This emphasis, as I will show in later chapters, has important consequences for the possibility of aesthetic empathy with the artist's work.

In part, this may be because the term has some distracting connotations. It is common, for example, to use it as a synonym for good taste in fashion, choice of decor, cuisine, and the like. However, there is a deeper *ontological* sense of style which these connotations express only superficially. This sense, indeed, is something integral to what we are as finite embodied subjects.

To explain. No such subject can occupy the same part of space at the same time as another person or material body. This means that, in terms of perception, activity, and self-understanding, we will always occupy the world in a way that is *different* from other beings. We have a personal history which cannot be shared by others. Indeed, no matter how much we share as members of the same species, the body's unique occupancy of space means that even motor and cognitive competencies will admit of some variation in functional scope and development (however slight) between individuals.

The differences in question here are not just logical ones. They find expression in the way people say and do things, their exercise of choice, and, in particular, in the things that they make. These active and positive existential differences are *style in its ontological sense*. They are especially important in relation to the making of images, since this activity expresses style in at least four different ways.

A first one is through *choice of a medium and facility in using it*. The fact that an artist has chosen one medium rather than another, is, in itself, an expression of style. And how he or she uses it allows this to be developed further. Such development involves decisions about what is amenable to the ontological structure of the particular medium, and what best expresses the artist's abilities. Of special stylistic importance is the fact that in making the work, the artist will idealize and exaggerate reference to some features of subject matter, and diminish or omit others.

The second key factor is choice of what kinds of subject matter to address, and when this has been decided, which aspects to focus on, in particular. These often will be determined by circumstances surrounding the image's production, but even if the creator is the prisoner of such circumstances there is always scope for some idiosyncrasy of choice (unless, of course, the image is meant to be no more than a mechanical *copy* of its subject).

A third aspect of style is that of composition. This involves the construction of narrative and other structures which allow the subject matter and its formal expression to cohere as a unity (within the constraints of the medium and the artist's own preferences). In one sense, this is the key aspect, for it is here that really sustained creativity comes into play as the artist connects, reworks, and develops his or her thematic material.

These three *intrinsic* aspects of style exist side-by-side with a *relational* fourth aspect. For just as a person can only define the nature of his or her individuality per se by comparison and contrast with other individuals, so an artist's style is only given its full character by virtue of its relation to the style of others.

There are many factors involved here. The making of images is a learned competence. It involves initiation into ways in which others execute the relevant practice, with a view to learning the possibilities which are available, and ways in which problems can be avoided. Characteristically this will involve negotiating norms and exemplars of achievement and excellence in the medium. This means, in effect, being initiated into its comparative historical context.

Of course, an artist can simply follow accepted formats and work in a style which is defined primarily by some geographical or cultural school. But even within this, idiosyncrasies can occur, and these can sometimes be developed as the basis of a more personal style.

In those cultures, indeed, where the making of images is practised for its own sake (rather than for informational, persuasive, or ritual purposes alone) an individual style can lead to important innovations which open up new possibilities for how the medium operates, or which show its limits, and thence the need for new formats. Style, in other words, is shaped by, and, in turn, serves to shape, historical practices in specific media. It is based on creative difference, and what can be learned from it. It is this dimension which has been substantially overlooked by anti-foundationalist critics of the canon (as subsequent chapters will show in detail).

Some broader points must now be made. The three 'intrinsic' aspects of style, in concert, show that the image does not simply reflect its subject matter, but rather interprets it, and, in so doing, changes and characterizes it from the standpoint of the creator. Such transformation allows us to see the subject matter and the artist's relation to it in new ways; and offers imaginative possibilities with which the audience can identify. As we shall see later, all this activity is of aesthetic import and constellates around factors which are fundamental to cognition. *It is the first axis of art's normative significance.*

Now whilst all images have aesthetic potential, they do not always manifest it. For such manifestation to occur, the image must stand out in terms of the fourth aspect of style—namely the comparative historical dimension. If a work has some individuality in relation to it, then our attention is engaged aesthetically, and we find that the artist offers us new ways of experiencing the world. A work *becomes* art, through its aesthetic significance being realized on the basis of a notable (and comparatively determined) superiority to formulaic artifice.

The latter superiority makes us attentive to, and clarifies, the first axis of normativity. It is, indeed, the reciprocity between art's intrinsic fascination and this comparative superiority which gives justification to the artistic canon. Stylistic originality in a comparative historical context, therefore, forms *the second axis of art's normative significance.*

In conjunction, these two axes define the nature of art and the basis of its value. However, it should be emphasized that whilst the making and aesthetic appreciation of artistic images has the cognitive content described by the two axes, the content is mainly experienced in *psychologically intuitive* terms, i.e. as a positive feeling which is enjoyed without us being explicitly aware of the factors which enable it.

By 'intuitive' here, I do not mean anything strange or mysterious. Most of our perceptual knowledge has this character. In simply walking down a street or scanning a landscape we process a huge quantity of information and judge and act on the basis of it without being consciously aware of the chains of inferences involved. Our sense of places and positions are constructed from a myriad number of items and relations whose individual characters are not noticed.

However, the intuitive character of most perceptual judgements does not prevent us from analysing their content and the factors which enable them, retrospectively. Intuitions are *explicable* in principle, even though they may turn out to involve issues of great complexity which do not allow a definitive analysis.[9] In the case of the making and aesthetic experience

---

[9] The relation between cognition and the aesthetic domain has not been given the attention it deserves in recent years. The great exceptions to this are Richard Shusterman and James O.

of art, such complexity is to the fore. This is, in part, because, as well as analysing the object, we have to find a vocabulary for the cognitive capacities involved, and for the relation between all these features.

It should be clear already that the content of our intuitions about art takes us beyond traditional notions of formal harmony and expressiveness. These notions serve a secondary function. A work can be described as formally harmonious or 'melancholy', 'joyous', 'serene', or whatever, but it is mainly originality of style in *how* these factors are exemplified which gives them a significant role in artistic evaluations. Formal and expressive properties contribute to judgements of merit and demerit *within* the sphere of art through *regulating* what is achieved through the image's stylistic originality. (I shall, of course, return to all these issues as my book progresses, and especially in Section 4.6.)

Having outlined my basic concept of art and its value, I turn now to the book's basic structure. Here is its central argument, in summary form.

Institutional definitions of art and anti-foundationalist approaches both misrepresent the nature of art's high cultural status. I justify its status on normative grounds. This involves explaining why art is intrinsically significant, and how this significance becomes an object of appreciation. I start from the fact that the image, qua sensible or imaginatively intended object, is an aesthetic configuration. *When an image's style of making is original (or, at the very least, individual) it characterizes its subject matter from the creator's viewpoint and thereby creates a distinctive kind of aesthetic unity which cannot be derived from other sources. This is art.* Embedded in the creation and appreciation of such unity are two broader dimensions. The first is an enhanced interaction of capacities which are fundamental to cognition. (Which capacities and interactions are involved is a function of the work's individual interpretation of features distinctive to the aesthetic and to the

Young. Amongst other important works, Shusterman's ground-breaking book *Performing Live: Aesthetic Alternatives for the End of Art* (Ithaca and London: Cornell University Press, 2000) shows how the aesthetic extends far beyond the interests of western modernism, and engages with many art forms which are not usually held in high cultural regard. His notion of 'somaesthetics' also links the aesthetic to complex bodily expression and style factors in a provocative way. Young's *Art and Knowledge* (London: Routledge, 2001) is close to the present work in terms of its convictions about the cognitive structure and scope of the aesthetic, and the possibility of providing a viable alternative to relativism. What separates my approach from both these thinkers is its specific emphasis on art and the aesthetic's modifications of the subject/object relationship. This separation is based on a contrasting philosophical lineage in so far as I am much closer to Kant, Hegel, and the phenomenological tradition than are the other two.

image per se, and also to the specific medium involved.[10]) The second dimension is that of creative difference in the way individual styles and works develop their medium of expression. This is the basis of canonic value.

My book embodies this complex argument in more specific terms, as follows. The opening chapters address art's aesthetic and cultural status in a contemporary context. Chapter 1 proposes that formalist and Institutional approaches to the definition of art are both conceptually flawed and culturally exclusive in an unacceptable way. I offer an alternative approach which emphasizes the image's interpretative style as a distinctive mode of the aesthetic. In Chapter 2 this is developed further through a critique which focuses mainly on relativist theory of the anti-foundational kind. I also offer a first detailed *defence* of the idea of canonic value, and art's justified high cultural status.

The next two chapters present the core of my general theory. Chapter 3 is a sustained phenomenological development of Kant's aesthetics and theory of art. This allows me both to characterize the aesthetic in depth, and address art's distinctive articulation of it. The importance of originality, exemplariness, and canonic meaning is also set out in more detail here. Chapter 4 develops all these themes further still through a sustained consideration of the aesthetic as it is developed through style in the making of artistic images. The scope of the image is shown to include even abstract works of visual art. In this chapter, I also make use of some important ideas from Gadamer to elucidate the ontology of the artistic image, and go on to consider how these involve important contrasts between artistic and other forms of making. Attention is paid then to the qualified role of formal and expressive values in judgements of artistic merit.

Having set out my general theory, the next group of chapters looks at some of the more particular ways in which it is embodied by the most important modes of imaging. Chapter 5, for example, considers the distinctive ontology of the pictorial image and the way in which its stylistic interpretation exemplifies a special relation to self-consciousness and imagination. In Chapter 6 it is shown that metaphor in the literary

---

[10] Peter Kivy has explored the difference between the art media in fruitful ways in his *Philosophies of Arts: An Essay in Differences* (Cambridge: Cambridge University Press, 1997). It does not, however, significantly encompass the visual arts, and Kivy's scepticism as to the worth of defining art also sets him apart from my approach.

artwork exemplifies a fundamental interaction between language and its perceptual origins. By means of a detailed case history (the Greek poet Archilochus) I also show how metaphor can make a powerful contribution to individual literary style, and through this, to what is canonic for literature.

In Chapter 7, I offer an extended analysis of musical meaning and value. This embraces the metaphysics of auditory experience, theory of the emotions, and the phenomenon of virtual expression. It is argued that, through style in virtual expression, music clarifies the narrative context of emotion, and is the source of distinctive aesthetic experiences. Attention is also paid to the continuing possibility of canonic values even in the sceptical postmodern era. In Chapter 8, I analyse the different and distinctive ways in which literature, film, music, and the visual arts preserve and communicate the momentary.

In my Conclusion, the central argument of the book as a whole is summarized and considered in relation to some broader questions, most notably artistic value's deservedly high cultural status, and its relation to controversies concerning the 'end of art'.

PART I
Culture and Artistic Value

1

Cultural Exclusion
and the Definition of Art

Introduction

It has been widely believed that art is an intrinsically valuable practice which improves human experience in a way that intercourse with other practices and their products do not. Art has a *normative* significance. In this chapter, I will offer an initial definition and defence of this belief.

Art's claims to normative value have been doubted and/or rejected with some hostility. The historical reasons for this reaction are complex. One major factor is the widespread belief that to assign art a privileged value entails various kinds of *cultural exclusion*.

Such exclusion (hereafter referred to as 'exclusionism') has two basic forms. Its *explicit* mode involves practices which affirm the superiority of one cultural group over others and either excludes those others from full and equal participation in society, or only allows inclusion to the degree that the participants give up the practices which are basic to their identity in favour of those of the ruling culture. These strategies are based on racial, class, and gender divisions, or on some combination of the three.

In its *unconscious* form, factors of the aforementioned kinds are involved— but as much broader attitudes embedded within social institutions and practices. Often they will be neither recognized nor intended as exclusionist, and may even sometimes take themselves to be of multicultural significance.

The political/ethical unfairness of both modes of exclusionism is a familiar theme in most feminist and post-colonial scholarship on aesthetics. Broadly speaking, such scholarship criticizes art and the aesthetic for not doing justice to the experience of women, and racial and sexual minorities.

In this chapter, however, I will show that exclusionism operates in other, rather unexpected ways.

Initially, I shall explore this by addressing unconscious exclusionism (of the racist kind) in the context of my two overriding concerns in this book. These are the normative status of art and the way in which art is defined—problems which overlap to a considerable degree.

Especially complex is the question of aesthetic *normativity* which consists, in the first place, of those qualities which enable us to distinguish art from, and elevate it over, other cultural practices, and in the second place, of those criteria which enable us to make distinctions of quality between individual artworks. Both these *axes of normativity* are brought into conceptual alignment by the definition of art, and it is here, indeed, that unconscious exclusionism operates both pervasively and in some quite surprising ways.

To justify these claims, Section 1.1 will investigate formalist approaches to the definition of art, and the way in which their unconscious exclusionism is closely linked to a problematic understanding of normativity. In Section 1.2, I will address the Designation definitions of art (i.e. the work of thinkers such as Dickie and Danto) which hold that what is fundamental to the creation of art is not the making of an artefact, but the artist designating something as art on the basis of some theoretical standpoint. These definitions allow that, in principle, anything can become art if it is appropriately designated. I, however, will argue that this conception of art is unconsciously exclusionist to a profound degree, and that again, its unconscious exclusionism is closely tied to more general conceptual difficulties concerning normativity.

In Section 1.3, I will move to a more positive approach by outlining the basis of a non-exclusionist normative definition of art which gravitates around the making of images. This will commence with a clarification of the role of mental images and imagination in cognition generally. On the basis of this, the image will be argued to have a distinctive aesthetic significance which can serve to define art.

Finally, in Section 1.4 I consider the way in which this value is *conceptually connected* to a work's place in a comparative diachronic horizon of other such works. The upshot is that, instead of making the definition of art gravitate around a few marginal and ambiguous western works (at the expense of those made-artefacts which are the basis of artistic practices in non-western culture), my theory reverses this unconsciously exclusionist dynamic. The made-artefact becomes the nodal point of definition with recent western works understood in their true light—as marginal, and parasitic for any claim to artistic status on the basis of their connections with the nodal centre of art.

1.1

There is a prima facie case for regarding the definition of art per se as unconsciously exclusionist on the grounds that the concept of art is itself a western construct. It has been organized around a canon of 'great works' from which non-western cultural groups and oppressed social formations within western society have been largely excluded. If they have been included, it is only to a degree that they can be assimilated within the margins of the canonic structure.

This unconscious exclusionism is a familiar object of analysis in 'post-colonial' and related studies. However, it must be emphasized that even though the very notion of 'art' is a western construct this does not, of itself, mean that there is nothing more to it. Indeed (as we shall see in more detail later), whatever the dominant historical patterns of its institutionalization, art has a transhistorical and transcultural significance that ranges beyond the recent preferences of western culture.

There is a flawed set of approaches to the definition of art which draw on this very possibility. I refer, of course, to formalism. Such a project has had a number of influential varieties, all of which affirm the centrality of formal qualities and unity, over and above issues of content. Monroe Beardsley, for example, has represented this approach very effectively in philosophical aesthetics.[1]

For present purposes, however, the more telling figures are the art critics Clive Bell and Roger Fry. The former is of special significance for his concept of the formalist project is one which seems—at first sight—to overcome the problem of cultural exclusivity. The key operative term here is that of 'significant form' which is defined as 'a harmony of lines and

---

[1] A useful presentation of his approach can be found in his *The Aesthetic Point of View* (Ithaca and London: Cornell University Press, 1982).

colours'. For Bell, this not only includes non-western idioms, but appears to actually give them the more privileged role in defining what art is. Indeed, Bell is bold enough to claim that no more than one in a hundred of the artworks produced in Western Europe between 1450 and 1850 can be described as art.[2]

Now if—as Bell (and the other formalists) hold—what defines art is formal properties, then it might be claimed that these features tend to be more manifest in works which have no insistent (and thence aesthetically distracting) narrative content. Works of this kind are especially common (according to Bell) in pre-colonial South America and other non-western cultures.

Now it is by no means intrinsic to formalist approaches that art outside the western canon should be regarded as having a privileged position. (Beardsley, for example, does not hold such a view.) I have emphasized Bell's point, however, in order to underline formalism's aspiration to inclusiveness.

Unfortunately, this inclusiveness comes at a great price. For to see non-western artefacts as aesthetically significant purely by virtue of harmonies of line and colour or organic unities or the like, is to implicitly degrade the often complex social and/or ritual context which determines the production of such works in the first place.

The work's real cultural identity is displaced in favour of a purely contemplative activity directed towards a narrow aspect of its phenomenal structure. A kind of western intellectual luxury goods consumer standard is made the criterion of aesthetic authenticity. For the 'natives'' work to be judged as 'art' the natives must satisfy criteria which define the interests of a western elite, rather than factors which are the basis of their own cultural identity. We have a clear case of unconscious exclusionism.

The formalist response to this, of course, would be to argue that in talking of art we are necessarily and exclusively dealing with criteria of aesthetic worth, and that factors other than formal harmony do not play a role in this. Formal harmony, indeed, despite being primarily theorized by western aestheticians, is something which is of *universal* significance. In principle, all cultures can become receptive to it.

[2] See his *Art* (London: Chatto & Windus, 1914), 154.

This is, however, an enormously problematic response. One great difficulty which it faces is the fact that the notion of the aesthetic extends far beyond formal qualities alone.[3] If this is so, then the formalist insistence on harmonies of lines and colour and the like, really does look like a particular cultural preference which assimilates the products of other cultures on its own exclusive terms.

Now even if it were insisted that the aesthetic is a function of formal qualities alone, a severe normative problem would emerge. This centres on the question of how we distinguish form which is 'significant' or 'unified' from that which is not. Bell's answer to this question is symptomatic of a general failing in formalism. He holds that the distinction in question can only be recognized by a sensitive few on an intuitive basis.[4] But if this is how significant form is recognized there again seems no more to it then the particular cultural preferences of a western elite.

This connects directly to the problem of what I shall call deep normativity—an issue which has scarcely been addressed by any formalists. In a thinker as sophisticated as Monroe Beardsley, for example, we are told that the *disinterested* experience of aesthetic form has extremely positive psychological effects.[5] The distinctive enjoyment of aesthetic form serves—in the very broadest terms—to unify experience.

But what neither Beardsley nor any other recent formalist [6] explains is *why* it should have this profoundly desirable effect. What is it that enables the experience of form to work in this normatively compelling way? To say that the enjoyment of such form has some universal intrinsic value tells us nothing at all unless we can explain the structure of such value. And to return to the other problem noted in the relation to Bell, formalists such as Beardsley are unable to specify *why* some forms are more significant than others in terms of having desirable psychological effects. To say that they are 'more unified' than others or whatever, again says nothing unless one can invoke and analyse a comparative historical horizon wherein the claim

---

[3] I discuss this at length in part I of my *Art and Embodiment: From Aesthetics to Self-Consciousness* (Oxford: Clarendon Press, 1993).

[4] See Bell, *Art* 29–30.

[5] For more on this issue see Beardsley, *Aesthetic Point of View*, ch. 5, pp. 77–92.

[6] The one partial exception to this is Kant. But Kant's formalist account of aesthetic responses is oriented primarily towards nature. His theory of art brings into play rather different considerations—as we shall see at length in Ch. 3.

to greater unity can be given a rational justification.[7] On these terms then the normative weight of formalism is located entirely in the domain of psychological effects. But if no deep explanation can be offered as to what makes these effects possible and why they are available from some formal configurations but not others, then it seems that the whole phenomenon of art has been defined around a few narrow phenomenal aspects which a few western observers find intuitively stimulating.

To construe the deep normativity of art in these superficial psychologistic terms embodies a failure to address fundamental conceptual issues. And it is this failure which leaves formalist definitions of art at the level of unconscious exclusionism.

There are two broad alternatives which remain. The first is to offer a definition of art which construes art in terms of 'non-exhibited' properties. This allows the concept of art to apply, in principle, to any kind of artefact, emanating from any cultural origin. Such a strategy informs the Designation theories of art. I shall now consider some of these theories, and their unconsciously exclusionist aspects.

I.2

In the twentieth century it has been widely held that making is no longer the basis of art, and cannot, therefore be held to be its definitive feature. This view arises through the development of Marcel Duchamp's 'ready-mades', i.e. items offered as art which *in toto,* or at least in part, consist of things which were not physically made by the artist. The items in question here are often highly mundane and commonplace, and would not normally be regarded as appropriate candidates for appreciation in terms of formal qualities.

The philosophical ratification of these works is provided by what I shall call 'Designation theories' of art. These share the belief that if a member of the art world designates something as art (usually an artefact), then that something becomes, thereby, an artwork.

---

[7] In Beardsley, *Aesthetic Point of View,* 46–64, we find a defence of intrinsic value which is orientated towards the aesthetic. However, whilst Beardsley tries to link such value to certain psychological effects (in an *extremely* qualified way) my point is that we must show what it is about form which enables positive effects, in order to establish its intrinsic value on a viable footing.

By far the most influential of these theories are the Institutional definitions of art, propounded by George Dickie and Arthur Danto.[8] Dickie holds that 'when we reflect upon the deeds of Duchamp and his friends we can take note of a kind of action which has until now gone unnoticed and appreciated—the action of conferring the status of art'.[9] A recent formalization of this as a definition holds that 'a work of art in the classificatory sense is an *evaluable* artifact of a kind created to be presented to an artworld public'.[10]

According to Dickie 'This definition of "art" incorporates evaluativeness in a way that does not guarantee any degree of value but leaves art open to the full range of evaluative assessment.'[11] But where do we draw the logical line between artistic evaluations and those concerning historical, theoretical, curatorial, and managerial issues? To say that it is the 'art world' which determines such criteria is of little help since it is composed of a complex network of practices each of which has its own distinctive criteria of evaluation.

And even if we reserve the decision as to what counts as art for the artists themselves, a normative problem then arises. For it is surely the case that even artists must be able to distinguish between correct and incorrect ways of understanding rules concerning the creation of art. In the absence of such a distinction art amounts to no more than that which the artist sincerely intends as art.

But if, as all Designation theories hold, the artist's pronouncing something to be art on such terms is a sufficient condition of its becoming art, then it is difficult to see how any artist could ever fail to apply the rule concerning what counts as art correctly.

Dickie would no doubt claim that this is not an apt characterization, and that the problem of artistic creation and evaluation go hand in hand. This would mean that the validity or otherwise of an act of artistic designation is a function of its acceptance by the art world—and this acceptance centres on questions of value.

---

[8] Levinson's 'historical' definition of art involves a similar sort of strategy in so far as what counts as fundamental to the creation of art is not a specific kind of making, but a kind of intellectual 'fit' between a work and historical precedent concerning what counts as art. His basic statement of this is in the classic paper 'Defining Art Historically', *British Journal of Aesthetics*, 19/3 (1979), 233–50.

[9] Dickie, *Art and the Aesthetic* (Ithaca and London: Cornell University Press, 1974), 32.

[10] Dickie, 'Art and Value', *British Journal of Aesthetics*, 40/2 (2000), 228–41, at 240.

[11] Ibid. 240.

However, such a response would be flawed on both empirical and conceptual grounds. Empirically, the way that the art world assigns value to designated works is one which (as far as I can see) rarely even considers their status as art. (The very fact that a work is presented as art seems sufficient for its acceptance in such terms.) And conceptually, to identify membership of the class 'work of art' with issues of value, would only be intelligible if we had criteria of which values were relevant to such identification, and which were not.

This, of course would take us straight back to the difficulty noted above, namely how to distinguish between artistic and other forms of value. If we are unable to determine which acts of designation are grounded on distinctively *artistic* criteria, then this reduces the normative dimension of art to no more than the preferences and fads of that distinctively western network of commercial, curatorial, and fashionable society interests which have colonized the art world.

We fare little better with Danto's more complex Designation theory. For him it is only by having its origins in an appropriate form of cultural practice and theory that artworks can be distinguished from real things per se. To use one of Danto's own examples,[12] we could not, on purely perceptual grounds, distinguish Rembrandt's *Polish Rider* from a mere 'real thing' such as an identical set of paint marks accidentally splashed on to a canvas from a centrifuge.

Even in the case of 'conventional' art, therefore, the distinction between artworks and mere things is taken by Danto to be grounded in the appropriate kind of cultural context. And it is this very origin which gives art its normative significance, in so far as the artwork is thereby invested with emergent properties of a complex kind. In this respect, Danto contrasts the mundane real thing and that 'transfigured' thing which is the work of art: 'learning it is a work of art means that it has qualities to attend to which its untransfigured counterpart lacks, and that our aesthetic responses will be different. And this is not institutional, it is ontological. We are dealing with an altogether different order of things.'[13]

Danto's theory is extremely problematic in some interesting ways. First, if the difference between artworks and real things is ontological rather than

---

[12] This can be found in his *The Transfiguration of the Commonplace: A Philosophy of Art* (Cambridge, Mass.: Harvard University Press, 1981), 31–2.

[13] Ibid. 99.

institutional then clearly we are going to need some very strong criteria which justify this distinction.

The nearest we get to this are Danto's arguments concerning the 'is' of artistic identification. In some respects, this is a catch-all term for the many varieties of emergent properties which pertain to art. Broadly speaking when we use the 'is' of artistic identification we do not mean that the work (or its component aspects) is literally what we predicate of it. For example, a dab of paint which 'is' Icarus in a Brueghel painting, is not physically identical with that mythical personage.[14]

Now for Danto there is one especially radical sense of the artistic 'is'. It occurs when an act of literal identification or predication has an artistic sense which constellates around emergent qualities that recontextualize how we should understand the literal identification.

Consider, for example, the statement 'that black paint is black paint'. This can be a literal identification of one of the physical aspects of a painting. Uttered by an artist, however, it can have a very different meaning. As Danto puts it,

He is not even uttering a tautology when he says that this black paint is black paint. Rather he is making an artistic identification by means of this 'is'—he is remaining within the idiom of art. He is saying, in effect, that a whole other class of identifications is wrong, relative to a theory of what art is. To see something as art at all demands nothing less than this, an atmosphere of artistic theory, a knowledge of the history of art. Art is the kind of thing that depends for its existence upon theories ... the artworld is logically dependant upon theory.[15]

On these terms then, art theory provides the factor which makes art meaningful in a way that mere real things are not. But why should this be regarded as ontological rather than just a different interpretative orientation? Ontological criteria relate, in part, to issues of dependence and independence between things, but how these operate in the art context is rather different from what Danto imagines.

Consider such emergent properties such as mental states and the content of pictorial representations. These are constituted by the state or content's exact mode of *embeddedness* in the material body or phenomenal structure from which it is emergent.

---

[14] The most sustained discussion of the 'is' of artistic identification is ibid., ch. 5.
[15] Ibid., p. 135.

Without inhering in just this 'real thing', the emergent properties would not have the exact character that they have, and without being configured so as to sustain just *these* emergent properties, the sustaining thing would not be just *this* particular thing. Emergent properties and the physical thing which sustains them are part of one another's full definition. They have an internal connection in terms of their respective identities.

In the case of Danto's understanding of the relation of artwork and theory, neither of these factors holds necessarily. The relation between the real thing and the theoretical intentions which make it into art, can, in principle, be logically distinct from one another. Indeed, this is hardly surprising, because theory by definition means *a general idea or set of ideas*. This means, in principle that the theory can be articulated without *any* necessary link to the physical means of its articulation.

If this is so, then, we are surely dealing with cultural interpretation rather than ontology. Indeed, the game is given away by Danto in this respect when he admits that 'As a transformative procedure, interpretation is something like baptism, not in the sense of giving a new name but a new identity, participating in the community of the elect.'[16]

For this 'baptismal' notion of identity to have ontological as opposed to merely interpretative significance Danto would have to embrace one or both of two further possibilities. The first is an epistemology which makes ontology relative to the 'social construction of reality'. Whether Danto could accept this relativism or not, it faces the gravest conceptual and ethical difficulties (as I will show in the next chapter).

A further possibility which he has affirmed is that in order to be meaningful, the artwork must 'discover a mode of presentation that is intended to be appropriate to its meaning'.[17]

This would suggest that theory alone is not enough to constitute the artwork, there must be some kind of appropriate fit (an internal connection of some kind, one presumes) between the material object or whatever, and the theory which transforms it into art.

Unfortunately, Danto does not offer any detailed criteria of appropriateness. Indeed, his stipulation concerning it is profoundly at odds with the general scope which he wants to allow to theory's transformative power.

---

[16] The most sustained discussion of the 'is' of artistic identification is Ibid. 126.

[17] Arthur Danto, *After the End of Art: Contemporary Art and the Pale of History* (Princeton: Princeton University Press, 1997), 195.

In this respect, for example, we are told that 'it is analytical to the concept of art that the class of artworks may always be revolutionized by admission into it of objects different from all hitherto acknowledged artworks'.[18]

It would follow from this that Danto must accept the possibility of radical externalist artworks whose very intention is to make the relation between theory and object wholly arbitrary and mysterious, and decidable only by reference to their circumstances of production. For such works, any 'appropriate' fit between object and intention would defeat the point of the exercise (and, indeed, tendencies of this kind have actually been around at least since the more radical phases of Dadaist and Surrealist activity from the 1920s and 1930s).

Given this, Danto's stipulation about the fit between theory and object is clearly inconsistent with a fundamental aspect of his own position. And even if we do allow his stipulation to hold, a decisive problem (already touched upon) then emerges with full force. For if it is theory which provides the content which constitutes art, this makes the connection between content and art object logically external. Theory is not the kind of thing which must be tied to the individual character of the idioms of its expression.

What is ultimately at issue here can be shown by considering a black painting in relation to which the artist says 'that black paint is black paint'. If this statement is taken to involve the 'is' of artistic identification, it might be interpreted in the following ways:

1. as an affirmation of the physicality of paint over painting's usual referential function (Danto's own gloss on the statement);

2. as an intensely personal rejection of white, and or/yellow, and/or [insert another colour or combination of colours, as appropriate ad infinitum ...];

3. as a gesture of indifference to all colours;

4. as a symbolic affirmation of the importance of ethnic blackness;

5. as a metaphor for darkness, or oblivion, or blindness, or infinity;

6. as an affirmation of the triviality of all things;

7. as a Zen-like affirmation of the wonder of all things;

[18] Arthur Danto, 'The Transfiguration of the Commonplace', *Journal of Aesthetics and Art Criticism*, 33 (1974), 141.

8. as the exemplification of supremely empty space;

9. as the exemplification of a space packed to a point of absolute density;

10. as an exemplar of boredom with painting;

11. as a metaphor for the profundity of painting;

12. as an affirmation of the need for stylistic economy;

13. as an ironic exemplification of a joyous state of mind;

14. as an exemplification of misery.

Now all these intentions would, in Danto's parlance, be 'appropriate' to presentation in black paint and thence to the statement 'that black paint is black paint' used in some supposedly distinctive artistic sense. But, of course, many of these intentions are inconsistent with one another; and there are many other possible theoretical intentions which could be added. (These, indeed, multiply further given the fact that amongst the relevant intentions, Danto includes choices which the artist *refrains* from making.)

It should also be added that if we were dealing with a black painting per se (rather than one whose meaning was partially decoded for us through the accompanying 'black paint' statement above) there would be infinitely many other theoretical intentions which might also be appropriate to the visual format in question.

On these terms, then, if a relation to theoretical intentions were genuinely constitutive of the artwork, this would entail an ontological nightmare which flagrantly violated Occam's Razor. For any object designated or created by the artist, there would be as many possible artworks emergent from it as there were theories which it could 'appropriately' present.

This means that *Danto's theory makes the identity of the artwork radically indeterminate*. Even if the object is 'appropriate' to a specific set of theoretical intentions, it is also, in principle appropriate to many others. And the intentions themselves, qua theory, do not have to match up with just this object. So we cannot recognize them just by looking at the work itself. What the work is 'about' remains systematically ambiguous. It lacks definiteness of sense.

The result of all this is to make artistic meaning fatally dependent on external factors bound up with critical and historical contexts of interpretation. Such external dependence reduces artworks to mere vehicles of theory about art, or at least provides no good reason for regarding such works in any other terms. The usual practice is for an artist to present an item and for it to be taken up by a loose combination of critical, curatorial, and commercial interests. The work's normative significance—its meaning in the broadest sense—is never exactly specified. It is little more than what can be read into it by western market and managerial classes.

There are three ways of avoiding this outcome. The first would be for the artist to stipulate exactly which theoretical intentions the work is meant to sustain. But this would involve each work being accompanied, in effect, by a Certificate of Due Intention, designating what is meant to be at issue in the work. But the fact that the work is made, thereby, dependent on external documentation reduces the object, in effect, to a mere exemplar of theory. (Indeed, the very fact that works which logically require this sort of back-up are taken to show the essence of art is further testimony to the ludicrousness of Danto's Designation theory.)

The only way round this embarrassment would be if the artist's accredited 'explanation' made no real sense without us having had direct perceptual acquaintance with the work itself. But if the sensible particularity of the work is meant to give us something which theoretical explanation cannot provide in itself, then it would surely mean that aesthetic factors over and above theory were coming into play.

This leads directly to the second possibility. If an artwork's embodiment of theory were, indeed, aesthetically significant, it might transcend the mere exemplification of intentions. Danto himself, seems to allow for this in some remarks noted earlier concerning the fact that our knowing a real thing to be an artwork makes our 'aesthetic responses' to it 'different'.

But why should the term 'aesthetic' be used at all in this context? What Danto may have in mind is something like appropriateness of the fit between object and theoretical intention noted earlier. However, whilst using an object to communicate one's intentions may have a successful outcome, this does not seem to have any intrinsic connection with aesthetic achievement and responses.

Danto wants to find room for the aesthetic, but offers no real principle of connection between a work's theoretical significance and the constitution of the aesthetic object. In the final analysis he seems to be saying no more than because theory is necessary to art it must have aesthetic relevance. But since ready-mades and the like are often phenomenally banal, we need to know how theoretical contextualization makes them meaningful in specifically *aesthetic* terms. Danto does not offer us any such account, and in the absence of it we are left with real things as vehicles for theory of art and no more than that.

I mentioned a third possibility. It is to identify the way in which art-works—in their making and reception—embody aesthetically significant cognitive structures, based on representational and cognate codes with a transhistorical and transcultural significance. This approach is the one which I shall explore throughout this book—even in relation to abstract art. It offers a systematic alternative to Designation theory.

Danto's—like Dickie's—Designation theory turns out, then, to be normatively empty and a function almost entirely of contextual factors. All that is required of the artist is that he or she present something as art. Rather than making an artefact or negotiating tradition, the artist is, in effect, able to create art by will-power alone.

This is a farcical return to one of the drearier stereotypes of western culture, namely the romantic genius. Far from—as is commonly supposed—consigning the 'masterpiece' to the dustbin of history, Designation theories can, in principle, consign the dustbin to the history of the masterpiece by pronouncing it 'artwork' and placing it in a display context.

Theories of this kind, then, offer wholly unviable explanations of why art has distinctive properties and why one work can be more significant than another. And this is done by reference to an ill-defined network or 'art world' of western market and managerial interests.

What gives this position its unconsciously exclusionist 'bite' is that the relation between objects and/or states of affairs and the 'art world' is seen by Designation theorists as the basis of art's definition per se. Rather than deal with ready-mades and the like as a marginal western activity (parasitic on expectations and display formats established by the making of representations), they redefine the entire concept of art to accommodate the 'ready-made', and, as a consequence, make a marginal and problematic western idiom into the arbiter of artistic meaning.

Of course, it might be that whilst the Designation theories are problematic, and whilst, indeed, their paradigm art examples are of recent western origin, the accusation of unconscious exclusionism is not justified. The celebrated Whitney Biennale of 1993, for example, shows how multiculturalism (and minority rights in general) can find expression through formats in the Duchamp tradition, in a way that they cannot through more conventional idioms.

This retort, however, is itself extremely problematic. For one thing, in the biennale in question it was difficult to separate art from mere political propaganda. And, indeed, even if the breakdown of this distinction should be seen as a good thing, what results is only a spectacle of viewing for the western gallery-going elite.

Those practices which (in part) define the cultural identity of participating ethnic groups are here recontextualized as objects of cultural consumption. They are assimilated within western display rituals and transformed into a mode of anti-exclusionist activity. However, even as such works preach multiculturalism their presentational idioms colonize and neutralize the message and thence enhance the unconsciously exclusionist dimension, which sustains their presentation as art.

Given the foregoing critical analyses, one alternative remains. It is to find a definition which offers an adequate grounding of the two normative axes of art, and which by so doing, offers a conceptually sound and non-exclusionist normative definition of art.

1.3

The basis of a normative definition will be developed in a sustained way as this text progresses. However, it is useful to provide an overview of it now, so as to indicate its particular strengths and to anticipate some familiar objections. In this section, therefore, I will link the making of art to the aesthetic manifestation of cognitive factors which are the basis of our knowledge of both self and world.

Art might be provisionally defined as a class of artefacts which centres upon the making of images. Their meaning is based on *isomorphic consistency*, i.e. the presentation of a range of phenomenal or imaginatively intended properties which are shared by the image and that which it is an image of. Which kinds of property are relevant here is not just determined by natural resemblance but the way in which this is conventionalized and mediated through the demands of the artistic medium in question.

Artistic images have intrinsic significance in terms of the first normative axis, by virtue of their active relation to mental imagery. By mental imagery,

I mean thoughts generated with a *quasi-sensory* structure. Such images are representations whose quasi-sensory character is consistent with a range of identifying phenomenal properties possessed by that which the image is 'of'. They can be generated as an aspect of memory, or to represent items or states of affairs (actual or hypothetical) which are not given in the immediate perceptual field. Imagination, in other words, is a capacity with various cognitive applications. Whilst we think of images as, primarily, visual, it also makes perfectly good sense to talk of auditory, tactile, olfactory, and gustatory images. Often, indeed, our images will involve several of the senses simultaneously—as when we imagine the pleasures of a good meal.

Mental imagery is, by nature, schematic and fragmentary. There are also significant variations in terms of how the capacity to imagine is developed by different individuals, and how it works even within the purview of an individual's life. The way in which we imagine *x* in our youth, for example, may be very different from the way in which we imagine the same *x* later on in life.

Now the schematic, fragmented, and variable character of the mental image means that it is not a reproduction of that which it represents, but rather a creative interpretation of it. The experiential idiosyncrasies of the individual lend a certain character or style to the images which he or she generates. And this has a remarkable role to play in relation to both personal identity and objective knowledge.

In terms of the former, for example, the intense stylization just noted has a profound implication. It means that the image always characterizes its content from the existential standpoint of the one who is generating the image. Even where we imagine what it is like to see the world from another's point of view, there is always something of our own which is at the heart of the imagery which is generated.

The importance of this concerns the unity of personal history. In relation to it, imagination has an existential primacy. All the things that happen to one are elements in the factual continuity of 'things that happen to one'. But a personal history is more than an inert continuum of facts. Imagination allows the generation of representations consistent with facts about what one has been, or things which one might experience, but—by virtue of the image's stylized form—these are always characterized by one's present viewpoint on life. They have an intrinsic 'as if experienced by me now' quality. The images so generated may be apt realizations; they may be idealized; they may be hopelessly inadequate to the facts they are endeavouring to realize; but in all cases, they bring the facts *alive* in and for the present.

Now empirical psychology analyses such things as the role of images in specific cognitive contexts, or the more exact structure of specific kinds of mental imagery. However, its methods are fundamentally quantitative, and/or localized, whereas what I am describing is a much broader qualitative unifying function which is not readily amenable to analysis through these methods. It is, rather, a *phenomenological truth*, i.e. one which describes a universal characteristic of human experience. Like most phenomenological truths, it can be supported by logical as well as shared introspective criteria. In the present case, this involves showing that objective knowledge and personal identity per se logically presuppose the capacity for imagination.

Of course, imagination's role in knowledge has, until recently, been significantly neglected in favour of the function of thought and language.[19] But its role can be justified on conceptual grounds.

This justification involves imagination's *trans-ostensive* function, i.e. its ability to represent times, places, and states of affairs other than those which are the objects of present experience. If the present was not informed by projections of what the past was like, what the future may be like, or what, counterfactually, might have been the case, then the notions of an objective world and, indeed, personal identity would not be possible. The criteria of unity presupposed by both, involves the making of unified connections between that which is immediately present to experience and that which—in terms of temporal and spatial location—is not. The unity of the objective world and that of the self and its history are correlated. As Gareth Evans puts it,

The capacity to think of oneself as located in space, and tracing a continuous path through it, is necessarily involved in the capacity to conceive the phenomena one

---

[19] This has now begun to change, even within the analytic tradition. Colin McGinn, for example, assigns imagination (viewed as a distinctive competence) a central role in many different aspects of cognition. See his *Mindsight: Image, Dream, Meaning* (Cambridge, Mass.: Harvard University Press, 2005). An earlier classic study is Mark Johnson's *The Body in the Mind: The Bodily Basis of Meaning* (Chicago: University of Chicago Press, 1990). There are also clear links to be made between imagination and that notion of 'simulation' which is central to some theories of personal identity. For an example of this see Jane Heal's *Mind, Reason, and Imagination* (Cambridge: Cambridge University Press, 2003). For an extended treatment of the links between imagination and objective knowledge, and personal identity, see chs. 5 and 6 respectively of my *Philosophy After Postmodernism: Civilized Values and the Scope of Knowledge* (London: Routledge, 2003).

encounters as independent of one's perception of them—to conceive the world as something one 'comes across'. It follows that the capacity for at least some primitive self-ascriptions—self-ascriptions of position, orientation, and change of position and orientation and hence the conception of oneself as one object amongst others, occupying one place amongst others, are interdependent with thought about the objective world itself.[20]

I would argue that mental imaging is a key condition of these correlations. Not only does it allow the projection of alternative objects, aspects, and states of affairs to those given in the present, but it does so in terms of *what it might be like* (in crude sensory terms) to perceptually experience them. The correlation of object and subject of experience is exemplified in the structure of the image itself.

This raises the decisive point. It might be claimed that the possession of language and concepts alone is a sufficient basis for linking the present to the trans-ostensive dimension. We do not *have to* bring in imagination as a conceptual precondition of the correlation of objective knowledge and personal identity.

However, the very capacity to learn and follow rules which is central to language formation—and especially to the learning of tenses—itself *presupposes* some more basic ability to project what things might be like, or have been like, in situations other than the present. *To suppose that this trans-ostensive capacity can be explained in terms of language and concept-use is to commit the fallacy of assuming the very factors which one is trying to explain.*

This approach works from another direction as well. For whilst one might learn to use a concept ostensively when the appropriate item was given in immediate perception, one would not have mastered it as a concept in the fullest sense, unless one knew *what it was like* for it to apply to other such items in other times and other places. One would need a sense of its extensional scope. But if we try to explain our comprehension of this scope through the use of other concepts then we must explain how, in turn, we become aware of their extensional scope, and so on and so on. This leads to a vicious infinite regress of concepts attempting to ground concepts.

---

[20] Gareth Evans, *Varieties of Reference* (Oxford: Clarendon Press, 1982).

The only way round this, is to posit a non-conceptual projective capacity (i.e. imagination) as a logical precondition of our comprehension of extensional scope.

It follows from these arguments, therefore, that we have some native (and cognitively fundamental) projective capacity which is not itself linguistic. Imagination is this capacity. It enables language acquisition and concept-use, and thereafter is strongly directed by both these factors (in ways which will be discussed in Chapter 3).

Of course, a person might insist that mental imagery plays little or no role in his or her conscious life. But by virtue of the foregoing arguments this claim cannot be true in absolute terms. It could, however, be accommodated by pointing out that whilst we *must* have imagination as a *disposition* which has been and will continue to be activated on some occasions, this does not entail that it is always occurent in *every* linguistic act or use of concepts. Its function, rather, is as a necessary factor in enabling, and then in generally sustaining, high-level cognitive processes. Indeed, it may also be that its function becomes so commonplace as to be scarcely noticed.

If this theory is correct, then, mental imaging is much more than a useful cognitive capacity. It is a conceptual precondition of our knowledge of objects, and forms the cohesive fabric of our personal identity, spanning and connecting objective location and experiential history.

Now since human beings can only acquire knowledge of themselves (and their own distinctiveness) on the basis of similarities to and differences from other people, it follows that a capacity to articulate the mental image in a publically accessible medium will be of the most vital significance in the understanding of self and the other.

Given this, it is hardly surprising that pictorial, literary, and musical imaging should have a profound *intrinsic significance*. As we have seen, mental images already have a kinship to artistic making in so far as they are creative and stylized. Hence, when images are physically made using a medium and its techniques, the artistic potential of imaging per se is both extended and made communicable.

This is not a case of 'externalizing' images which are already in the head. Rather the image is generated in a physical mode which allows its creative *stylistic* aspects to be explored through working the medium—a possibility, of course, which is not available to the mental image. (The stylistic factors in question include choice and handling of the medium, selection and emphasis in subject matter and in the construction of narratives and composition.) Such working also enables the fragmented and transient character of mental imagery to be compensated for through an alternative creative idiom which forms enduring physical entities.

The public character of such entities also means that the audience is able to encounter another person's style of experiencing and interpreting the world in its sensible aspects. And the fact that the physical image's existence—once made—is no longer tied to that of its creator, allows us to identify with the artist's way of experiencing on our own terms too. Knowledge concerning who created the image may enhance our enjoyment of it but such knowledge is not presupposed in order for us to appreciate the image's way of sensuously articulating the world, per se. There is a negotiation, or play, between what the artist presents and what the recipient is able to find in the work.

We have, then, an account of the intrinsic significance of making images. This account proceeds from the cognitive centrality of mental imagery—with its inherently creative, stylizing aspects—to the fuller development of these stylistic aspects in the physically made image. In later chapters, I will show that the aesthetic dimension is not only involved in the latter, but many other aspects of self-consciousness and the unity of the self. Whatever the case, it is brought to full expression in the physically made image.

This intrinsically significant aesthetic 'for its own sake' character is the basis of the first normative axis of art. By showing the intimate connection between the cognitive centrality of imagery and its sensuous embodiment in art we can explain why such works have a fascination over and above that accruing to their practical employment.

They make basic features of our knowledge of both self and world perceptually available in an enhanced—aesthetic—mode. Formalism reduces this to the disinterested appreciation of those harmonious lines and colours so beloved of the sensitive western elite. My point is that the object of disinterested aesthetic enjoyment is bound up with much deeper elements of style and interpretation in the image. These elements reach to the very roots of the self.

Let us now consider some putative objections to the theory. The first one concerns the relation between physically made images and functional utility. If the definition of art is to avoid unconscious exclusionism then surely its normative significance—if such it has—must be located firmly in the functional sphere, i.e. in terms of those contexts or rituals which give it its culturally specific meaning.

This objection, however, overlooks a fundamental fact which has scarcely been addressed in aesthetics or anthropology. It can be put in the form of a question. Given how culturally widespread the functional use of visual, literary, and musical imagery is, what is it that enables it to be so used? What is it that makes artefactual images *so* effective in functional contexts?

An easy answer is to say that the quasi-sensory aspect of imagery makes it more vivid, and thence more communicatively efficacious. This, however, would be to read the image exclusively in terms of the means/end rationality of western instrumental reason. Functional reductionism of this kind completely underplays the depth of non-western involvement with images. In such involvement the image is often taken to give power over, or identity with, that which it is an image of.

Is this just superstition? I would say not, and that it is an unconscious recognition of the image's profoundest dimensions. For as well as reaching to the very roots of the self (in the senses described earlier) the making of images is a volitional act, and thence subject to the will. Through being rendered in an image reality is symbolically remade on our own terms and in a way which also affirms the creator's or creative ensemble's individual and cultural identity.

The ontology of the artefactual image, in other words, is one which is empowering in its own right. It has a fundamental *aesthetic* power which—it is reasonable to assume—would encourage belief in its broader functional and ritual potency.

However, this leads directly to a second putative objection. For if—as was argued earlier—disinterestedness is a key aspect of aesthetic responses to art, surely this criterion cannot encompass such things as tribal masks and war dances. To regard them in terms of disinterested attitudes is surely to strip away the social context which makes them intelligible, and to transform them into mere objects of western contemplation. This, of course, is exclusionist.

Now if one subscribes to formalist notions of disinterestedness it is, indeed, hard to assimilate the more Dionysian artistic idioms. However, this difficulty only arises because the formalist criterion of disinterestedness is a psychological one, i.e. involves the active taking-up of a contemplative attitude. But the criterion of aesthetic disinterestedness is more aptly regarded as *logical*. On these terms, whilst some image may have significant practical use-value, it may be possible to enjoy it without taking this value into account, or in such a way that it figures primarily as a decisive element within some broader aesthetic unity.

This by no means entails any psychological state of contemplative detachment. For example, whilst the desire for victory may impel a tribe to perform a war dance it is surely possible for the participants to be caught up in and to enjoy the rhythms and drama of the dance for its own sake, rather than in terms of its anticipated practical consequences.

In such a case the logical ground of the dancers' rapture is disinterested, even if their feelings are Dionysian. Indeed, as I have already argued, it is the very power of such *aesthetic* rapture which can explain why dancing and other forms of artefactual imaging are taken as having effect on practical outcomes.

Disinterestedness, then, is a valid criterion of the aesthetic as long as it is tied to the logical ground of such responses rather than the kind of psychological attitude which they are taken to involve. Interpreted in this way it is free of unconsciously exclusionist western elitism.

However, a third putative difficulty for my position must also be considered. It is a simple one, which holds that whilst image-making may have the intrinsic aesthetic significance which I have assigned to it, not all artworks are images. The realms of abstract, applied, and conceptual art, for example, clearly stand outside it.

Despite this, there are grounds for holding that image-making is the central core of various overlapping modes of sensible representation which include the aforementioned putative counter-examples.

In terms of this overlap, I will consider the case of abstract art at length in Chapter 4. For immediate purposes, however, it is worth addressing architecture and functional artifice in general. Most works of this kind are engaged with primarily on the basis of their use-value. However, some such artefacts exceed this significance. They not only fulfil their function but do so in an exemplary or unusual way. The relation between form (in the broadest sense) and function is one which attracts attention in its own right.

We are engaged by the way in which form creatively interprets or even (in the case of highly decorative works) overrides the function. In such cases, the work's style operates, in effect, as an image of its function as well as being, literally, an instance of it. One might call this an *exemplificational image*.

There is another significant but more peripheral variety of image to be considered here. It is a realm of artefacts whose status as images is logically and historically parasitic upon the nodal core of artefactual imaging (non-western in its origin) which I have already described. More specifically, it consists of the Duchamp 'ready-made' tradition associated with Designation theories, and which finds expression in 'Conceptual art'.

In Section 1.2 I showed how Designation theories use this tradition so as to redefine art on the basis of western art market and managerial interest. By so doing they marginalize non-western participation except in so far it can be dressed up in the guise of 'multiculturalism', i.e. ethnicity and the like presented as a consumer spectacle for the western elite.

If therefore, we wish to jettison this unconscious exclusionism we must either reject the Designation tradition altogether, or else, show it to be a marginal variant of productive imaging. The latter course is the more viable one for works in the Designation tradition can stake a claim to artistic status in so far as they adopt the presentational formats of the nodal art practices.

This leads to an interesting possibility. For even if work in this tradition is comprised entirely of elements which were not actually made by the artist, there are two tests which might locate a work in relation to the first normative axis. These are: (1) a work's having a phenomenal structure or physical presence which is engrossing in its own right, (2) its having a specific connotative significance (or range of such significance) which is recognizable on the basis of shared cultural stock without reference to accompanying explanatory texts.

If a work can satisfy these criteria, then it would declare its own distinctive way of articulating visual space, and the imaginative skill of the artist is selecting such an item (or configuration of items) for display. And if the work has a range of specific connotational meaning which is recognizable on the basis of shared cultural stock, then this will mean that the work embodies something like an 'aesthetic idea' in the Kantian sense (a concept which will be discussed in Chapter 3). It is important to emphasize, however, that such works are of only marginal 'honorific' artistic significance, and are parasitic for their appreciation upon the expectations and presentational formats of artefactual imaging. For reasons noted earlier (and for others which will be considered in the next chapter) they cannot be used legitimately to redefine art on a western-orientated Designation basis.

In the foregoing arguments, then, I have clarified the intrinsic significance of the image and presented it as the basis of the first normative axis of art. I have also shown how it can encompass even some Designated works.

However, the definition is not yet adequate as a definition because not all images succeed in engaging our aesthetic attention; and, of course, even if they do, they will often figure only as elements within broader practical contexts. In order to complete the definition, therefore, one must explain how it is possible for art and its institutions to emerge from the non-western matrix of image-making.

1.4

This emergence is conceptually connected to the 'second normative axis', i.e. the realm of distinctions of merit between one work and another. If a work is to exceed its practical documentary or ritual functions, this entails that it is *positively different* from images which remain only at the functional level. We need a comparative historical horizon wherein such differences can be recognized.

Now the great bulk of works in any tradition of art will be wholly unremarkable. The vast majority of paintings, poems, songs, and the like, quickly disappear from attention, never to be noticed again. This is because most of them have no stylistic characteristics that are not simply derived from other works. In literal terms they are different from one another, but this difference does not have any positive significance.

The question arises, then, as to what positive as opposed to mere difference might be. What makes difference *creative*? And the answer is *originality*, or, in its simpler form, *individuality*. In terms of making images and diversifying their formats, some works refine or extend the scope of both these factors, however minimally. Consider, for example, when an artist or creative ensemble not only has stylistic idiosyncrasies (such as a fondness for certain words), but has a style that is recognizably his or hers, or theirs, i.e. *one which can be identified (in at least a provisional way) purely by reference to its manifestation in the artwork*. Such achievement means that the style of the artist(s) has expanded the scope of the medium in a very small way by opening up a new mode of sensibly interpreting the world.

This is originality in its primary artistic sense. We do not expect, however, that every work produced by an artist will be like this. Once primary originality has been attained, many artists spend their entire career exploring its possibilities. They may maintain a secondary level of originality (at the level of individual works) through refining the style in some respects or by producing formally strong expressions of it. Alternatively, an artist's individual works may be entirely unoriginal in secondary terms, if they maintain his or her style in highly formulaic terms only, or are unable to create anything other than formally weak individual variations of it.

The artists who creatively refine and develop their style and/or maintain high formal standards are, of course, the more likely to achieve canonic status. This is because by opening up new possibilities for themselves they also open up new ideas for other artists working in the medium in question. Indeed, as well as their *oeuvre* having canonic significance per se, it may become possible to identify key works within it as canonic in an individual sense, i.e. as *masterpieces*.

Whatever the case, the most decisive criterion of canonic worth is influence. Some artists who achieve an original style, and creatively sustain it, often spawn direct imitators. If there is also evidence that their influence extends in more subtle ways, i.e. other artists use the style without simply copying it, then this means that their role in the canon is more creative. They become exemplary—a concept which I will explore in Chapter 3.

When the individuality of an artist's style is achieved through significant refinement of, or innovation in relation to, some factor which is absolutely fundamental to a medium, then we would expect that artist to have very high canonic significance.

The development of rigorous perspective by Italian Renaissance artists is a case in point. This is not just a technical invention. The syntactic organization of pictorial space is a problem faced by anyone who wishes to do a picture involving more than one item or state of affairs. Those artists who make important contributions to its development, accordingly, are adding new possibilities to the scope of the medium in the most radical sense. And this in turn means new ways of interpreting the visual world.

Stylistic individuality of any kind, but especially in this fundamental context, prompts us to attend closely to how the particular artist achieves these effects and thence to enjoy his or her style for its own sake. Other artists, of course, may simply do no more than repeat existing idioms or do little more than what is required in order to communicate some basic message. In such cases the image does not stand out so as to attract sustained aesthetic scrutiny.

All these points will be developed further (especially in the outer sections of Chapters 3 and 4). Suffice it to say now that *it is a comparative horizon of historical difference—based on the relation between individuality of style and the nature of the medium—which is central to the canon of artistic merit.* This merit may remain embedded at the level of ritual and practical existence, but in some circumstances may be recognized in such a way as to allow the making of images to be pursued for its own sake as a distinctive form of social life.

Western culture is, of course a key example of this. The normative axis of the comparative historical horizon has been of decisive significance here. For whilst the much reviled 'canon' of western art may strike fashionable cultural relativists as simply a reflection of a ruling elite's interest, it is much more than that. Once a *critical* tradition of production is established in a culture, then it enables those individual works which extend the scope of a practice to be distinguished from those which merely repeat established procedures.

In the context of making images, this means that by occupying a significant position in the comparative historical horizon, a work invites us, thereby, to explore and aesthetically enjoy the phenomenal means which makes this achievement possible. The artefact which represents a content or exemplifies a function, can now be enjoyed aesthetically as art. The first normative axis—imaging's deep cognitive significance—is energized by the latter. What was merely a representation or merely functional now becomes accessible as an instance of fine or applied *art*.

I am arguing, then, that at the basis of the definition of art are two axes of normativity—namely a transcultural and transhistorical value (bound up with the intrinsic cognitive and aesthetic significance of making images), and a comparative historical horizon whereby works stand out through their role in developing a medium's scope. The latter axis allows the former's potential to show through. It allows the image to be recognized as art.

This normative definition of art resolves the omissions and obscurities of formalist and Designation theories, and, by so doing, resolves those conceptual difficulties which are so deeply bound up with their unconscious exclusionism. It is true that the two normative axes have only been explicitly developed (albeit in a somewhat misunderstood way) by western culture and those which it has influenced.

However, it is vital to emphasize and acknowledge that this emergence is logically dependent upon a normatively significant set of practices—image-making and artefactual exemplification—which pre-date and extend much further than the western viewpoint. The recent western art world, however, has not acknowledged this parasitic and wholly marginal status. It has preferred rather to redefine the concept of art and the basis of artistic creativity in terms of the exclusive interests of a western philosophical, critical, and curatorial elite.

The normative definition of art, in contrast avoids such unconscious exclusionism And we are thus led to a final delicious irony. For by resolving those normative problems which are implicated in the other theories' unconscious exclusionism, my approach is also able to provide solid criteria for assessing the significance and worth of Designated works. The normative definition of art does not simply criticize but rather creates possibilities as well. And in organizing the definition around the two normative axes we have, thereby, criteria of art which are even—dare one say it—of a *common-sense kind*.

2

Defining Art, Defending the Canon, Contesting Culture[1]

Introduction

At first sight, it might seem that defining art is one of those specialist activities with few reverberations outside aesthetics itself. Actually, the task has explosive epistemological and cultural implications which have scarcely received the consideration they deserve.

One of the reasons why is because the normative dimension of aesthetics has been eclipsed by a fashionable cultural relativism which is sceptical about the objectivity of aesthetic and canonic values. The possibility of such objectivity is central to the normative aesthetics proposed in this book. Such an approach argues that some idioms of representation[2] are more deserving of cultural prestige than others, and that some broad dimensions of culture itself have an intrinsic value which other areas do not.

In this chapter I will develop further my normative approach to the definition of art. The strategy can be initially formulated in terms of a fundamental methodological conflict between normativity and relativism. The viewpoints can be succinctly stated as follows: normativity—'art' and the 'aesthetic' are forms of representation and experience (respectively)

---

[1] The arguments in this chapter came together through a reading of Parul Dave Mukherji's unpublished paper 'Visual Politics and the Binary Logic of Art History: From Maillard's "Western Misunderstandings" to Bryson's "Gaze and the Glance"'. This was presented at a symposium hosted by the Slovene Society of Aesthetics in Oct. 2002.

[2] By 'representation' I mean a mode of reference where the sensible or imaginative dimension of the sign has a logical bearing on its meaning. In this sense the term can encompass abstract art and even some Conceptual forms.

with universal validity and a justified claim to cultural privilege; relativ-ism—'art' and the 'aesthetic' are merely western forms of signification, with no universal validity or justification for their supposedly privileged status.

This conflict can be resolved from various directions. My own approach will be to show that the relativist position is self-contradictory in terms of its substance and implications, and that there is no compromise position between it and the normative approach. I will, accordingly, defend norm-ativity through arguments which link it to a creator-based transhistorical, transcultural, aesthetic theory of art and value.

In more specific terms, Section 2.1 will expound the hard 'genealogical' version of relativism in relation to its treatment of art and the aesthetic. It will also expound the softer relativism associated with Institutional definitions of art.

Section 2.2 will criticize the former view at length, showing that it is unconsciously racist and conceptually problematic in its implications for non-western representation. The basis of these problems will be shown to lie in hard relativism's consumerist exclusion or suppression of the importance of making and the creative process. Section 2.3 shows further that the aesthetic is, in fact, an integral part of the making and perception of non-western representational artefacts. On the basis of this, the soft relativism of the Institutional definitions of art will be criticized.

In Section 2.4 I shall trace the significance of western culture's specialized pursuit of art as an aesthetic activity independent of functional contexts. It will then be argued that this pursuit has significantly developed the logical scope of art media, and that by relating such developments to the horizon of diachronic history, it is possible to establish the idea of a canon and to justify aesthetic judgements on an objective, universalist basis. I will extend this position by considering a number of potential relativist objections, at length.

Section 2.5 will address possible reservations about my use of the term 'unconscious racism' in relation to hard relativism, and the Institutional definitions. Finally, I will draw some vital general conclusions concerning the definition of art as a way of contesting relativism.

2.1

Cultural relativism comes in varying degrees of hardness and softness. The hardest version is the genealogical approach—which is the basis of that transdisciplinary *mélange* sometimes called 'Theory'. It is inspired in general terms by Foucault, but has also become mixed up with many other fashionable strains of postmodern thought (so much so that it is sometimes simply called 'postmodernist'). Keith Moxey summarizes genealogical critique very lucidly as follows:

These perspectives subvert previously established knowledge claims by characterizing them as unavoidably tainted by the values that inform the circumstances of their production. The voice from nowhere, the objectivity posited by foundational epistemology, has come to be seen as suspect because of its identification with Western culture, with the dominance of white races, with masculinist bias, and with middle-class prejudice.[3]

Applying this to art,[4] it would follow that art and the aesthetic are social constructs which cannot be legitimately applied to forms of representation outside specifically western contexts. To do so would be (at least unconsciously) racist for two related reasons. First, it would involve the appropriation (or in some cases exclusion) of indigenous symbolic practices on the basis of western interests; and second, such appropriation would sever the indigenous practices from that context of ritual and societal value which is the real basis of their meaning.

The genealogical approach also holds (characteristically) that normative conceptions of art and the aesthetic are problematic even *within* western culture.[5] This is because their dominant canons and forms do not significantly reflect the experience of women, or socially disadvantaged classes, or marginalized racial groups.

---

[3] Keith Moxey, *The Practice of Persuasion: Paradox and Power in Art History* (Ithaca and London: Cornell University Press, 2001), 126.

[4] The genealogical approach is massively influential across most of the leading journals of art history, literature, and cultural theory. Moxey seems to be setting himself up as something of an ideologist for the tendency. Other influential exponents include Victor Burgin, J. Hillis Miller, Judith Butler, and most feminist writers on the arts.

[5] This angle is especially emphasized by thinkers such as Griselda Pollock and, in more general terms, Pierre Bourdieu. See e.g., the former's *Vision and Difference: Feminity, Feminism, and the Histories of Art* (London: Routledge, 1988); and the latter's *The Field of Cultural Production* (Oxford: Polity Press, 1993).

In respect of this issue, Moxey points out as a warning:

the scholar who affirms the notion of aesthetic value, the idea that there is some spiritual sustenance to be found in works of art which sets them apart from the rest of the paraphernalia of everyday life, without recognizing that such an understanding of aesthetic value is a characteristic of a social elite with the cultural capital to appreciate it.[6]

On these terms, art and the aesthetic are, in effect, a function of the fetishization of luxury commodities and their consumption. They reflect the tastes and interests of the dominant white male middle-class patriarchy. In so far as the disempowered do figure in western art, it is in roles defined by the dominant class rather than by themselves.

The hard relativism of the genealogical approach, holds, then, that art and the aesthetic are culturally specific terms which not only lack transhistorical value and significance, but are, in fact, implicated in various forms of social oppression.

A rather softer relativist approach to this issue is found in those Institutional definitions of art[7] which I discussed in the previous chapter. They hold that art can be defined, but that aesthetic criteria are not involved (unless by definition, one defines 'aesthetic' as that which pertains to judgements about art[8]). This means, in effect, that any kind of object or state of affairs can become a work of art if it is designated as such by an artist on the basis of some theoretical position.

The advantage of this approach is that by dispensing with the restrictive necessary link to aesthetic qualities, it *seems* to democratize art in a way which can encompass hitherto marginalized or excluded idioms. Art thus becomes universally significant by giving up its traditional normative base.

This approach has putatively strong empirical support. For it is a fact that, in the course of the last century, the range of artefacts counted as art has gradually expanded until there are no limits on what kind of thing or states of affairs it can encompass. What we *mean* by art now involves this expanded field.

---

[6] Moxey, *Practice of Persuasion*, 132.

[7] The major representatives of Institutional theories are, of course, Arthur Danto and George Dickie. However, a similar strategy is also found in theorists such as Jerrold Levinson, Robert Stecker, and even in Nelson Goodman's late work.

[8] Thierry de Duve's *Kant After Duchamp* (Cambridge, Mass. and London: MIT Press, 1997) takes this approach. It also seems to be Danto's approach, also (as I suggested Ch. 1).

It might seem that Institutional definitions offer us, accordingly, a promising way of dealing with the conflict noted at the start of this chapter. On these terms, the Institutional approaches would form a 'synthesis' which resolves the antagonism between the universalist thesis and the relativist antithesis by retaining the concept of art as universal but cutting its connection to normative and aesthetic dimensions of meaning. The 'strong empirical support' noted above, suggests, indeed, that this synthesis is gradually establishing itself in common usage as what we now mean by 'art'.

There is, however, a problem with this imagined resolution of the conflict. It consists in the fact that the Institutional synthesis and hard relativism are both internally problematic and/or contradictory. I will now show this in relation to the hard relativist approach.

2.2

Hard relativism holds, characteristically, that art should be understood as a *discursive practice* whose meanings are generated on the basis of context-dependent social activity. How meaning is *produced* rather than objective 'foundational' categories is what is decisive to cultural analysis. The emphasis on production serves to emphasize the shifting and unstable nature of meaning, and the fact that it is given its character by changing power relations (pertaining to race, class, and gender).

On this approach, the artwork is interpreted primarily from a *consumerist* (i.e. spectator or reader) viewpoint as something created as a means to socially meaningful ends. The ends in question constellate around the presentation of information or narrative, or the use of these for persuasive purposes. Representations document, clarify, or distort the experience of the communities who produce and receive them. They centre on the social 'production' or 'construction' of meaning.

In relation to art, this viewpoint is as radically distorted as it is influential. However, to judge the full scope of its error requires that we explore it, initially, in a non-western context. In this respect, it is clear that the hard relativist position involves a *general* theory about meaning, rather than one which is confined exclusively to the interpretation of western culture. Indeed, its heavy contextual emphasis might seem to protect against any temptation to judge other cultural products in terms of western standards.

If applied to non-western representation, however, we find a surprising outcome. The discursive practice approach is profoundly—if unintentionally—racist in terms of what it implies for such artefacts. Its status as a consumer-orientated variety of western instrumental reason becomes apparent.

At the heart of this is the way in which the process of *making* is relegated to an entirely secondary role, or suppressed altogether, and the audience's involvement is located at the level of *consumer* rather than *participant*. These points need great emphasis. The primary significance of art in non-western cultures is as an activity which is *formative* both from the producer's viewpoint and from that of the audience. In terms of this, the process of making the object as well as the finished product are sources of significant value. Indeed, Chantal Maillard observes that the purpose of traditional Indian art is 'to embody the canons, rhythms and matter-spirit life lines of which the universe is made for the intimate participation of those who contemplate the object'.[9]

This metaphysical complexity of creator and audience involvement is equally pronounced in much far eastern and African work. Vis-à-vis the latter for example, Susan M. Vogel notes in relation to tribal art of the Baule,

To approach art from the Baule perspective entails speaking of experiences that are not primarily visual, and of art objects that are animate presences indistinguishable from persons, spirits, and certain prosaic things. Even when the Baule people are clearly talking only of a wood sculpture, they may describe it as capable of volition and action that most western readers will find incredible.[10]

In this and many other cases of non-western art,[11] the whole *special* role which representation characteristically plays is *much more* than a means to some ritualistic end of communication or persuasion, and the social 'production' of meaning. The work is more akin to a living and creative

---

[9] Quoted in Mukherji, 'Visual Politics'.

[10] Susan M. Vogel, *Baule: African Art / Western Eyes* (New Haven and London: Yale University Press, 1997), 83.

[11] See e.g. the debates in Michele Marra (ed.), *Modern Japanese Aesthetics: A Reader* (Honolulu: University of Hawaii Press, 2003).

force based on its physical presence as a made artefact or on what that presence embodies.

Hard relativism, of course, could insist that all this is analysable in terms of 'polyvalent' layers of signification. But if anthropology, art history, and other analytic disciplines approach representation in these terms primarily, they lack the conceptual wherewithal to make sense of the primacy of making and participation. They are locked into the consumer dimension of experience.

Of course, all *analysis* by definition can only articulate its object at a relatively abstract level, but when we are dealing with sensibly or imaginatively specific artefacts such as pictures, sculptures, poems, dances, and music, this becomes an especially distorting factor which must be compensated for.

Unfortunately, in treating representation as a discursive practice, hard relativism reduces it to just one form of cultural production amongst others. And even if its special status is recognized, this is usually taken to involve no more than descriptions of the relevant ritualistic beliefs and social values which surround it, rather than those sensible and imaginative factors which are also implicated in representation's privileged status and which, indeed, *enable* those ritualistic beliefs and social values (an issue which I addressed in Chapter 1 and will return to at length in the next section).

The underlying problem here is that whilst any intelligent activity and its outcomes might be said to involve the 'production of meaning' this is not a sufficient characterization of representational practices. They, and cognate areas of experience, involve *much* more by virtue of complex processes of making. Ironically, whilst the 'production' metaphor has its origins in artifice, its application to the semantic domain actually distorts our understanding of the artefact. Far from assimilating meaning on the model of artifice, the strategy has the effect of recontextualizing artifice as a variety of signification.

The details of this are very revealing, and worth dwelling upon. First, it is clear that the metaphorical linking of 'production' and meaning is driven by a contemporary western interest. For if meaning is understood as something which is 'produced' or 'constructed', then it seems close to middle-class fantasies of natives and workers, fields and factories. It appears earthy and made, and far removed from the despised ivory towers of pure knowledge. Meaning, in other words, is here articulated through a 'politically correct' metaphor which presents intellectuals, natives, and workers as sharers in the same kind of productive process.

Interestingly, this fantasy engenders an even stronger reverse dynamic. For to understand meaning on the metaphor of production or construction, is to reduce it to the means/end model of western instrumental reason. But at the same time, through this reduction, it now *appears* that artifice and meaning amount to very much the same kind of thing. They can, accordingly, be analysed on a common methodological basis as modes of signification. Ironically enough, *by linking artifice to signification the latter is able to dictate the terms in which the former is understood.* Complex forms of making are thus reduced to the status of signifying practices, and adapted, thereby, to the special interests of western academic relativism.

The notion of 'discursive practices' involves a globalization of this approach. Such practices are presented as a general way of understanding *all* cultural products. Every activity—including artifice and representation—is cleansed of its concreteness and/or physicality and repackaged as a mode of meaning or signification. It is, in other words, reduced to an informational schematic within the consumerist discourse of academic relativism. The western empire of signs enters its most complete Imperialist phase.

We find, then, that when thought through in the context of non-western representation, hard relativism's 'discursive practices' emerge as unconsciously racist. Such notions embody a distorted version of western instrumental reason as the global basis for understanding cultural activity per se. In its very eagerness to be politically correct, in other words, hard relativism achieves the opposite.

And the contradictions do not stop here. For hard relativism's theory of discursive practices is conceptually tied to an anti-foundationalist epistemology which has its own major logical problem.[12] It consists of the fact (familiar to analytic philosophers but apparently unknown to postmodern thought) that any absolute or hard relativism will always be in contradiction with itself. On these terms, then, we must ask whether or not the theory of discursive practices is itself a discursive practice, or something more.

Its protagonists are logically committed to the view that—despite its global application—the theory cannot claim definitive objective status.

---

[12] The systematic critique of anti-foundationalism is a major theme of my book *Philosophy After Postmodernism: Civilized Values and the Scope of Knowledge* (London: Routledge, 2003).

It is just another form of discursive practice. This, however, leads to a broader contradiction. In epistemological terms the theory wants to affirm the primacy of historically specific or (in Moxey's terms) 'local knowledge'.

But this, in itself, is a claim about the universal conditions of knowledge formation. As such, it logically presupposes some meta-theory which can explain the, in effect, *foundational* role which is here being unconsciously assigned to the historically specific (and its component notions such as 'perspective' and 'difference').

If such a meta-theory insists that all conceptual schemas merely have truth-value relative to contexts of production and use and that *this is a brute unanalysable fact about the world*, then the act of 'closure' in the italicized clause of the sentence contradicts the openness which is affirmed in the first part. If, however, we affirm the first part of the sentence alone, then this requires a meta-theory to explain how diversity of perspectives is possible, and why it should have a decisive epistemological role. This, of course, restores the foundational dimension.

Hard relativism's notion of representation as a discursive practice is, therefore, not only problematic in both racist and epistemological terms through its unrecognized western consumerism, but is also part of a more general self-contradictory discourse.

2.3

As one might expect, these and related problems carry over into hard relativism's critique of art and the aesthetic. At first sight, however, this might appear *not* to be the case. For when describing the special status of representation in non-western cultures earlier on, the complex processes and experiences involved *seemed* to be metaphysical or religious rather than aesthetic. If, therefore, 'art' and the 'aesthetic' do not figure in the special status of such representation and the responses to it, then the case for them being fetishized exclusively western cultural constructs remains intact.

The case is, however, terribly mistaken. Superficially, it sets up non-western representation as an authentic 'other' against which we can criticize the fetishized western concepts of art and the aesthetic. However, through its implied marginalization of making, hard relativism also conceals or distorts non-western representation's *aesthetic* core.

It is true that the terms 'art' and the 'aesthetic' are western concepts, but what they conceptualize is something of transhistorical and transcultural significance. It focuses on what follows from representation's sensible and/or imaginative specificity.

These factors can be clarified by asking a question which is steadfastly avoided by hard relativism, namely how is it possible for non-western representation to be invested with the extraordinary levels of 'ritual' metaphysical and religious significance noted earlier? What is it about the making of such representations which facilitates the belief that they can bond the creative process, the work, the world, and the audience in an intimate living relationship?

An easy answer is that processes of mimesis are often accompanied by the belief that it enables one to become the object of imitation, or at least share in its being. But why should beliefs of this kind arise? Is it just a case of the poor non-westerners being wholly deluded by superstition, or is there something about mimesis *in itself* which can act, at least in part, as the ground of such belief? The ubiquitous high regard in which representation is held suggests, of course, the latter.

Now it might be argued that the sensory or imaginative vividness of mimesis simply give its meanings more immediate cognitive impact than those of mere linguistic reports. Such vividness represents its objects as if (however vaguely) they were immediately present to the body—and thence potentially amenable to manipulation. In principle—the argument might continue—this is a sufficient explanation of why representation can engender and sustain broader networks or metaphysical and religious belief. It is grounded in a sense of control of the object which arises through the process of making. There is, accordingly, no need to bring in the aesthetic.

However, (unless the creator is genuinely deluded) qua representation, the work must also be understood to have at least some difference from that which it represents—if only through the artist and audience's knowledge that the work was created. This means that it cannot be *sufficiently* characterized as an indirect expression of control.

There is always an additional element involving the dialectic of cognitive proximity to, and distance from, the represented object—a dialectic mediated (in the audience's case) by the activity of another individual or creative ensemble. Indeed, in representation all the factors in this relationship mutually enhance one another. There is *formative power* at work in and through the sensible and/or imaginative particularity of the medium.

This extraordinary bonding—or 'at homeness' with the sensible world—is intrinsic to the making and direct perception of representations, *and is composed of varieties of aesthetic experience* (issues which I will explore in Chapters 3 and 4).[13] These intrinsically valuable experiences facilitate the belief that representation is the kind of privileged activity which can realize the metaphysical and religious effects noted earlier. Through the power of aesthetic embodiment, these abstract ideas find an appropriate and distinctive sensible manifestation. Belief in their ritual potency is thus *enabled* by their aesthetic power.

To those who imagine that the aesthetic amounts to little more than 'significant form' this analysis may come as a surprise. The surprise is understandable in that most thinkers in the analytic tradition have been content to use 'aesthetic qualities' or 'expressive properties' and the like as logically primitive terms. Even twentieth-century formalism has tended to stress those 'felt' effects arising from the contemplation of harmonies of line and colour etc., rather than the ontological structures whose aesthetic embodiment makes those effects possible.

However, the most substantial and profound theories of the aesthetic do engage with such structures. Kant,[14] Schiller, Schopenhauer, Hegel, Heidegger, Gadamer, and Merleau-Ponty (amongst others) all have a cognitive emphasis in their theories of art which allows clear connections to be made with the non-western avenues of meaning described above.

Most notably, all these thinkers see the aesthetic as an enhancement of our cognitive powers which can only be achieved through the reciprocity of sensible form, powers of understanding, and, in the case of

---

[13] I also expound the complex relation between aesthetic experience, the artwork, audience, and creator at great length in chs. 8 and 9 of *Art and Embodiment: From Aesthetics to Self-Consciousness* (Oxford: Clarendon Press, 1993).

[14] There is a crude stereotype of Kant's which treats his aesthetic of nature as if it were a theory of art. On these terms art is taken to involve formal qualities alone. Kant, however, explicitly and emphatically separates the aesthetics of nature and art. His theory of the latter is very much a normative one. I will address it in Ch. 3.

art, creative transformation. As such, the varieties of the aesthetic make at least indirect connections with other fundamental areas of experience. (Astonishingly enough, even Clive Bell takes us in this same direction. His extreme formalism is underwritten by a much neglected—albeit somewhat vague—account of its broader metaphysical significance.[15])

We find, then, that the hard relativist approach to art utilizes an analytic framework which grossly distorts the significance of non-western representation by implicitly degrading the importance of making. Additionally, in its reductive eagerness to stigmatize the aesthetic as a merely western construct, it attacks a notion which is fundamental to non-western traditions, and which is, indeed, probably many thousands of years older than its western conceptualizations. It is this which constitutes real *cultural* contradiction.

Matters fare equally badly with soft relativism as found in the Institutional definitions of art. As we have seen in the previous chapter, they dispense with making and aesthetic formation in favour of acts of designation which can accommodate the western Duchampian tradition. Such theory, indeed, implicitly makes that tradition into the paradigm of artistic creation in so far as ready-mades (and the like) focus on the art-constituting act of designation, rather than mere distractions such as aesthetic formation.

The logical grounds on which I criticized this approach in the previous chapter can now be supplemented by some ethical points (aimed mainly at Danto).[16] First, I noted the 'strong' empirical support for Institutional definitions which I mentioned earlier. This consists of the de facto truth that, throughout the last century, the concept of art has developed in a way which allows any item or state of affairs, in principle, to be designated 'work of art'. To put this more bluntly—like it or not, it is a fact that artistic meaning has now been entirely colonized by specifically western theory and its managerial support structures.

Now whilst the art world may assume, thereby, that colonization by the west has been ratified by the sheer passage of empirical history, the moral dimension argues otherwise. The fact that western cultural colonization has evaded the exposure of its unconscious racism for so long, is a philosophical

---

[15] See his chapter on 'The Metaphysical Hypothesis', in *Art* (London: Chatto & Windus, 1914).
[16] See Sect. 1.2 of the present work.

scandal of the highest order. And even if we cynically allow that the passage of time deadens our sensitivity to established moral turpitude, there is no guarantee that this will remain so.

In this respect, we should recall that at the start of the last century the British Empire encompassed about a third of the world. In de facto terms, its truth seemed unchallengeable. In terms of *de jure* issues, however, things changed, its subjects articulated their anger, and its aspirations were gradually destroyed by events. The Institutional and cognate theories of art would do well to be mindful of this example of overthrown hegemony. However naturalized an intellectual position may seem to be, there is always the possibility that it will be destabilized by an accumulation of logical and ethical critiques. (The present work, of course, seeks to offer just such a critique in relation to artistic relativisms.)

A second ethical problem arises from the fact that designation theories make theory of art into an essential element of art itself. But what of cultures that do not have a concept of art? The clear implication is that they are marginal through only having an understanding of how art can be used, and not of what it is in reality. They are undeveloped in contrast with the achievements of western modernism and its revelation of the true essence of art. (It is noteworthy, indeed, that in Danto's writings this revelation is tied specifically to the development of the Duchampian tradition by American Pop Artists such as Johns, Rauschenberg, Lichtenstein, and Warhol. In both its iconography, and broader cultural setting, such art involves a celebration of consumer society.)

Now of course, western art has its own distinctive and epochal achievements which must be acknowledged. But in Designation theory some of these are unwarrantedly presented as the culmination of art itself. Danto even holds that, because of this culmination, there can be no new radically innovatory art. Art, in a sense, has come to an end.

Danto's position here is a sincere one and is not intended in any Imperialistic sense, of course, but it would be difficult to find a grosser case of unconscious racism. Around thirty thousand years of worldwide artistic creation is redefined and made secondary to the supposedly definitive status of western modernism's 'ready-made'.

2.4

I shall now consider an important objection to my arguments which will also allow me to introduce some further positive features of the normative definition of art.

It has been acknowledged that art and the aesthetic are concepts of western origin. But if this is the case, to describe them as having being colonized by the west in unconsciously racist terms might appear to make no sense. Unfortunately, it makes perfect sense. For whilst the terms 'art' and the 'aesthetic' are western, that which they articulate is not. However, it is important to clarify what is involved here in more detail.

I earlier described the significance of a complex zone of experience which is intrinsic to representation. This experience—whatever name we give to it—is distinctive to the perception of sensible or imaginative representation, and is presupposed by the complex bodies of association and belief which different cultures are able to derive from such representation. The production of artefacts grounded in such experience cuts across historical and cultural boundaries and needs a name of its own—even if it is not pursued separately from functional or ritual contexts.

In the west, the term 'aesthetic' names the relevant area of experience, and the term 'art' names the productive activity in which it is embodied. Now whilst *what* these terms name exists independently of western interests, the fact that they have been named at all independently of function is indicative of a special relation to them. Through its political and economic expansion, the west has developed cultural contexts and techniques whereby art and the aesthetic have been developed as specialist interests in their own right. This has enabled the respective representational media to have their logical scope developed to a quite extraordinary degree.

Now, as we have seen, the consumerist mind-set of hard relativism negotiates such media primarily on a western means/end model addressed exclusively to what their social meanings are. This not only diminishes the significance of making in general, but, in particular, the way in which individual representations are positioned in relation to the *logical scope* of their medium. Such positioning involves a complex negotiation between the medium as a semantic and syntactic code and the way in which meaning focuses, fundamentally, on the individual artefact's way of embodying it.

We are thus led to the decisive point. The example of non-western art shows the centrality of making. This is equally important for western art. For to develop the logical scope of a medium is—literally—to *make* new idioms of representation.

As we have already seen in the previous chapter (and will continue to see, as this work progresses) a work's individuality can refine or innovate in relation to the scope of its medium. When this occurs, then (over and above any broader social functions it may serve) the work can have an objective value which representations that merely repeat established patterns and formulae of production do not. By virtue of its *creative difference* from other representations, it opens up new possibilities of aesthetic experience. *This is the basis of an authentic canon of major works and artists or creative ensembles.*[17]

These arguments invite four important questions. First, why should the medium-based creative differences just noted be regarded as anything other than mere technical innovations? Second, why should they be of any interest to anyone other than a western audience? Third, who decides which differences are creative and which are not? Fourth, why is the 'logical scope' of a medium not simply relative to the cultural context in which it is produced?

The answer to the first two questions is broadly the same, and has yet another interesting paradoxical outcome for relativism. By developing the logical possibilities of a medium, the artist opens up new ways of presenting the world. This means that the relation to medium and audience is renewed and developed in complex aesthetic terms.

Such aesthetic renewal and development is almost a model of what life (in its positive modes) symbolically aspires to, and it also connects, of course, with the fundamental experience intrinsic to perceiving representation which I described earlier. It is, accordingly, transcultural and transhistorical in terms of its significance. In most cultures, this aesthetic experience remains closely integrated with metaphysical and religious ritual. In the west, however, it has been gradually developed independently from this context, to both its advantage and disadvantage.

The advantage is the fact that the variety of idioms in specific media has been more diversified in the west because of the development of

---

[17] The idea of a canon of visual art is argued in detail in ch. 4 of my *The Transhistorical Image: Philosophizing Art and its History* (Cambridge: Cambridge University Press, 2002).

art and aesthetic culture as specialist practices. The disadvantage is that this specialization has been so intensive as to exhaust the possibility of further revolutionary innovation—whilst leaving the expectation of such innovation in place.

In respect of the latter, there are conceptual limits to what communicative codes such as pictorial representation can sustain in terms of their logical development.[18] When those limits are reached, art pushes in new directions—such as the development of abstracting and abstract tendencies. When these have reached their limits, the expectation of continuing innovation leaves only one more possibility, namely ad hoc signification wherein an item or state of affairs is designated as art by an artist on the basis of his or her specific interests.

Unfortunately this entails that artistic meaning is now almost exclusively directed towards, and consumed by, the western art world's managerial structure, i.e. a loosely defined network of critics, art historians, curators, collectors, and journalists. This gives us our paradox. Whilst the arguments rehearsed a little earlier show the potentially universal significance of innovation or refinement in relation to the logical scope of the medium, recent western 'Conceptual' art practice collapses this. 'Artistic' meaning is locked into the world of managerial and market interests. It becomes exclusively an object of concern to western cultural fashion or those who have been colonized by such fashion.

We are thus led to the third question posed earlier, namely *who* decides which differences are creative in terms of how the logical scope of a medium is developed? Hard relativism (especially in its feminist and post-colonialist forms) holds that this *canonical* question is decided by white male middle-class patriarchy on the basis of its preferences and interests. Its affirmation of this, however, is characteristically based on an almost fanatical consumerist viewpoint.[19] If, however, we opt for the non-racist medium-and-making-based approach which hard relativism suppresses or marginalizes, rather different conclusions must be drawn.

---

[18] These limits are explored in *Transhistorical Image*, and in my *The Language of Twentieth-Century Art: A Conceptual History* (New Haven and London: Yale University Press, 1997).

[19] e.g. the great bulk of Griselda Pollock's work treats pictorial art as though it had, in effect, no significance over and above its role as visual documentation or in relation to the disclosure of social, race, and gender 'positioning'.

The most important point is that developments of a medium's logical scope can, in principle, be identified on the basis of analysis and rational argument based on the evidence of comparative history. Masaccio's importance, for example, is based primarily on the aesthetic effects which are enabled through his 'clinching' of mathematical perspective as a method for integrating pictorial space, plastic values, and narrative meaning.

Likewise, whilst an avant-gardist like Gauguin may represent women in a way that conflicts with the moral standpoint of western feminism, his way of articulating pictorial space opens up possibilities which any other artist can work with. In this respect, artists such as Paula Modersohn-Becker and Frida Kahlo are able to build on these possibilities and articulate them on their own terms. The innovations and refinements which an artist adds to a medium's logical scope, do not remain essentially tied to any race, class, or gender interest. They can be used, abused, and creatively transformed according to circumstances.

Of course, women and non-western racial groups have been institutionally excluded from participation in the development of the canon. But if, as I am arguing, the canon is conceptually connected to the logical scope of art media as modes of making, then this has no necessary bearing on the validity of canonical judgements.

If world history had been matriarchal in its direction, the same structural possibilities would have been open for development. We would be talking about different individuals involved in the developmental process, but *what* was developed would involve reference to the same criteria of making. Canonical judgements, in other words, would be determined by the kind of productive activity being judged, rather than by the identity of the judges.

And again we are led to a paradox. One of the great relativist precepts is that a work's meaning is historically specific. It is determined primarily by the societal conditions of its production, the audiences to which it was originally addressed, and the subsequent history of its reception. Any alternative to this is deemed 'ahistorical'.

However, this consumerist standpoint actively suppresses the other great dimension of cultural history, namely diachronic transmission—the way in which what is *made* at one time serves to enable and/or contextualize what is *made* at other times. It is this comparative horizon which allows canonical judgements to be made on an objective basis. Such judgements can aspire to objectivity through arguments concerning the diachronic history of art media as developing *modes of* creative artifice rather than as sources of consumer gratification or resentment alone.

In this way, indeed, aesthetic judgements concerning art are themselves authentically historicized. For whilst one can simply make arguments as to why one artist or work is objectively more important than another (vis-à-vis the logical scope of a medium), in the final analysis what really counts is something more. It is the fact that *these judgements centre on achievements which open up new perceptual or imaginative ways of engaging with the world.* If one artist does it first and others are able to take it further, then interpretational perspectives, in the broadest sense, are transformed. The world is aesthetically different.

I shall now consider the fourth and final objection noted earlier. Surely what counts as representation is culturally specific, and thence the development of a medium's logical scope will likewise be culturally determined. It should also be emphasized that in many cultures what is most important about representation is that it aspires to repeat the time-honoured idioms rather than 'develop' them in new ways.

In response to this, one must note that in many cases the same communicative code operates across great historical and cultural divides. Pictorial and sculptural representation, for example, is based on the conventionalized use of visual resemblance to achieve reference to *kinds* of three-dimensional items or states of affairs.[20] (If such a work could not be recognized as depicting at least one such three-dimensional visual kind there would be no grounds for calling it a representation.)

This code of visual reference is found worldwide. What differs radically is the cultural iconography of the code. What the 'likenesses' or kinds of depicted subject matter mean in more specific terms, and how they are used, will admit of the most extreme variety.

If, however, we are talking about the logical development of a representational code qua code, then we are dealing with ways in which its basic modes of reference and idioms of physical articulation are extended, rather than how it is used in specific cultural contexts. Such culturally specific

---

[20] For an elaboration of the logical basis of pictorial representation see Robert Hopkins's *Picture, Image and Experience: A Philosophical Inquiry* (Cambridge: Cambridge University Press, 1998).

usages may be instrumental in stimulating a medium's logical development, but they are not constitutive of it.

This means that if a culture focuses on a medium's logical scope (in terms of semantic, syntactic, and phenomenal structure) then what it develops in that respect has a genuine transhistorical and transcultural validity through opening up new ways for the code to be applied.

Now if a culture places emphasis on repetitions of the same it will not have a universal canonic significance, unless its mode of representation contains a logical element or elements which have not yet been developed elsewhere. This does not mean that such a representational practice is 'inferior', for it may well be that its practices—however repetitive—have a genuine individual distinctiveness from which other cultures could learn.

The upshot of all these arguments is that we can distinguish art from mere representation on a normative basis. The term 'art' is *necessitated* (as a universally significant category) when representations are able to achieve something distinctive by extending the logical scope of a specific medium through innovation or refinement. The normative definition of art, in other words, is bound up with both the intrinsic aesthetic significance of representation, and the comparative historical relations of its specific instances. Historical distinctiveness is, in part, constitutive of a work's aesthetic value.

2.5

Before moving to a conclusion, I shall address a further objection which might be raised. It involves a querying of my use of the phrase 'unconscious racism' in this and the previous chapter. This usage might be doubted on the basis of three (overlapping) points, as follows:

1. A link has been established between [global] consumerism and various relativist doctrines in art and broader theory. However, this link does not warrant the term 'unconscious racism'. Global consumerism may indeed be strongly associated with western power, but it is not an exclusively western phenomenon. Many other cultures have, at least, strong mercantilist and commercial traditions. Indeed, the oppressive effects of global consumerism are genuinely global. They

are destructive of local identity and cultural values in the west as well as beyond. Non-western peoples are not singled out here—either intentionally or unintentionally—for oppression.

2. Far from anti-foundationalist relativism being unconsciously racist, it has the opposite significance. For it explicitly aims to put different cultural interpretative schemas on a par with one another. The idea of their being some universally valid conceptual scheme is a mere hangover of the discredited western 'Enlightenment project' whose outcome (as opposed to intention) is the privileging of western epistemology. This is exactly what anti-foundationalism contests.

3. The understanding of art as a discursive practice, and the Institutional definitions of art, have as their 'other' specific reactionary or conservative approaches within western art. They criticize *them*, and not the practices of non-western peoples.

These three points may appear sufficient to rebut the accusation of unconscious racism. They are not; in fact, they exacerbate the problem. This can be shown by a mixture of empirical and conceptual points.

First, we must recall (from Chapter 1) that unconscious racism is unintentional, and sometimes takes itself to have the opposite significance. To recall the old saying—'the road to hell is paved with good intentions'. With this in mind, I will now address the three points in turn.

The first one is true at one empirical level, but overridden at a second one. Global consumerism is indeed destructive for all. However, the particular form which it has taken since the 1960s (if not before) is that of an aggressive *westernization* of other cultures which leaves no significant alternative space for indigenous cultural realizations. De facto, global consumerism's workings are unconsciously racist, even though this is no part of its loose programme of economic 'modernization' and free trade.

Indeed, the theoretical tendencies which I have shown to be complicit with globalization are not 'guilty by association'; they are *active protagonists* in the process, and—much, much worse—by extending the consumerist mind-set into 'oppositional' spheres, they, in effect, negate real opposition to the process. They expand the scope of western oppression.

In relation to anti-foundationalism's supposed anti-racist hostility to the Enlightenment project, it is actually nothing of the sort. It merely narrows the scope of that project, by seeking for equality at the level of collective rather than individual agency—all cultural viewpoints and values are equal, and they are all, in effect, taken to be based on class and gender power relations within those cultural contexts.

This, in itself, has a disturbing unconsciously racist outcome. Anti-foundationalism's crude equalizations have the effect of *not* taking non-western epistemologies and value systems seriously. They locate such systems within an overriding western 'grand narrative' of equality, which devalues their individual claims to truth (a key point which I will explain in more detail in the conclusion to this chapter).

What, finally, of the claim that the discursive practice approach to art and the Institutional definitions have, as their targets, developments within western culture, rather than practices outside it? This is true in terms of their immediate objects. My point, however, is that it is manifestly not true, in terms of their *effects and implications*. All these approaches treat the *making* of art—a factor which is fundamental to just about all non-western work—as though it were just one unexceptional, or, at worst, contingent, element in a field of signification, rather than *the factor which drives and coordinates the field*.

Again, in terms of western art and its dominant managerial interests, this diminution of making is the result of 'local' preoccupations. But its upshot is to make a culturally specific and logically parasitic set of practices into the criterion of what is art for all places and times. Indigenous art in other cultures, is, thereby, unconsciously demeaned, and, literally, *degraded*. It becomes little more than the cultural stuff of tourist brochures...

The reason why all this tends to actually exacerbate unconscious racism is, ironically enough, precisely because of a key feature of global consumerism. Despite its immediately negative cultural effects, globalism has created a worldwide network of communications which allows any informed scholar to become aware of non-western art practices, and their 'otherness' from western relativist ways of thinking about art. This avenue of awareness, however, is serenely ignored. *Unconscious racism is, thereby, taken to a higher level*.

Conclusion

At the beginning of this chapter I claimed that the task of defining art raised 'explosive' epistemological and ethical issues. By now it should be clear that the dramatic tone of this observation is entirely warranted. The conflict between normative worth and relativism has been resolved in favour of the former.

This was done by showing that hard relativism and the Institutional definitions of art entail various contradictions and unconsciously racist attitudes which radically problematize their theories. Both turn out to be surfaces of a narcissistic western globalism which colonizes the cultural world with its distorted consumerist mind-set (whilst imagining that it is doing something with the opposite significance).

Relativism's problems centre on the exclusion or marginalization of making and its profound connections with aesthetic experience. I restored the importance of these factors in relation to non-western art, but also showed them to have a transhistorical and transcultural significance. Indeed, by further emphasizing the significance of works which make refinements or innovations that extend the logical scope of a medium, I was able to offer the basis of objective justification for art historical and aesthetic judgements concerning the 'canon' of art.

The strategies and arguments summarized here have a much more general significance. For varieties of relativist anti-foundationalism pervade all aspects of contemporary culture. From Geography to Cultural Studies, recent continental Philosophy, and the Social Sciences, we find anti-foundationalist sentiments professed almost to the degree of an orthodoxy in some areas. What makes these so dangerous is that—whilst nominally being radically opposed to it—they unconsciously perpetuate the mind-set which is at work in global consumerism and the aggressive neo-conservative politics which sustains it.

This all converges on a 'master narrative' which holds that conceptual schemes are culturally specific and have no validity outside their individual contexts. At first sight this is extremely egalitarian. But it takes away a supreme right, namely the right to be true or false, right or wrong in objective terms.

In this respect, consider the First Pillar of Islam which holds that there is no God but God, and his prophet is Muhammad. For Muslims this is not a social construction but rather a truth about the nature of things. And this is how conceptual schemes mainly work outside the western anti-foundationalist appropriation of them. They are intended as universal truth-claims concerning the objective nature of reality. To recontextualize them as culturally specific social constructs is, in effect, *to degrade them and their believers*. It is to define them within a new global world-order where they cannot be what they take themselves to be. They are, rather, elements in a conceptual zoo whose keeper is western anti-foundationalism and its global consumerist infrastructure.

We are thus led to a final and extremely positive paradox. For in so far as relativism, unconscious racism, and global consumerism are manifestations of the same *market-driven* western mind-set, this carries an extraordinary critical implication. It means that *cultural conservatism* of the normative kind advocated here, can now, in principle, be a *left-wing* project.

Having shown the inadequacy of other approaches to the cultural status of art, the time has come to give my normative theory of art a much more sustained development. In both historical and conceptual terms, Kant's aesthetics offers the decisive starting point.

PART II
The Aesthetic and the Artistic

3

From Beauty to Art: Developing Kant's Aesthetics

Introduction

At first sight, with all his talk of 'faculties' of imagination and understanding, and his use of terms such as 'taste' and 'genius', Kant is marked out primarily as a man of his times. And the times in question are those of the Enlightenment and early Romanticism.

Another first impression is that, in the emphasis he assigns to the 'disinterested' character of aesthetic judgement, Kant is, at best, talking about a kind of luxury contemplative activity which is the historical province of white male middle-class taste, and which has now been swept into the dustbin of history by the massive cultural transformations of twentieth-century society.

The effect of these superficial impressions is to invite the question 'why bother with Kant as the starting point for a new theory of art?' He may have had a huge influence in aesthetics, but this could even be claimed as a malign one.

Now in my first two chapters I introduced a normative definition of art. This is not only Kantian in its origins, but is one which can now be developed much further by reference to Kant's aesthetics. He offers continuingly powerful insights concerning the central questions in aesthetics, and especially those bound up with the cognitive significance of beauty and art. In contrast to the formalists discussed in Chapter 1, he is able to explain how the aesthetic—in both beauty and art—achieves its distinctive effects, through a special relation to competences which are the bases of cognition per se. Indeed his treatment of art takes us far beyond the limits of formalism as it is customarily understood.

In the present chapter, therefore, I expound and considerably extend Kant's approach to beauty and art so as to bring out its normative significance. My main strategy is to develop Kant's basic insights in detailed *phenomenological* terms, i.e. to show how notions which he spells out only schematically or opaquely, might be made much more concrete and compelling.

The more exact structure of the chapter is as follows. Section 3.1 addresses Kant's basic definition of beauty, and the notion of disinterestedness. Section 3.2 offers a very detailed analysis of the phenomenology of beauty, attending, in particular, to the role of imagination and understanding, and to their broader experiential significance. In Section 3.3, Kant's theory of fine art is outlined and developed in relation to all these factors.

3.1

Kant observes: 'We can easily see that, in order for me to say that an object is beautiful, and to prove that I have taste, what matters is what I do with this presentation within myself, and not the [respect] in which I depend on the object's existence.'[1]

Kant's point here, is that our pleasure in beauty (which he also describes as a mode of 'pure aesthetic judgement') is a function of how the object *appears* to the senses. What kind of thing the object is; its relevance for our practical interests; indeed, whether the object is real or not; are questions which have no necessary bearing on our enjoyment of its mere appearance. Through its rootedness in the immediate sensible particular our pleasure can be characterized as disinterested.

Disinterestedness is, on these terms, a *logical* characteristic which separates pure aesthetic judgements from those of the agreeable and the good. Pure aesthetic judgements are, in logical terms, indifferent to the real existence of the object.

It is, however, important to be clear about the scope and significance of this claim. In respect of it, Kant has been very badly served by subsequent

---

[1] Kant, *Critique of Judgement*, trans. W. Pluhar (Indianapolis: Hackett and Co., 1987), 46.

tradition. As we have already seen in Chapter 1, formalists such as Monroe Beardsley and Clive Bell (and others who I have not previously mentioned, such as Edmund Bullough and Harold Osborne) have, in effect, interpreted the disinterested aspect of aesthetic judgement, as though it were in essence *psychological*—a kind of detached attitude or mental stance wherein one purges oneself of all considerations deriving from 'real existence'. Many critics of disinterestedness such as George Dickie, Richard Shusterman, and manifold Marxist and feminist theoreticians, have interpreted it in similar terms.

This has led some of them to the view that there simply 'ain't no such thing' or, indeed (in the case of Marxists), that the very idea of a detached 'disinterested' standpoint, is itself ideologically 'interested' to the highest degree.[2]

Now there are elements in Kant—such as his additional characterization of the pure aesthetic judgement as 'contemplative'—which lend some weight to this interpretative tradition. These, however, pale into insignificance alongside Kant's—wholly valid—logic of negation. The key *logical* significance of the pure aesthetic judgement lies in what it does *not* presuppose in order to be enjoyed.

To take a pleasure in the way things appear to the senses is *just* that. We may find that our being in a position to experience such pleasure has required a certain path through life; it may also be that lots of factual knowledge and practical considerations impinge upon our pleasure. However, such factors are not *logical* preconditions of our enjoying beauty: they are contingent elements. We do not *have to* take account of them in appreciating formal qualities for their own sake.

On these terms, then, the aesthetic experience of beauty is autonomous in logical terms. This is its definitive trait. However, such experiences occur under historically specific circumstances which means that their significance is mediated. By virtue of both the context in which it occurs and the kind of objects which bear it, beauty can be ethically and politically neutral or rendered negative or positive.

In a healthy society, for example, the enjoyment of beauty should not become an obsessive aim overriding broader responsibilities to both self

[2] For a critical discussion of some of the general issues involved here see my review article 'Sociological Imperialism and the Field of Cultural Production: The Case of Bourdieu', *Theory Culture, and Society*, 2/1 (1994), 155–69.

and other. But likewise, in a society such as ours, imprisoned as it is in the obsession for money and power, the 'useless' aspect of beauty—a simple pleasure in the structure of appearances per se—is one whose pursuit can have broader ramifications. It exists in a state of determinate negation to the instrumentalist values of a consumer society.

Given, then, this analysis of the logical characteristics of beauty, the time has now come to address the more significant question of its ontological structure.

3.2

First, Kant sees our pleasure in the pure aesthetic judgement as arising from a harmony of the cognitive faculties. He observes that 'if a presentation by which an object is given is, in general, to become cognition, we need imagination to combine the manifold of intuition, and understanding to provide the unity of the concept providing the [component] presentations'.[3]

This, of course, is a familiar tenet from the first *Critique*.[4] The particular act of judgement involves the subsumption or discrimination of sensible particulars under a concept or concepts. This itself is only possible through the exercise of our imagination's powers of attention, recall, and projection. The capacity to generate images enables an item or concept to be related to its past, present, and possible appearances or applications (respectively). It is, thereby, the basis of a unified temporal horizon which enables the understanding to form and apply concepts. By means of this, we are able to identify particulars, and kinds of things, and thus have knowledge of self and world.

---

[3] Kant, *Critique of Judgement*, trans. Pluhar, 62.

[4] See esp. the first edition version of 'The Deduction of the Pure Concepts of Understanding', in Kant's *Critique of Pure Reason*, trans. N. Kemp-Smith (London: Macmillan and Co., 1973), 128–50. Kant's theory of the imagination is now receiving an impressive level of sympathetic treatment in both analytic and 'Continental' approaches. See e.g. Rudolf Makkreel, *Imagination and Interpretation in Kant: The Hermeneutical Import of the Critique of Judgment* (Chicago: University of Chicago Press, 1990); Wayne Waxman, *Kant's Model of the Mind: A New Interpretation of Transcendental Idealism* (New York: Oxford University Press, 1991); Sarah Gibbons, *Kant's Theory of Imagination: Bridging Gaps between Judgement and Experience* (Oxford: Clarendon Press, 1994); Patricia Kitcher, *Kant's Transcendental Psychology* (New York: Oxford University Press, 1994); and Henry Allison, *Kant's Transcendental Idealism: An Interpretation and Defense* (New Haven: Yale University Press, 2004).

Now even if one does not accept Kant's general epistemology *in toto*, there are good reasons for accepting the decisive role which he assigns to imagination. I have addressed these in Chapter 1, and will develop them further in Chapter 5. Central amongst them is the fact that concept formation and application presuppose that we can engage with factors which are not immediately present in the perceptual field. We must have some sense of what it is like for terms to apply to the same or similar items and contexts in different places and times.

This cannot be explained through learning language and concepts as such, since it is these terms whose very possibility we are trying to explain. And even when we have learned to apply concepts ostensively, we do not comprehend them as concepts in the fullest sense, unless we can countenance how they might apply also to similar items and contexts in other places and times.

Given these various trans-ostensive requirements, we must assume—as a matter of conceptual necessity—some cognitive capacity which can project possibilities beyond those which are present in the immediate perceptual field.

Kant calls this capacity the 'productive imagination'. In its normal highly specific employments, it is tightly directed by a relevant concept, and functions in a fundamentally 'reproductive' way. For example, in conceptualizing something as a 'dog', our application of the concept will be informed (unconsciously or explicitly) by expectations based on associations which we have made (or could make) between the present creature and our previous experience of doggy-type appearances and behaviour.

Cooperation between the understanding and imagination in its repro-ductive function, then, is the basis of what I shall call *normal specificatory judgements*. These are acts of subsumption or discrimination which affirm that specific relations hold. Such judgements have definiteness of sense, and are the basis of everyday cognitive life. They exemplify and exist in a context which might be characterized as discursively rigid, in so far as they locate us in a realm which involves the application of definite concepts to definite objects on the basis of definite practical interest or physiological needs.

It should be emphasized that whilst Kant describes understanding and imagination as 'faculties', my reading emphasizes their role as basic aspects of cognition—*competences without which our recognitional activity would not be intelligible.* Such a viewpoint is, of course, consistent with Kantian epistemology, but it is not tied to it. (An epistemological realist could, in principle, also subscribe to the position.)

Now, the role of these competences in the pure aesthetic judgement is very different from that found in the normal specificatory mode. In engaging with a beautiful form, Kant suggests that 'the cognitive powers brought into play by this presentation are in free play, because no determinate concept restricts them to a particular rule of cognition. Hence the mental states in this presentation must be a feeling, accompanying the given presentation, of a free play of the presentational powers'.[5]

This raises two question, namely, what exactly is involved in this free play, and why should it be pleasurable? I shall address these questions in turn.

First, we will recall from Section 3.1 that Kant characterizes the pure aesthetic judgement as 'apart from any concept', but in the foregoing remark he claims that it involves 'no definite concept'. Now if Kant's theory is to do any useful philosophical work, we must read these contrasting characterizations as differences of emphasis rather than substance. For whilst (in order for Kant to be consistent with his overall account of judgement) the pure aesthetic mode must have some conceptual content, it must also have much more than *just* conceptual content.

This means that judgement must here function in something other than its normal specificatory mode. On these terms, the 'apart from any concept' characterization should be taken simply as an overstated emphasis of the pure aesthetic judgement's exceptional status. A better way of putting it would be to say that such judgements focus on the possibility of a manifold's conceptualizability per se, rather than its relation to a definite concept.

But how are we to make this more specific? One important clue is provided by Kant's emphases on the role of the productive imagination. Consider the following passage: 'this power is here not taken as reproductive, where it is subject to the laws of association, but as productive and spontaneous (as the originator of chosen forms of possible intuitions)'.[6]

---

[5] Kant, *Critique of Judgement*, trans. Pluhar, 62.
[6] Ibid. 91.

To make sense of this, we must recall how in the normal specificatory judgement, the relation between imagination and understanding is discursively rigid. Now a phenomenal form—such as a bird of paradise's plumage or an arabesque—can be described in just these rigid terms. We identify them as formal configurations which are characteristic of this particular kind of bird, or this particular kind of ornament.

To judge them as *beautiful*, in contrast, entails that these forms have relations of unity and diversity which are amenable to sustained cognitive exploration. In discriminating the relation between parts and whole in the bird's plumage, for example, what may engross us is the way the overall shape contains and directs sequences of colour and texture, and other contours within the manifold. We explore the various phenomenal sub-unities in relation to both one another and the structure of the whole.

In the case of the arabesque, matters can be even more complex. The visual rhythm of the pattern may suggest continuations beyond that which is immediately given. We find formal cues which enable us to, as it were, rhapsodically continue the rhythm in imagination. Again, in exploring the way in which one colour limits or tends to negate or neutralize other colours, we might see and develop this as a *process* of formal interaction, taking the given configuration as one moment in a continuous movement which might be traced back to imaginary previous stages, or forward to future ones.

Yet again, the gestalt character of specific forms within the ornament may be such that we can see them as either foreground or background elements. With each switch from one to the other, the whole structure of virtual space is reconfigured into new possibilities.

Now, as Kant's celebrated example of the house in the first *Critique's* Second Analogy shows, the unity of an object—as opposed to that of an event—can be perceptually apprehended in a random order. As he puts it: 'my perceptions could begin with the apprehension of the roof and end with the basement, or could begin from below and end above; and I could similarly apprehend the manifold of the empirical intuition either from right to left or from left to right'.[7] Kant further suggests that whilst the subjective succession of perceptions here is 'arbitrary', 'it does not prove anything as

---

[7] Kant, *Critique of Pure Reason*, 221.

to the manner in which the manifold is connected in the object'.[8] Hence, whilst the order of our perceptions in relation to an object is arbitrary, this arbitrariness has no bearing on its specifically objective unity.

However, in perceiving the beauty of a bird's plumage or an arabesque, very different considerations hold. For the *aesthetic unity* of the object is a function of the interplay between phenomenal form and the different *possible* avenues of cognitive exploration and development which it can open up.

An element of randomness in judgement, in other words, is partially *constitutive* of aesthetic unity. In contrast with the objective form of manifolds of sensible intuition, we are dealing here with 'chosen forms of possible intuitions'.[9] The imagination is not tied to the retention or projection of appearance on exact associational lines dictated by a specific concept. It is involved, rather, at the level of its definitive being—as a productive capacity which creates possibilities of unity in the manifold.

This extraordinary contrast between the discursive rigidity of empirical perception and the freedom of aesthetic judgement, has not, I think, been at all properly developed in the existing interpretative literature.[10] One reason for this is that in the third *Critique* Kant has hardly anything explicit to say about those 'pure concepts of the understanding' or 'categories' which are so decisive in the first *Critique*. However, they do play a crucial implicit role, to the degree that the pure aesthetic judgement serves to 'refer a given representation to cognition in general'.

It is for this reason, earlier on, I suggested that such judgements focus on the possibility of a manifold's conceptualizability. The evocation of the productive imagination noted above, demands not empirical concepts, but the categories—and, especially, the quantitative and qualitative ones.

[8] Kant, *Critique of Pure Reason*, 222.

[9] Kant, *Critique of Judgement*, trans. Pluhar, 91.

[10] This is true even of such thorough and impressive treatments as are found in Paul Guyer's book *Kant and the Claims of Taste* (Cambridge, Mass. and London: Harvard University Press, 1979) and Hannah Ginsborg's *The Role of Taste in Kant's Theory of Cognition* (Cambridge, Mass. and London: Harvard University Press, 1988). Interestingly, Dieter Henrich does take an approach with some similarities to mine, in terms of his notion of 'the conditions of a possible conceptualization in general'. See his *Aesthetic Judgement and the Moral Image of the World* (Stanford: Stanford University Press, 1992). However, he does not bring in fully the role of the categories. Indeed, like Guyer and Ginsborg (and many others) his interpretative attentiveness to the details of Kant's text is not matched by a corresponding *phenomenological* attentiveness to the concrete experience of beautiful configurations. If, however, we are interested in the *validity* of Kant's claims, this latter consideration should be of decisive importance.

These are (respectively) unity, plurality, and totality, and reality, negation, and limitation. One may dispute the membership and relevance of Kant's list of categories, but the aforementioned six seem to be fundamental to our characterizations of reality.

Indeed (although Kant does not remark on it), the categories also play a role in pure aesthetic judgements. In judging beautiful form—as I tried to show in my examples—the categories are engaged in loose, experimental, explorative ways, allowing a similar flexibility in the way imagination orientates, and projects the manifold. In one sense the beautiful configuration is cognitively unstable.

However, this is not a loss of intelligibility—a kind of cognitive breakdown. Rather, we have, as it were, cognition *in the making*. Imagination and understanding here function in their primordial form as free formative powers, which, in concert, organize sensory inputs. This is, in effect, a repetition of the ontogenesis of experience itself, and it indicates an even deeper significance to the aesthetic which goes beyond what Kant himself would have countenanced.

One might put it like this. An infant interacts with its environment on the basis of curiosity, searching out and exploring different patterns of relation and order. In this it is guided by a propensity to mimic, and the encouragement (or otherwise) of adults. The motives for this exploration, cannot, I think, be reduced to these guiding factors. Mimicry, for example, may be an innate propensity, but the complex uses to which it is put, bespeak a deeper motive—namely the exploration of possibilities of order for their own sake.

Adult guidance and, indeed, the desire to please adults, are important factors in determining infant behaviour, but they do not exclusively determine it. Left to itself, the infant will want to do things other than simply satisfy its physiological needs, and the demands of adults.

What I am suggesting, then, is that the motive for non-determined infant behaviour is aesthetic. It is a curiosity-for-its-own-sake which can be characterized as disinterested in so far as the infant has not yet fully articulated the categorial basis of either the world or its own self. It is playing with possibilities of order and appearance, which, in conjunction with the other mediating factors, enable a sense of reality—a systematic calibration of understanding and imagination—to be eventually achieved.

Through free aesthetic exploration in concert with other natural and socializing factors, the infant gradually correlates its body with both the unity of the world and the unity of its own perspective upon it as an individual self.

Now if this account is correct, the aesthetic judgement is a natural factor in the infant's development, and is deeply implicated in the formation of a categorial framework. It is crucial to emphasize, however, that we do not find the pure aesthetic judgement pleasurable *because* it repeats the formative stages of experience. Rather it is the free formative activity itself which is pleasurable. The significance of the repetition consists in the way the individual moment of aesthetic pleasure, *exemplifies* intuitively a mode of experiential formation, which reaches back into, and is decisive for, the origins of individual self-consciousness.

One might say that the aesthetic responses of the mature subject (as opposed to the infant) are experientially framed. For given that the adult's cognitive and sensory-motor capacities are fully coordinated, this means that the free formative activity of the aesthetic response here occurs within, and defines itself against, a 'surround' of completely calibrated reality. As well as being intrinsically pleasurable, the enjoyment of beauty is ontologically discontinuous from the normal (discursively rigid) order of events.

It is this 'break' indeed, which allows aesthetic form to function as a kind of self-sustained experiential image of the origins of embodied self-consciousness. The reasons for this have already been broadly indicated. However, it is worth giving them further illustration by reference to the notion of depth. (Again, this is not a topic considered explicitly by Kant, but it is one which illuminates the surprising scope of his approach.)

In physical terms, depth is the three-dimensional space in which the body inheres and acts. It is structured around a foreground of items and relations amenable to immediate perception and manipulation, and a background which is accessible to such inspection only through bodily repositioning.

The passage through depth involves not only acts of mental discrimination. Rather the body itself must become habituated to specific styles and modes of positioning in order to negotiate depth. This means in effect habitual coordination in both spatial and temporal terms. Through this latent schema of possible bodily actions, depth is given a discursively rigid structure. It is opened up in terms of quite specific patterns of negotiation with the world.

Let us now consider the case of pictorial and optical illusion. In the former case, to greater or lesser degrees (according to the pictorial format) we are dealing with a virtual realization of depth which has some affinity with a possible physical experience of it. In a perspectivally highly calibrated work, the fact that the picture has an edge or limit serves to declare the virtuality of its space and thence its apartness from physical depth.

This apartness is also emphasized by the fact that the limit of the picture can also manifestly determine the disposition of the internal pictorial elements. The more pronounced this is, indeed, the more our tendency to see affinities between the virtual depth and real depth, will be scrambled. And, of course, there are other destabilizing factors—such as a strong sense of the picture's style or general compositional structure.

When these factors are operative in a positive sense, even the most emphatic virtual depth is flexibly reordered as an element in a high-level aesthetic unity. The nature of the virtual depth and the items within it switch to and fro between their extensible status and that of forms, masses, shapes, groups, textures, densities of colour and light, etc.

If our appreciation centres on the relation between these factors *and* explicit awareness of the work's artefactual status, it will involve an aesthetic experience far more complex than that of mere beautiful form as such. (And I will consider this at length in the next section of this chapter.)

However, it is also possible to look at nature and decorative pictorial and ornamental art forms in the terms just described—at least in so far as such forms involve phenomenally variegated items or relations.

In the visual context, illusion is always operative here. For once a colour is given a specific shape, or a line is brought into relation to another line, or a colour is read against a surround, or a pattern is distributed across a surface, then in the structure of these forms (or in their relation to the immediate perceptual context), we find a basic figure/ground structure or structures. This is a schematic analogue of the foreground/background relation which defines physical depth. We are, as it were, placed at the threshold of such depth in virtual terms. But we are unable to cross in a straight line.

Consider even so simple a structure as evenly hued red dots, individually equidistant from one another, and distributed evenly over a white surface. Here we might see the dots as forms upon a white ground, or as punctures which allow a red ground beneath the ostensible white one, to show through. Again we might see the white ground simply as a ground or as an infinite recess, or indeed, as a void. The dots themselves might be characterized as a series, a cluster, a group, a sequence, or even as a constellation.

Now, of course, with structure as simple and unappealing as this, we simply describe it as red dots on a white background and leave it at that. But the point is that this basic description is subtended by many different possible aspects, and that in the case of more poignant or sophisticated configurations the multiplicity of aspects provides the primary basis for our perceptual engagement with them.

I am arguing, then, that whereas the body's relation to physical depth is projected in rigid habitual schemata, in the case of aesthetic configurations it is not. In the former we find a cognitive continuity between physical and virtual depth (be the latter pictorial or purely optical) but in the beautiful configuration depth becomes ambiguous. We have experience not of clear directions through it, but rather of alternative constitutions. Unity, plurality, and totality, reality, negation, and limitation, are all *at issue*.

The aesthetic engagement with depth is one which invokes an unstable order of spatial and temporal unity. As embodied beings, we are in space and time, but they are unified in systematic terms only when the body has both habituated itself to the exploration of physical depth, and when, on the basis of this, it has developed the capacity to recognize itself as having inhabited, and being able to inhabit, different regions of a spatio-temporal continuum. The aesthetic configuration both relates to, and differs from, this. It invokes, in virtual terms, that proto-encounter with depth wherein lie the origins of self-consciousness.

My basic claim, therefore, is twofold. First, the experience of beauty has its own intrinsic pleasure through being grounded in the enhanced interaction of understanding and imagination—two capacities which are essential for communication between humans. Second, this interaction is one which, in its contrast with the discursive rigidity of normal embodied experience, offers a virtual exemplar of our proto-encounters with depth, and the ontogenesis of self-consciousness.

For a finite subject, this symbolic re-enactment of its own genesis, offers a massive degree of existential security. Given such factors, the human propensity to arrange, embellish, and adorn, and to formalize gesture (as in dance) is hardly surprising. For this—as Ellen Dissanayake puts it—'making special'[11] impregnates the resistant material world with the *ur*-form of self-consciousness. Indeed, in the dialectic of making and medium, with its resistances and failures, compromises and reworkings, and new possibilities and techniques, the ontogenesis of self-consciousness is internalized in the process of physical labour itself.

The importance of all this is that, as we have seen, much contemporary writing treats the aesthetic as if it is a mere class- or gender-based preference which has been unwarrantably privileged as a higher pleasure through its role in the social power structure of certain western societies. (Pierre Bourdieu's well-known critique of Kant is a paradigm case of this approach.[12]) However, the impulse to embellish, to ornament, to adorn, and to formalize gesture seems to be a ubiquitous feature of all human societies.

Superficially this might seem to favour the reductionist view just noted. On these terms, we would argue that aesthetic embellishments and adorn-ments (etc.) are found pleasing because of their efficacy in certain kinds of functional or ritual context. But against this, we must ask, why should aesthetic elements be regarded as efficacious in such contexts? Why is it that they are taken to add something to their contexts of occurrence? If it is because of some putative magical significance, again we must ask what is it about the aesthetic which *lends itself* to being invested with such magical powers?

At some point in this analysis, we will be returned to the brute fact that the aesthetic is both a mode of pleasure inherent in the fabric of self-consciousness itself, and one which (however vaguely or intuitively) discloses and deepens our sense of free-belonging to the world. Kant's basic aesthetic theory enables us to think both these aspects through. As we shall now see, his theory of fine art can extend them even further.

3.3

To start with, it is useful to do something which Kant himself does not explicitly do—namely to modify the pure aesthetic judgement so that it

---

[11] This is a basic theme in her book *What Art is For* (Washington: Washington University Press, 1988).

[12] See e.g. Pierre Bourdieu, *Distinction: A Social Critique of the Judgement of Taste*, trans. R. Nice (London: Routledge & Kegan-Paul, 1984), 485–500.

can involve explicit and positive knowledge of the artefactual character of certain beautiful forms. Earlier, I described in detail the way in which beautiful configurations including artefactual ones aesthetically engage our cognitive capacities. In the case of artefacts, our sense of them qua artefacts, is not always involved in our appreciation of their beauty. Ornaments, embellishments, and many decorative idioms can be enjoyed without us having to take account of the fact that they are products of artifice.[13]

With artworks, in contrast (for reasons which will be made clear a little further on), our experience of beauty is actively mediated by knowledge that the work is a human creation. This, of course, can be purely factual knowledge. However, it can also be a constitutive factor in our enjoyment, in so far as the configuration's properties emerge in a distinctive way—through our perception of the artist's or creative ensemble's style.

Here what emerges qua aesthetic form—in all the complex ways described in Section 3.2—does so through, at the same time, emerging from, and manifesting, the distinctiveness of another human being's or ensemble's style of working sensible or imaginatively intended material. The beauty of phenomenal form and the distinctiveness of the creator(s) exist in a mutually enhancing and inseparable state. Each is part of the full definition of the other. Without the specific creator(s) this particular form would not be unified in the way that it is; and through this unification, the creator(s) have achieved a distinctive way of articulating sensible phenomena.

This artistic variety of beauty is, I think, of some significance in our enjoyment of art. Kant himself, however, does not develop it to the degree that I just have. This is hardly surprising. For such artistic beauty is by no means the only aesthetic factor which is relevant to art. Indeed, it is not even the most important one. Artistic beauty in the sense just described is a modification of the pure aesthetic judgement, and is, accordingly, in part derivative from the aesthetic appreciation of natural form. Its central aspect is not, in other words, unique to art.

Furthermore, since artistic beauty must be distinguished from mere decorative beauty, this logically presupposes a horizon of comparison which

---

[13] Sometimes—in the case of what Kant calls 'appendant beauty'—what kind of thing an artefact is can be so significant in itself, that it makes accompanying ornament or embellishment perceptually or morally inappropriate.

enables a work to stand out as artistically beautiful (by virtue of having a more individual character than decorative works). Such a comparative horizon is more decisive for artistic status than beauty per se.

These issues are probably why Kant develops a theory of fine art which goes considerably beyond his general formalist aesthetic. Indeed, he identifies a factor which is absolutely unique to art. Understandably, this forms the centrepiece of his theory.

To comprehend it, consider the following passage: 'By an aesthetic idea I mean a presentation of the imagination which prompts much thought, but to which no determinate thought whatsoever ..., can be adequate, so that no language can express it completely and allow us to grasp it.'[14]

For Kant, works of fine art present aesthetic ideas, and the images wherein they present them are irreducible to linguistic paraphrase. The reason why is made clear in the following remarks:

A poet ventures to give sensible expression to rational ideas of invisible beings, the realm of the blessed, the realm of hell, eternity, creation, and so on. Or, again, he takes (things) that are indeed exemplified in experience, such as death, energy and all the other vices, as well as love, fame, and so on; but then, by means of an imagination that emulates the example of reason in reaching (for) a maximum, he ventures to give these sensible expression in a way that goes beyond the limits of experience, namely with a completeness for which no example can be found in nature.[15]

This complex passage focuses on the interplay between imagination and the artist's style in handling a specific medium. Kant defines imagination as the capacity to represent that which is not immediately given in perception.[16] This has two aspects. On the one hand, we can imagine things which happen not to be immediately present in perception but which could become present and, on the other hand, we can imagine things which are not encounterable in perception under any circumstances by virtue of their being wholly fictional.

As we have already seen, Kant holds that imagination is not merely some, as it were, luxury cognitive capacity, it is, in fact a precondition of any possible experience (in so far as our sense of the present and our mobile occupancy of space are only intelligible in so far as we can project what it is

---

[14] Kant, *Critique of Judgement*, trans. Pluhar, 182.   [15] Ibid. 183.
[16] Kant, *Critique of Pure Reason*, 111.

like to occupy times and places other than the one which we are presently occupying). Imagination allows the projection of a phenomenal continuum wherein other cognitive factors such as the acquisition of language and concepts are enabled.

Given this, the fact that art centres on making images would, in itself, go some way towards explaining its intrinsic value and fascination for us. However, there is another important issue here. For in the last quotation Kant makes much of the fact that the artist's imaging ranges beyond the actuality of experience. What he has in mind here is probably not just art's capacity to represent things which do not exist in reality. Rather he is also voicing late eighteenth-century sensibility's preoccupation with the Ideal. On these terms the work of art improves upon reality by eliminating phenomenal and, where appropriate, psychological and moral defects. In this way the subject matter exists in art with a completeness which it does not enjoy in reality.

I do not propose to defend this notion of the Ideal. There is no need to; for it is a dispensable historically specific embodiment of *more general* features of the aesthetic idea. These converge on the fact that art represents kinds of, and particular, items or states of affairs. We recognize that this is a picture *of*, or a poem *about*, such and such a subject matter.

Now when an artist represents such a subject, he or she does not simply reproduce it. All the vital stylistic factors outlined in the Introduction to this book, come into play. Through working in a medium the artist must adapt the subject in relation to the specific demands of the medium, and work it so as to accommodate the specific demands of the subject matter. His or her style of writing or whatever will emphasize some factors, omit others, and be shaped by a particular history of negotiating the medium in question.

This means that the aesthetic idea, of necessity, involves stylistic interpretation. By means of it the artist presents the subject in a way which clarifies its scope through imaginative enrichment. Consider, for example, Sartre's novel *Nausea*. This narrates an individual's gradual turning away from the established social and natural order of things, through a growing sense of the metaphysical absurdity of Being in all its aspects. Alienation and estrangement are common themes in literature, but Sartre's style gives these an unusual and extremely striking interpretation.

The upshot is that our attention is powerfully engaged in realizations of the narrative as it is developed by the author. We do not simply follow the plot as one might an extended set of factual descriptions; rather, its various aspects—in terms of plot, characterization, and evocation of actions, events, and places—are made vivid in imagination.

In this way the artist's guiding subject ideas are explored imaginatively. We learn more about the scope and different ways in which concepts such as alienation and estrangement can be instantiated according to different circumstances of place, time, and personality. Of course, the content of Sartre's novel could be described to us in detailed factual terms, but in the novel we are invited to share the narrative *as if* we were direct witnesses of it, or were seeing events as if we were actual protagonists in the narrative.

This imaginative enrichment then is in harmony with our understanding of the scope of those concepts which are the artist's major themes. It makes them cognitively significant for us at the level of perception and feeling rather than that of abstract understanding alone. Indeed, their expression of conceptual content is inseparable from their identity as this particular sensible object or (in the case of literature) this individual imaginatively intended manifold. One cannot enjoy or appreciate what is at issue in the work without direct engagement with it.

The free play of understanding and imagination in the experience of beauty is here replaced by a more focused form of harmony. But one must emphasize nevertheless that this *is* a genuine mutually enhancing harmony between how we understand and how we imagine, rather than a mere conformity of competences wherein imagination provides bare exemplars for concepts.

Now it is interesting that Kant does not apply the notion of disinterestedness in relation to the art's embodiment of aesthetic ideas. Within the strict terms of his philosophy this is disallowed because to recognize something as art means that we must take account of its artefactual status.

However, it is surely possible to appreciate art's embodiment of aesthetic ideas for its own sake—i.e. without having to suppose that such enjoyment will be of practical or informational benefit. Our enjoyment may have these outcomes, but the point is that we do not *have to be* thinking in terms of them in order to enjoy the aesthetic idea. It can therefore, be justly characterized as relatively disinterested. (This is a topic I shall return to in more detail in various other chapters in this book.)

Kant, then, is able to direct us towards that which eludes Designation theorists, namely a viable notion of distinctively aesthetic ideas embodied in the work. This establishes a basis for the first normative axis of artistic value. He also makes the most vital contributions towards justifying the second axis. This centres, we will recall, on explaining how distinctions of canonic merit can be made between artworks. Kant offers a two-level approach to this. His first step is as follows:

If art merely performs the acts that are required to make a possible object actual, adequate to our *cognition* of that object, then it is *mechanical* art; but if what it intends directly is (to arouse) the feeling of pleasure, then it is called aesthetic art. The latter is either agreeable or is that the pleasure should accompany presentations that are mere *sensations*: It is *fine* art if the purpose is that the pleasure should accompany presentations that are *ways of cognizing.*[17]

In these decisive observations, Kant makes key normative distinctions. Some representations are made so as to do no more than give simple information or serve definite practical functions. Others are made to do no more than be decorative, or to look 'nice'. Fine art in contrast is made so as to present those modes of formative imaging outlined earlier.

What Kant is, in effect, offering here, is a distinction between art with a small 'a' and art with a large 'A' (a distinction which I will explore in the next chapter), on the basis of a difference between mere function and intrinsic significance.

He then takes this distinction to an even more important second level. In this respect, we are told that fine art is the product of 'genius'. There are two especially important aspects to this:

Genius is a talent for producing something for which no determinate rule can be given, not a predisposition consisting of a skill for something that can be learned by following some rule or other; hence the foremost property of genius must be originality.... Since nonsense too can be original, the products of genius must be exemplary; hence, though they do not themselves arise through imitation, still they must serve others as this, i.e. as a standard or rule by which to judge.[18]

Recent feminist thought makes it almost an article of faith to reduce the question of genius to issues of gender, on the basis of historical associations.

---

[17] Kant, *Critique of Judgement*, trans. Pluhar, 172.   [18] Ibid. 175.

Kant's notion of genius in the *Critique of Judgement*, however, is based on conceptual factors and carries no gender connotations.[19]

It centres, rather, on two points of the most far-reaching significance. In relation to the first, for example, whilst Kant presents originality as bound up with the psychology of creation, it also has *necessarily* a logical and objective aspect. This is because in order to recognize originality of style we must be able to compare its products with those of others. Stylistic originality emerges only through reference to a horizon of—in the broadest terms—*historical difference*.

However, Kant shrewdly notes that since there can also be original nonsense, the originality at issue in genius must be of an *exemplary* character. It must act as a stylistic model for producers and interpreters of art.

Interestingly, Kant does not develop the notion of exemplariness in any substantial further terms. But it is possible to do so, and to do so, indeed, in surprising depth. The decisive factor here consists in developing the logical scope of specific art media, i.e. the semantic and syntactic codes which are the basis of their formative articulations.

It is important, however, to note one factor which does not satisfy this criterion, namely those acts of artistic designation which I have discussed in my first two chapters. It is possible to designate any item or state of affairs as having such and such meaning in relation to art and art theory. But if this meaning can only be generally recognized through reference to some supporting documentary or critical discourse, then it is merely yet another illustration of the western dogma that the artist can, in principle, designate anything as art. It does not expand the semantic and syntactic scope of the medium in a way that can be exemplary for other artists qua artist. In many cases, we have no more than the 'original nonsense' noted above.

To see what exemplariness really centres on, we must focus on those factors which are part of the full definition of a specific medium's logical scope. In Chapter 1, I introduced the notion of artistic originality in primary and secondary senses. The former involves the achievement of a style whose distinctive features can be recognized by comparison and contrast with other works in that medium, rather than by external documentary

---

[19] In Christine Battersby's insightful *Gender and Genius: Towards a Feminist Aesthetics* (London: The Women's Press, 1989). Kant's theory of genius is somewhat misrepresented, through the author focusing on his more populist lecture courses, rather than on the conceptually grounded theory proposed in the *Critique of Judgement*. The former courses pre-date and are largely eclipsed by his Critical philosophy.

evidence. Secondary originality concerns the way in which individual works refine this style, or maintain high levels of formal achievement in relation to it.

Now a work which attains these modes of originality is already a contribution to the canon. It has added something new to the medium of which it is an instance. Other artists can learn from it, even if this amounts to no more than simply working in, or exploring, that style.

In canonic terms, however, exemplariness can amount to much more than this if it explores and clarifies possibilities basic to the medium in question. Consider, in this respect, the distinction between the linear and painterly emphasis in pictorial style. The former emphasizes outline and clearly defined plastic contours, whilst the latter blurs edges and is orientated instead towards broad masses, and foreshortening achieved by graduated and diffuse effects of tone and shadow.

Now it might be thought that these two tendencies merely describe aspects of how certain western paintings from the Renaissance onwards *appear* to the viewer. Their significance however, is much deeper—in transhistorical and transcultural terms.

This is because they express the two logically basic ways of acting upon a plane surface in order to create a three-dimensional image. One can either incise it, characteristically to delineate contours; or one can place marks upon it, so as to gradually build up an impression of the represented object's plastic substance. It is of course, also possible to combine these and, in effect, *all* pictorial creations can be positioned along a notional continuum with incised markings at one extreme, and the accumulation of marks upon a surface at the other.

And this is the real significance of the linear/painterly pairing. As stylistic emphases they look back towards these primal alternative possibilities of pictorial formation. This is why, in principle, they can be applied to any historical or cultural context. There is always, accordingly, the possibility that a pictorial practice will become orientated to one of these basic formative possibilities, and will significantly renew it, or innovate in relation to it.

We can now understand the key meaning of exemplariness. This takes on its most canonic importance when a style significantly develops factors which are basic to the semantic and syntactic scope of the medium concerned (as in the case of the linear/painterly pairing just described). I say 'scope' rather than 'structure' here because many semantic and syntactic factors require a great deal of historical development—in diachronic terms—before they are fully articulated.

Such technical transformations and aesthetic achievement are necessarily (though not sufficiently) correlated. It is this correlation (rather than the preferences and interests of dominant power groups) which explains and justifies the notion of a canon. As I argued in Chapter 1, any body of work that has a significant individual style gets a foothold in the canon. If other artists find this style attractive, it may become exemplary through being copied or otherwise adapted—albeit in a historically (and sometimes geographically) limited way.

But those works which are canonic in the most important sense are those whose individuality is achieved through refinement or innovation in relation to factors which are fundamental to their medium's syntactic and semantic structures. They are exemplary in recurrent, transhistorical terms. In terms of the visual arts, for example, Poussin's articulation of linear values and Rubens's articulation of the painterly are so fecund, that, for the next two centuries, the terms *Poussinisme* and *Rubenisme* are used to describe the two dominant formal vectors of European painting.

These considerations embody the most important criterion of artistic merit. If an artist is original, not just, say, in his or her colour schemes but in terms which innovate or refine so as to expand or illuminate the medium's basic logical scope, then the formative power of the medium is also enhanced. Far-reaching possibilities are opened up for other artists and for their audiences. Literally and metaphorically new ways of seeing the world aesthetically are opened up.

The great virtue of developing Kant's approach, then, is that by emphasizing the semantic and syntactic codes of art, it reorientates the analytic standpoint towards the art object and the history of its modes of creation, rather than towards the art consumer and the conditions of critical reception.

Kant's aesthetics proves enormously fruitful in terms of clarifying the normative significance of the aesthetic per se, and of the particular claims of art in this respect. It would be possible, in principle, to write the remainder of this book as an extension of the ideas from Kant which I have expounded and phenomenologically developed in this chapter.

However, whilst being broadly consistent with his position, much of what has been argued already goes considerably beyond what Kant explicitly countenances. And since the cognitive structures of the arts are so individually rich, it will be necessary to go much further still. Kant will, accordingly, hereafter feature episodically in my arguments, rather than as their fulcrum.

4

The Scope and Value of the Artistic Image

Introduction

Having identified the key characteristics of aesthetic experience and art in the previous chapters, it is now time to clarify the general nature and scope of the artistic image. This involves analysis of the role of style, and its complex relations to cognitive aspects of experience and canonic value.

In Section 4.1, I further elaborate how the image involves a stylistic interpretation of its subject matter, and that the notion of 'image' can encompass literature and music, and even abstract art. In Section 4.2 I clarify further the dynamic role of style in the image through an analytic appropriation of ideas from Gadamer. In Section 4.3 I introduce some points concerning the structure of experience,[1] and, in Section 4.4 link these to my treatment of Gadamer. This linkage illuminates the extraordinary ways in which art (and the aesthetic experience of it) exemplifies fundamental cognitive competences and relations.

Section 4.5 considers the way in which this meaning is activated. The focus of attention here is the particular artwork's achievement of indi-viduality in terms of the comparative history of its medium. This allows a fundamental normative distinction to be made between art with a small *a* and Art with a large *A*. Finally, Section 4.6 will address the problem of making judgements of merit or demerit within the realms of *art* and *Art*. Formalist approaches to this will be given critical scrutiny.

---

[1] By 'structure of experience' I mean those competences and relations which are necessary conditions of objective knowledge and personal identity. As we have already seen, imagination and understanding are of decisive significance in this respect.

4.1

Suzanne Langer was famously wary of the term 'image' because of its strong visual connotations, but no alternative to it has become established. Pictorial and sculptural works remain prototypes, accordingly, of what it is to be an artefactual image. Given this, it is worth considering briefly why music and literature also have a prima facie case to be counted as artefactual images. And then to consider (at somewhat greater length) the rather more startling possibility that abstract art has a distinctive artefactual image-character.

Langer has suggested that 'the tonal structures we call "music" bear a close logical similarity to the forms of human feeling—form of growth and of attenuation, flowing and stowing, conflict and resolution, speed, arrest, terrific excitement, calm ... Music is a tonal analogue of emotive life.'[2]

The final remark here is unnecessarily parsimonious. As I will show at great length in Chapter 7, music has the character of virtual expression of both emotional characteristics of a gestural kind, and the narrative developments which sustain their emergence. It is a distinctive image of these things. The most important code involved (in the west at least) is that of tonality. In western cultures the tonal system is learnt from childhood in terms of associations of the aforementioned sort. Likewise the quasi- or neo-tonal scales of non-western cultures. Such associational logic even permeates our hearing of serial or aleatory pieces.

The image-character of literature is rather more complex than those of the visual arts and music, since here elements of a pre-given symbolic formation—namely language itself—are made into a sensible manifold. But what is it that gives literature a sensible or sensuous meaning that the merely descriptive levels of language do not have?

Let us consider first the example of poetry. It is one thing, say, to describe the experience of love or a visit to Slovenia, and another thing entirely to make these experiences—real or imagined—into a poem.

The crucial point is that in making a description we are consuming the description in its referential function; but in writing a poem, in contrast, we are seeking to articulate and preserve an actual or possible personal

    [2] Suzanne K. Langer, *Feeling and Form* (London: Routledge & Kegan Paul, 1953), 27.

experience of love or Slovenia, or whatever. In poetry we are concerned not just with ideas and relations but with the poet's personal experience of these, and, in particular, his or her *style* of language.

We are invited, in other words, not just to recognize a meaning or set of meanings, but to *inhabit* the poet's experience of them—to share a way of seeing the world. This solicitation, indeed, is a necessary part of the meaning.

Similar considerations apply in the case of narrative literature. The world is projected for us in terms of imagination—an address to the feelings, senses, and intellect in concert—rather than the factual schemas of the intellect alone.

Now what makes these various literary sharings of the author's experience more than metaphorical is the fact that they are embodied in language. The words are the author's; but the way in which they are articulated is one which engages the reader or audience's imaginative involvement. We are not simply presented with a factual description of events or experiences. Nor is the work a simple reference to the artist's intentions. Rather the literary format allows us to experience the events or experiences described *as if* we were the subject of them, or, at least a protagonist in the action described. It is our own distinctive imagining which is involved but its form (to put it crudely) is the author's own experience *as exemplified in the format and style of the work.*

In this respect, for example, the novelist does not simply present us with a narrative and then (as it were, in parenthesis) indicate the various significant events, actions, and motives which determine the structure of the narrative. Rather he or she welds these together in a unified succession of images. Style, in the senses described in the Introduction to this book, *interprets* its subject matter. We encounter the salient events of the plot, hatched out from a matrix of other events. As Merleau-Ponty observes: 'The function of the novelist is not to state … ideas thematically but to make them exist for us in the way things exist.'[3]

Further aspects of the image-character of literature will be made clear in Chapter 5. However, we must now address a much more problematic issue. It is that of extending the scope of the image to abstract art.

---

[3] Maurice Merleau-Ponty, *Signs*, trans. Richard C. McCleary (Evanston: Northwestern University Press, 1964), 46.

By abstract art, I mean non-figurative paintings, sculptures, earthworks, and some installations. For these to be understood as a mode of imaging, their meaning must be orientated mainly towards the work's phenomenal structure, and its interpretation of some subject matter.

But there is an immediate problem of ambiguity. In Chapter 1, I explained the extreme difficulty faced by Danto's 'is' of 'artistic iden-tification' whose exact application in the particular case—even when the object or whatever is appropriate to the theoretical intentions which sustain it—remains fatally open. In order to make abstract works meaningful other than through their relation to external contexts, then, we must take a very different approach to that of Designation theory.

A good starting point is the fact that abstract works—and even most Conceptual ones—are presented in display formats (e.g. being framed, put on a plinth, or simply placed in a gallery per se). They are thus parasitic upon the expectations raised by more conventional modes of visual image-making. And this means that we will tend to ask what, in visual terms, they represent.

Designation theorists can go along with this as a general point, but give no concrete meaning to 'represent' over and above vague reference to the artist's theoretical intentions. However, just as pictorial representation achieves reference through its use of a codified natural phenomenon, namely visual resemblance, abstract art also does so—albeit in a much looser, and much more complex, way. The basis of this is *a presumption of virtuality*. By virtue of its presentational formats, the abstract work is taken to be 'about' some visually significant item or state of affairs other than itself, or (more unusually) about factors involved in its own particular way of being visible.

Now of course, blank canvases, and minimal works, by the likes of Yves Klein and Agnes Martin might be offered as counter-example to this, in so far as they literally contain nothing, or just about nothing. They might even be taken as attempts to resist 'aboutness'. However, even in such denial, the work's visual features can be strongly evocative of emptiness, desolation, and the like. They have a virtual loading. In fact, once an abstract work is placed in an appropriate display-context, none of its immediately visible properties are virtually inert.

This leads us to the main point. *Abstract works have intrinsic properties of optical illusion*—and thence virtuality. Colours and shapes, masses, and textures, and the spaces constrained or declared by them create illusions of depth, and, in some cases, motion. A single line or dab of colour upon a plane appears to cut into it or to emerge from it—depending on the nature of the specific line or dab. In the case of minimal idioms, the figure of emptiness, absence, or whatever, emerges from a ground which consists of the physical edge of the work. To make a mark on a surface, is constitutive of such illusionistic relations whatever one's other intentions might be.

Such illusions provide a point of orientation whereby abstract works can be approached. Because they are constitutive of the work qua visible object, *one cannot choose not to see them.* One might focus on some illusionistic properties rather than others, but one cannot describe the work in visual terms without reference to some of them.

Of course, an artist might say that optical illusion is simply not relevant to his or her intentions in the work. But if this is so, then it amounts to saying that a factor which is necessary to the work's *specific visual character* is irrelevant. In which case, the work is merely relegated to some kind of generalized 'prompt' for accompanying theoretical intentions. Should this be the case, there are no grounds for calling it art at all.

We now reach a key point. Optical illusion is encountered in many contexts, but to encounter it in abstract art is special. The presumption of virtuality means that we take it to be about something other than itself. But the question is, what?

If we are reading the work *purely in terms of the presumption and the work's immediate phenomenal character* there is only one general possibility available here, as far as I can see. The abstract work's shapes, colours, lines, textures, and volumes must be taken as representing possible modes of three-dimensional space-occupancy or as exemplifying two-dimensional modes. These modes of space-occupancy are not those described by ordinary pictorial representation, but rather the space of details and broader visual possibilities which subtend the ordinary appearances of visible things. The work is a stylistic interpretation of varieties of visual item and/or relation, which usually go unnoticed.

To explain. Given a three-dimensional item in the visual field, what enables its specific visual character is not only the immediate detail of its appearance but also its hidden aspects, or its possible transformations or relocations and indeed its relation to things beyond those which are immediately given. An embodied subject's objects of visual attention are not inertly registered. They emerge from a context of hidden visual aspects and possibilities which reconfigure in correlation with the subject's changes of perceptual orientation. This not only extends to factors which are literally hidden from view, but also to ones which are present only as possibility or fantasy.

I am arguing, therefore, that there is a *contextual visual space* which subtends and makes the immediately visible world intelligible to us qua visual. It is the factor which enables us to inhabit visual space rather than have encounters with a two-dimensional field of the proverbial (but only notional) 'raw givens'.

The description of this contextual space is, in any terms, massively complex. This is probably the main reason why it has not been fully invoked before in the explanation of abstract art (or at least, not in the relatively comprehensive way in which I am presenting it).

In what follows, therefore, I will analyse seven basic dimensions which structure contextual space. As far as I can see, these are comprehensive. (It may be, however, that they could be very usefully subdivided, or that there are combinations of them which are so potent and important as to be considered dimensions in their own right.) The dimensions are:

1. those adventitious correspondences or associations which occur when colours, shapes, or textures resemble specific visible forms other than themselves (e.g. seeing faces in clouds);

2. visual forms suggestive of gestural correlates for particular kinds of states of mind (e.g. 'violent' shapes or 'melancholy' colours);

3. items, relations, or states of affairs which are inaccessible to visual perception under normal circumstances, e.g. small or microscopic surface features, internal configurations, highly evanescent atmospheric effects, and unusual perceptual perspectives (e.g. aerial viewpoints);

4. possible visible items, relations, or states of affairs which might exist in alternative physical and perceptual environments to our usual one;

5. visual configurations arising from the destruction, deconstruction, reduction, reconstruction, or variation of familiar items, relations, or states of affairs;

6. visual traces or suggestions of past, future, or counterfactual items or states of affairs;

7. the structural features of spatial appearance—emphasized individually or in combination; these features comprise such things as colour, shape, volume, mass, texture, density, geometrical structure, and changes of position;

8. dreams, and cognate fantasy phenomena.

We now reach a decisive point. Any abstract painting opens up a virtual space. If this space does not consist of familiar visual items, then—in so far as we take the painting to be 'about' something—its optical properties *must* be referred to some aspect of the contextual space just outlined.

It might be objected that we cannot insist that a work 'must' allude to some aspect of this space. Perhaps the artist intends something which is not itself visual (for example, 'inner states' of feeling or other 'dimensions' of reality). Indeed, the allusion to contextual space cannot be inferred without evidence that such meaning is intended. The recognition of such meaning, of course, would involve reference to factors external to the work itself (such as the artist's writings).

Against these objections we must insist that art is primarily a social, and only secondarily a private, activity. Hence, if an artist wishes to represent some non-visual meaning through a visible configuration, he or she must *utilize* idioms which draw on a shared visual cultural stock with an associational range which encompasses the intended sorts of non-visual meaning.

Aspects of contextual space provide this. In the case of states of feeling, indeed, whilst their visceral components may be purely psychological, their behavioural criteria often encompass the visible dimension. We ascribe such and such a state of mind on the basis of how people look, and the things which they choose and do in relation to social and other visual environments. These criteria enable that correlation of visual form and appropriate states of mind which is level (2) of contextual space.

The role of the artist's intentions in abstract art must also be thought through in relation to art as a social practice. A painter may create a frenzied and gloomy-looking work, for example, that generally suggests, say, a position within a storm at sea, but never actually thinks of the latter association, and actually intends the frenzied appearance of the work as a life-affirming harmony of complex formal elements.

Now if this work is created so as to be viewed by an audience other than the artist, then it is self-defeating. Objectively, the work is frenzied and gloomy, and can, thereby, be rightly regarded as referring to an appropriate aspect of contextual space. The suggestion of a viewing position within a storm at sea—even if not noticed by the artist—is also a 'valid' association as long as it is visually consistent (however loosely) with the possibility of how things might appear from the midst of such a storm. We expect abstract works to utilize visual forms which evoke other such forms through adventitious resemblance. This is an established aspect of abstract art as a social practice.

This social context of expectations, precedents, and the presumption of virtuality in effect, *informally codifies* contextual space as the basis of meaning in abstract art. It gives it a social intelligibility which allows it to function as an established practice even though the nature of its code is so elusive. Everyone involved with this practice—creator or audience—has at least some unconscious understanding of aspects of contextual space.

Of course, the correlation between abstract work and contextual space is nothing near as determinate as that which holds between pictorial and sculptural images, and their referents. There is more openness and *positive ambiguity*. The work *alludes to*, rather than depicts, a specific subject matter. Contextual space defines the scope of possible virtual 'subject matter' here, but which of its aspects might be relevant to a particular work is only suggested.

Now it might be objected that the link between abstract works and contextual space takes us no further than Designation theories. Just as they leave artistic meaning systematically ambiguous, that is surely the case also with the approach just described. The notion of contextual space is so broad that we can make any work mean whatever we want in relation to it.

However, whilst there is openness of meaning involved, it is not at all arbitrary. And most importantly, *questions concerning it can be addressed at the level of the work's visible appearance, rather than at the level of external theoretical contexts.*

Suppose, for example, that a certain work evokes a sense of being a piece of striated rock magnified to an unusually large size. One can debate about the appropriateness of this characterization by comparison and contrast with other visual configurations. One can also suggest more appropriate associational content for this optical structure. The work may surprise and delight, indeed, through drawing on more than one possible aspect of contextual space, simultaneously.

In this latter respect, for example, it will be recalled that in Chapter 1 I offered a number of different intentions which might explain the description 'that black paint is black paint'. Amongst these were:

1. a metaphor for darkness, or oblivion, or blindness, or infinity;
2. the exemplification of supremely empty space;
3. the exemplification of a space packed to a point of absolute density.

These three possibilities are actually rather more than mere 'intentions' to be inferred from the work. Their deeper significance is to describe different optical gestalts in terms of which a person with imagination might see the painting, irrespective of whether the artist intended such meanings. The viewer could switch from one gestalt to the other (or see the work in terms of some other possibility) simply on the basis of visual consistency between the painting's configuration and a relevant aspect of contextual space.

One might, of course, try to pin all this down more exactly by reference to the artist's writings or whatever. In so doing, however, something important would be lost. For it is abstraction's *allusiveness* which gives it a distinctive evocative power that is congruent with the complexity of contextual space. This space is familiar enough to give us a general immediate orientation to such works—even if we have not explicitly formulated that space's general structure. (And this is true also of our general visual orientation. The visual field is only intelligible by virtue of latent space but we do not need a systematic theory of such space in order to operate within the visual field.)

The abstract work, accordingly, is of unexpected cognitive significance. It is an exploration of a level of vision which structures all aspects of the visual field, but which is usually unnoticed. It is an *allusive image*. This is one which selects and explores possibilities of contextual space from the artist's stylistic viewpoint. It is visually consistent with a range of such possibilities without being absolutely tied to any of them, individually.

I have argued, then, that all art—even abstract modes—has an image-character. It is a stabilized and enduring mode of representation, wherein a sensible or imaginatively intended manifold and a symbolic content are inseparably combined. And at the heart of this is the way in which it is done, i.e. the artist's *style* of articulation.

The image status of art requires careful further analysis to bring out the dynamic role played by style. This role, indeed, is one which focuses many complex cognitive features in the making and aesthetic experience of art. To understand these factors, I will make use of some important ideas from Gadamer's monumental *Truth and Method*.[4]

4.2

First, Gadamer's major positive strategy is to explain the essence of art by articulating its ontological structure. He finds the clue to this structure in the phenomenon of *play*. By play, Gadamer has in mind such things as children's games, sport, chess—any activity, in fact, which is both pursued for its own sake, and self-enclosed (in the sense of carrying rules to which the players must conform).

He further holds that whilst play is founded on behaviour tied to the realization of specific goals, its meaning cannot be reduced to such goals. It is rather a function of the event of playing itself. The game takes hold of the players, and, through them, achieves a kind of 'self-representation'. In this narrow sense, of course, all play is representational, but, as Gadamer points out, some games are representational in a stronger mimetic sense—for example, children's make-believe.

There are, no doubt, some grounds for disputing that play is a self-representational activity (or at least for claiming that it is no more so than any other form of human activity). However, this objection would not affect Gadamer's basic strategy. For given that there is such a thing as representational or mimetic play, the key step which he must make is to show how this illuminates the ontology of art.

---

[4] Hans-Georg Gadamer, *Truth and Method*, trans. William Glen-Doepel (London: Sheed and Ward, 1979). The most relevant area of this work is part I, sect. II, subsections a) and b). The best writer on Gadamer in English is Nicholas Davey. For a useful essay which offers a general perspective on hermeneutic aesthetics see his 'Hermeneutics and Art Theory', in P. Smith and C. Wilde (eds.), *A Companion to Art Theory* (Oxford: Blackwell's, 2002), 437–47. A more detailed and challenging approach to a central aspect of Gadamer's theory of pictorial representation can be found in Davey's paper 'Sitting Uncomfortably: Gadamer's Approach to Portraiture', *Journal of the British Society for Phenomenology*, 34/3 (2003), 231–46.

The step is taken as follows. Gadamer claims that art is the highest form of representational play, and in it, play achieves 'ideality' and 'transformation into structure'. Now whilst his arguments in relation to this are, unfortunately, rather unwieldy, their substance amounts to the following ...

First, mimetic play in general can be defined as a rule-governed activity which achieves reference to some aspect of the world other than itself. For Gadamer, artistic representation is an activity of this kind, but one which issues in the production of symbolically significant artefacts.

It is this latter fact which gives art its special status for it embodies a threefold relation between the artist, the world in general, and the audience. When representational play issues in an artwork, it is no longer an unstable event in progress, but rather a concrete set of mimetic relations which have become autonomous from the specific conditions under which they were produced, and which are now permanently accessible to a general historical audience.

This amounts to a 'transformation into structure'. The reason for this is not only that the artwork's content is embodied in a material concrete form, but also because the content is clarified. In representational play 'what is, emerges. In it is produced and brought to light what otherwise is constantly hidden and withdrawn.'[5]

For Gadamer, this involves a process of recognition, wherein 'what we know emerges, as if through an illumination, from all the chance and variable circumstances that condition it and is grasped in its essence'.[6]

Now in the case of content's essence, it is not simply a case of recognizing what kind of content is being referred to; nor is it a case of Heideggerian disclosure. Rather the artist's particular *style* of articulating his or her medium is decisive. As Gadamer puts it,

the presentation of essence, far from being a mere imitation, is necessarily revelatory. When someone makes an imitation, he has to leave out and to heighten. Because he is pointing to something, he has to exaggerate whether he likes it or not. Hence

---

[5] Gadamer, 'Truth and Method', 101. Kendall Walton has addressed some similar issues in his *Mimesis as Make-Believe: On the Foundations of the Representational Arts* (Cambridge, Mass. and London: Harvard University Press, 1990), 11–69. Walton emphasizes the continuity between play and make-believe and the complex functions of representation in pictures and literature. He is not concerned with the specific conditions of *artistic* representation, nor indeed, with how the ontology of image-making involves a transformation of the subject matter. These, in contrast, are the major issues which Gadamer addresses, and which I wish to develop.

[6] Gadamer, 'Truth and Method', 102.

there is an unbridgeable gulf between the one thing, that is a likeness, and the other that it seeks to resemble.[7]

The *crucial* implication of these remarks is that, in art, the revelation of essence centres on the artist's stylistic interpretation of content. The finished work refines content in the direction of what the artist takes to be its essential features vis-à-vis his or her relation to the world and to the artistic audience. Indeed, Gadamer sees the artwork as exemplifying the essence of experience itself. For example, in relation to the aesthetic reception of art, we are told that: 'Precisely because it does not combine with others to make one open experiential flow, but immediately represents the whole, its significance is infinite.'[8] And that the experience of art is the 'perfecting of the symbolic representation of the whole of life towards which every experience tends'.[9]

Now before considering what is problematic about Gadamer's position, I shall indicate something of its great strength. First, Gadamer's account is one which enables us to significantly develop the Kantian 'aesthetic idea'. It preserves a sense of the continuity between creative process, art object, and audience and declares the fact that all art has an event–character wherein the concreteness of the work qua work mediates the different interpretative horizons of creator and recipient.

More than this, Gadamer's account broadly indicates art's vital function in the continuity of what—in the previous section—I called *world-projection*. Let me explain this notion further and thence develop Gadamer's position.

To be self-conscious is a function of the coordination of our sensory and linguistic capacities. This means that any moment of awareness and cognition has both a sensuous and a conceptual/symbolic dimension. In most cognitive situations these dimensions will be very evenly balanced, in other situations one or other of the two elements will preponderate.

For example, in making mathematical calculations, or in problem-solving (in both practical or theoretical contexts) the conceptual element is to the fore, in so far as we are striving to deductively analyse or inductively generalize about items and their relations. Here, in other words, our capacity to comprehend instances of sameness and difference per se is the decisive element in cognition.

---

[7] Gadamer, 'Truth and Method', 103.   [8] Ibid. 63.   [9] Ibid.

There are other states of consciousness, however, where the conceptual core is much more weighted by the sensory dimension. For example, every moment of awareness is informed by latent knowledge concerning ability to recall past experiences, and to posit future ones, and to project possible perceptual situations coextensive with, but beyond the reach of, our immediate position in the phenomenal field.

Now whilst the ability to project beyond immediate perception in these terms, can be purely a process of thought, its more fundamental mode is *the image*. As we saw in Chapter 1, an image is a mental state which refers—and thence has a symbolic or conceptual content—but which does so on the basis of isomorphic consistency between aspects of itself and its referent's phenomenal structure. It has something of the sensory vivacity of immediate perception itself. Indeed, it may be that thought itself has its phylogenetic origins as a refinement of image-mimesis. The realm of imagery—be it exercised in memory or imagination—is the zone from which rationality emerges.

As we also saw in Chapters 1 and 3, imagination has an existential primacy. This does not mean that it is the basis of conscious life as such. Rather it is a disposition whose exercise is logically presupposed by our ability to acquire and apply language. Once the acquisition has taken place, images will be generated to assist cognition as and when required. In the case of desire and fantasy (including, but extending far beyond, sexual factors), indeed, imagery will play a dominant role. Imagination is the capacity which makes elsewheres and elsewhens live in, and enrich, the present.

On these terms, then, the cognitive life of self-consciousness finds its very flesh in imagery. Through memory and imagination, we project a quasi-sensory world of past actualities and alternative perceptual possibilities—a latent existential space—which informs and shapes our actual passage through the world. Games, sport, make-believe, and the like are play-activities where cognitive world-projection finds expression and development in publically accessible idioms.

Now we will recall that Gadamer sees play as the clue to the ontological structure of art. This is a major insight. For in linking play to art, he is, in effect, showing that art has its origins and structure in an element which is fundamental to self-consciousness itself. In affirming this, Gadamer is preparing the ground for a proper understanding of what separates artistic truth-claims from those which characterize other forms of knowledge.

The key point here is that art stems directly from the experience of shared subjectivity—from a mutual recognition of common forms of relatedness to the world. Such recognition involves a kind of seeing the world from where the other sees it.

At the heart of this experience is the fact that, in art, sensuous embodiment and symbolic content are necessarily related. In effect, Gadamer is following up and redirecting Hegel's most general position on art—namely that it is a mode of knowledge midway between the sensuous immediacy of material things and the abstractness of pure thought.

This is correct. What is distinctive about art as a form of knowledge is that it is not a body of abstract truths derived by generalization or deduction from sets of relations; nor is it a simple item present to the senses in purely material terms. Rather it is a function of the zone of imagery—of world-projection—where abstract thought itself emerges from a mode of more corporeal and sensuous mimetic reference.

Whilst Gadamer's theory directs us towards art's distinctive status as a form of knowledge, it has, nevertheless, some shortcomings. For a start, the points which I have just made vis-à-vis art's relation to self-consciousness and world-projection are only indicated by him in the most general and schematic terms. A more serious worry concerns his claims about the artwork exemplifying the essence of experience. A claim of this sort is necessary; in so far as art transforms play into 'structure', i.e. it is a full realization of tendencies which are only hinted at in play and games. Only in art, in other words, does image-mimesis attain the status of knowledge.

But why is this so? We will recall that Gadamer suggests that in the artwork we find a revelation of essence, which, in our experience of it, does not simply combine with other experiences in an 'open experiential flow'. Now the very fact that the artwork is a symbolically significant artefact means that we do not experience it as we would an ordinary material thing.

This, however, does not, of itself, explain why—as Gadamer also holds—the artwork is a symbolic presentation of 'the whole of life, towards which every experience tends'. Until this point is clarified, the exact determination of art's distinctive symbolic form remains incomplete.

In this respect Gadamer does offer us one further illuminating clue in the course of his discussion of the visual arts. Consider the following remarks concerning picturing: 'now that the original is represented, it experiences, as it were, an increase in being... if it represents itself in this way, this is no longer any casual event, but is part of its own being. Every such representation is an ontological event and belongs to the ontological level of what is represented.'[10]

Gadamer is here making a metaphysical point derived from Neo Platonism. The subject of the picture is a 'one' from which the picture itself is an emanation of overflow. Given this, 'if what is originally one, does not grow less from the overflow of the many from it, this means that that being becomes more'.[11]

Now stated in this metaphysical way, there is much about Gadamer's point which is puzzling and obscure. Not least of his problems is the fact that whilst by definition pictures are of a recognizable *kind* of subject matter, this does not presuppose that the subject is an original in the sense—which Gadamer clearly intends—of being actually existent. Many pictures for example, are of imaginary subjects.

However, if we interpret Gadamer's metaphysical point in an ontological or existential sense, a clearer set of possibilities emerge. By treating the artist's *experience* of a subject matter (be it real or imaginary) as the original, then we might see the artwork which results from this as a kind of 'increase in being' for the original. This interpretation indeed, would also allow Gadamer's point to encompass artworks in addition to the visual.

---

[10] Ibid. 124. Gadamer's approach to picturing is very different from that of the literature in the Analytic tradition. He focuses primarily, on the picture's ontological implications for its subject matter, i.e. how the representation literally re-presents its subject matter, in stylistic terms. Analytic approaches, in contrast, tend to dwell upon the logical basis of picturing's referential function, or the conditions under which the picture is perceived. The vast Analytic literature on this topic includes Dominic M. Lopes, *Understanding Pictures* (Oxford: Clarendon Press, 1996); Robert Hopkins, *Picture, Image, and Experience: A Philosophical Inquiry* (Cambridge: Cambridge University Press, 1998); Andrew Harrison, *Philosophy and the Arts: Seeing and Believing* (Bristol: Thoemmes, 1997); Flint Schier, *Deeper into Pictures* (Cambridge: Cambridge University Press, 1986); and David Novitz, *Pictures and their Use in Communication: A Philosophical Essay* (The Hague: Martinus Nijhoff, 1976). All of these works give special attention to a key problem deriving mainly from Nelson Goodman's *Languages of Art* (Indianapolis: Hackett and Co., 1976), namely that resemblance is *not* a necessary condition of visual representation. Lopes's book has considerable scope and insight vis-à-vis understanding the many different forms of picturing, and their historical being. Hopkins and Schier pay special attention to the conditions of spectatorship. Further approaches with this latter emphasis include Richard Wollheim, *Painting as an Art* (London: Thames & Hudson, 1990), and Ernst Gombrich's *Art and Illusion* (London: Phaidon, 1978).

[11] Gadamer, 'Truth and Method', 124.

In order to develop this approach, it is first necessary to consider some basic facts about the ontology of experience.

4.3

First, every moment in human experience is determined and given its specific character by its relation to *all* the moments which preceded it, and by anticipations concerning non-immediate experiential possibilities and the future in general. It is an intentional state—in the sense of being directed towards some object of consciousness. But the emergence to consciousness of this intended object and, indeed, the state's particular characterization of it, depend on its relation to other such states. Indeed, an experience's own identity as a particular experience, is *defined* in relation to the totality of the subject's other experiences and projections of possibility. To explain further. It is difficult to determine how intentional states from our past causally affect those of our present. Some past events are much more significant than others in how they influence current decisions. But, if one were to remove even the smallest previous intentional element from the network of past states, then it would follow that the causal network upon which our present is founded would be transformed. Given one small change, an accumulating wave of other such changes (increasing exponentially) would have to be posited, thus completely changing the character of the whole. On these terms, who we are now would not be possible.

This conclusion could only be avoided if it were possible for some past experiences to be totally inert in terms of their causal role in our personal history. It might be argued that certain *conditions* of our conscious activity—such as breathing or perspiring—might be exempted from this role in so far as their occurrence does not presuppose the mediation of intentionality, but these are, at best, exceptions rather than the rule. Experience occurs within a broader physical continuum of causal regularity between our intentional acts and is necessarily subject to the rules of this continuum.

In consequence, even the smallest intentional state from a specific time in someone's personal history must have some knock-on causal effect on those states which take place after it. Now whilst the psychological narrative continuity of experience may be different from that of the physical order, its causal basis is necessarily bound to that order. This means that the character of any particular experience must be dependent on all those which have preceded it—whether or not we can explain the exact pattern of influence.

The identity of any present experiential state is also influenced by our beliefs concerning things which are not present in the immediate perceptual field, and by anticipations of the future. It should be emphasized that the latter does not involve any notion of backwards causality in so far as it is determined by what we believe the future to hold rather than by its actual content.

On these terms, then, our present experience is shaped in causal terms by the totality of intentional states from our previous history, and by a more abstract, notional sense of the totality of events which awaits us.

However, it is one thing to imply the totality of life, and another thing entirely to *symbolize* it. True, there are privileged moments in any person's experience, wherein one feels oneself to be at a crucial stage in existence—one towards which the totality of events in one's life so far have been, as it were, pointing; and around which future events will constellate.

This awareness of totality is, however, fragmentary, and quickly submerged in the general experiential flow. Hence, if the whole of a person's experience is to be symbolized in a full sense, it must be through a medium which, whilst being something directly present to the experiential subject, is also in some sense autonomous from his or her experience. It must, in other words, be made into an artefact.

Now (as I noted in the preceding section) for Gadamer the artwork is, in effect, a continuation of that capacity—necessary to all self-consciousness—which I called world-projection. The work is a made image—a sensible manifold wherein overt symbolic or referential content is stylistically interpreted, on the basis of learned techniques and communicative codes.

It is thus ontologically akin to the world-projection aspect of experience, whilst, at the same time, being physically autonomous from its creator. The significance of this, of course, is that in artefact form, the image endures. Indeed, it embodies an overt symbolic content which (in a way that a mundane artefact does not) *invites* interpretation from the audience. Already, therefore, we can see how in art experience might be said to enjoy an increase of being. However, this is only the most basic level. I shall now consider its further possibilities.

4·4

The first one concerns the subjective aspect of the artist's creativity. It must be emphasized that the artwork is not simply an external analogue of some completely pre-given private experience. Again, Merleau-Ponty usefully observes: 'As for the novel, although its plot can be summarized and the "thought" of the writer lends itself to abstract expression, this conceptual significance is extracted from a wider one, as the description of a person *is* extracted from the actual appearance of his face.'[12]

What is decisive here is not the 'what' of representation, but the style in which this is done—the artist's interpretation of appearance. The creator has an intention to create, to produce an image addressing such and such an area of his or her experience, or imagined experience. This intention guides the creative process, but in the course of working the material, it may be changed, reinterpreted, or even totally transformed. Style is paramount.

The finished artwork is, thereby, more than a sensible surface which addresses a certain range of experience. For the artist knows that his or her work did not simply happen as the sum of an accumulation of discrete moments. Even if the work is formally or technically simple, through style it condenses and preserves data drawn from experience reaching deep into the artist's past and projections of the future, and embodies them in the unity of the present finished artwork. The work is thus, subjectively speaking, a symbol of the whole of the life which informs it.

This subjective increase of being for the artist's experience has an objective counterpart for his or her audience. In this respect, the audience recognizes that sensible form with such and such a significance is being addressed. However, the artist's particular style is one which interprets this significance. It serves (as Merleau-Ponty says in a fine phrase somewhere) to 'carve out relief in things'. It is a made *image*, i.e. one which interprets its subject matter through style in dealing with a medium.

---

[12] Maurice Merleau-Ponty, *Phenomenology of Perception*, trans. Colin Smith; rev. Forrest Williams (London: Routledge & Kegan Paul, 1974), 151.

Now it is often remarked upon by formalist aestheticians that the enjoyment of organic unity per se is fundamental to the aesthetic experience of art. This is true, but it is by no means the whole truth. For given the fact that the artwork *itself is* an event of stylistic interpretation in the sense just described, its organic unity takes on a deeper significance. The artist has articulated his or her subject in just *this* way. He or she offers us a personal vision of what is of aesthetic worth or broader human significance in the subject.

However, this vision is not something simply imposed on, or translated into, the work. Neither is it simply the sum of the parts. Rather it emerges as a unity from the parts, even as (qua organizational principle) it determines the particular character of those parts. The audience knows further that this emergence is of futural significance. It may change the way we experience our own lives. It may even be subjected to radical reappraisal by generations yet to come. All genuine interpretation is *effective history*.

Now the point to gather from all this is that at an objective level the artwork symbolizes the totality of human life in a kind of qualitative sense. It exemplifies the way in which particular experience necessarily emerges from a network of broader relations—both subjective and objective—to which it gives a determinate character, and which it situates in terms of anticipations of the future.

On these terms the artwork embodies experience's basic reciprocal structure. It presents that structure not in abstract factual terms but as an object at the level of perception. This means that in the experience of art, a fundamental structure in experience itself is grasped at the ontological level that is fundamental to self-consciousness—namely the embodied subject's reciprocal interactions with the sensible realm in which it inheres. In art, experience increases in being in the sense of attaining a mode of self-possession.

There is also one final sense of increase of being which is pertinent to art. In fact, it is the most decisive of all. Every event in one's life knits together in a web of finite, mainly contingent decisions. What we decide and what we do may be explicable in broad terms, but we have no vantage point from whence all the factors involved can be exhaustively and definitively computed. From a finite perspective all our deeds, individually considered, have a contingent aspect. We can never fully realize or preserve all the causal routes which give form to our present position in life.

But through art we can, at least in a symbolic way. This is because of the active relation between the physical process of making and the finished work. In the process of making, each decision and act—no matter how logically connected—occurs within a broader matrix of contingent choice and happenstance. The accumulation of choices and acts takes the creative process further forward, but qua finite, the artist cannot recall the exact sequence of them as individual factors. In the physical act of making, writing, and composing, or whatever, the individual creative steps retain a substantially contingent aspect. They are mainly lost in the flux of accumulating experiences.

In relation to the finished artwork, however, the situation is transformed. Even though the artist does not retain knowledge of every step in the creative process, he or she knows that—vis-à-vis the end product—these are all *individually necessary* to the identity of the finished work. Not one tiny step or aspect of the process can be removed. To do so would mean that the exact causal nexus which gave rise to the finished work would have followed a different route, and thence would not have been able to issue in just the work that it did.

This has an existential as well as causal meaning. For it means that in relation to the finished work all the individual steps of the creative process are *notionally preserved and declared* in the sensible particularity of the finished work, even if they cannot be individually identified in exact terms. They are redeemed from a mere passage into oblivion precisely through being embodied in the identity of the work. Every element in the process becomes meaningful in terms of the completed artefact.

Both artist and audience know this, intuitively. When one attends to the relation between whole and parts in the phenomenal or imaginat- ively intended artistic manifold, one deals with a passage from individual contingency and loss to necessity and redemption. The whole and parts are embodiments of experience and not *just* pleasing formal elements and structures. In the making and reception of art, the work acts upon exper- ience and increases its being through the preservation and declaration of individual aspects, in the necessity of the finished work's structure.

Of course, it might be claimed that any individual experience, or indeed, any made artefact per se, has exactly the same character as this, logically speaking. Its own character as an individual preserves and declares the preceding states which enabled it.

However, what is true logically speaking, is not true ontologically speaking. For whilst individual experience has the bare logical character just described, it cannot exist independently from the person who sustains it, whereas the artwork can exist independently of its creator. Indeed, the very fact of it being physically discontinuous from the artist gives it an ontological self-sufficiency and completeness which individual personal experiences do not have. Through being embodied in a *finished*, physically self-contained, and publically accessible form, the work enables the creative steps which informed its making to be ontologically preserved and declared rather than simply be present in unconscious form, as a network of, as it were, logical traces.

In the case of non-artistic artefacts, slightly different considerations apply. One of the reasons why we attend to the way in which art engages experience is because of its image-character. As we have seen, the image is a stylistic interpretation, and the details of its appearance can, accordingly, be a source of interest in their own right. In contrast, when a work is produced through formulaic artifice, and the specificity of its appearance (or imaginatively intended structure) has no necessary bearing on its meaning, or does nothing except in relation to some practical function, then that work is simply used. There is no reason to look for any additional dimension of significance.

This is true even if the formulaic artefact happens to be an image. If it is *too* formulaic, we receive the 'message' alone, and completely ignore the particular means which enable its communication (a point which I will return to in more detail in the next section).

The increase of being which I have been describing here, represents a kind of self-congruence of meaning in experience. Experience by definition involves a search for meaning in both particular and general terms. But that search is always on-going. There is no literal sense in which experience stops, and we can climb outside it so as to gather up and make ourselves at home with the complex causal nexus of events which have made us who we are, or which is implicated in the most significant episodes in our lives, or in our understanding of less momentous things.

In art, however, the creator finds a form for embodying experience which preserves and declares the conditions of its meaningfulness as a part of its own meaning qua particular. *That which makes meaning is sensibly exemplified, rather than understood in logical terms alone.*

I have argued, then, that art is to be defined as that mode of artifice which is embodied in stylistically significant images. Through this embodiment it exemplifies structures which are necessary to self-consciousness, in a unique way. This is the first major axis of art's normative significance. Earlier in this book, however, I also indicated a second normative axis, and it is this which we must now consider in more detail.

4.5

The issue can be focused initially in terms of the distinction often drawn (and also frequently denied) between the products of mass culture and those of 'high art'.

For present purposes, one could put the problem like this. Kitsch paintings, pop songs, TV soap operas, and the like, are all kinds of image, but the term 'art' would seem travestied if applied to them.

The task, then, is to clarify the conditions under which art in the sense of image per se becomes art in the sense of the second normative axis. This means specifically that we must consider the way in which general historical relations mediate the production and reception of art qua aesthetic object. For it is only under such conditions of mediation that the reflective significance of art—its distinctive power of experiential illumination—fully emerges.

In what follows, I will pick up and significantly develop some key aspects of Kant's theory of fine art (as broached in Chapter 3). I start with the decisive notion of originality.

First, production in all fields of art-making—indeed artifice in general—involves the following of rules. Similar considerations pertaining to methodology, rigour, the gathering of evidence, and verification procedures, also guide the pursuit of forms of knowledge in general.

Now in the case of artifice (in industrialized societies at least) the bulk of production is effected simply by following rules. The criteria of functional efficiency which determine work processes and end products, make the particular identity of the producer into something contingent. Who one is as a person and one's particular interests, are abilities that may lead to one doing one job rather than another; special aptitudes, indeed, may mean that one does the job rather well; but these personality factors are only significant to the degree that they promote or are conducive to efficiency. They do not figure as a necessary element in either production or end product.

Similar considerations hold (albeit more controversially) in relation to theory or discovery in most forms of knowledge. Odd personality traits, good luck, or untoward conjunctions of circumstances, all play their role in the formulation of theory and the making of discoveries.

However, this role is entirely contingent. Given any body of knowledge in the human or physical sciences, it is entirely conceivable that some person or group of people *other* than those who formulated the knowledge in question, could have done so.

The essential features of Kant's philosophy, or Einstein's theories of Relativity, for example, could have been formulated by others—given, of course, that the historical framework and precedents which informed the formulation of such theories, had already been laid down. Likewise in the field of technological invention, someone other than James Watt could have invented the steam engine; someone other than Frank Whittle could have invented jet propulsion.

In the case of art, in contrast, matters are much more complex. Kitsch works, and most products of mass culture, are produced according to fairly distinct formulae of functional efficiency. Even here, however, the role of individual creativity can be more than simply a contingent one.[13]

The hugely successful TV soap opera *Coronation Street,* for example, was devised by Tony Warren in 1960. The idea for a drama series

---

[13] In his book *The Philosophy of Mass Art* (Oxford: Clarendon Press, 1998), 196, Noel Carroll argues that one can talk of 'mass art' if and only if three criteria are satisfied. First, the work must be an *artistic* instance of a multiple-instance format or type. Second, it must be produced and distributed through mass technologies (such as television). Third, it must be intended—through the appropriate narrative structures or symbolism—to allow access to its content through minimum effort on the part of a maximum number of untutored recipients. Carroll regards this tripartite structure as classificatory rather than evaluative. But the third criterion is, to say the least, ambiguous in this respect. On my terms, it is necessarily in conflict with artistic status through its stipulation of, in effect, a formulaic character for mass art. But surely a work can achieve artistic status using mass technologies and accessible idioms without necessarily adopting 'lowest common denominator' idioms? Indeed, I indicate how this is possible in the body of my text. My own sense is that the term 'mass art' should be treated, at best, as a synonym for what I call art with a small 'a' (i.e. images or decoration which serve basic communicative or entertainment functions). It would be better still to dispense with it altogether. For if a work in a mass medium transcends itself towards artistic meaning in the fullest sense, then it *is* art—no matter what medium or technology it happens to be embodied in. Hence, whilst the term 'mass art' might seem to strike a blow for marginalized idioms, the prefix 'mass' actually perpetuates the marginalization by qualifying the artistic status of those cases where such status is actually achieved.

based on northern English working-class life, of course, could easily have been devised by someone else; but the possibilities of plot and characterization presented by his original idea—the, as it were, flesh of *Coronation Street*—are very much a function of Warren's idiosyncratic original formulation.

In the case of 'high art', the role of individual creativity—expressed through style—is utterly and absolutely central, and should be stated in the strongest possible terms. The key concept here is *originality*. It has two basic dimensions—refinement and innovation. A work which refines is one whose style takes up established motifs and idioms and articulates them to an unprecedented degree of excellence. The innovatory work, in contrast, is, in some respects, unprecedented in the way it departs from existing motifs and idioms, and introduces new ones.

Now artistic originality is unique. For that which is original here, is style in a sensible material particular—viewed in relation to the traditions which inform production in that medium. This means that the original artwork is internally related to the identity of its creator or ensemble of creators. It is not produced by following a rule, but (at the very least) by varying the way in which a rule or technique of production within a medium is applied.

Of course, it is logically possible that two artists might produce two perceptually indiscernible paintings, or that two writers might produce two novels which are identical with one another, word for word. However, the point is that (even in this scarcely imaginable scenario) the works are created on the basis of the artists' own special gifts rather than by merely following rules. The conceptual connection between the identity of the creator is still presupposed.

A rather different 'marginal' issue arises in those cases where a work has multiple authorship based on direct cooperation between individuals. Many works attributed to Rubens, for example, were in fact done by him with major cooperation from studio assistants. In music, the Maoist *Yellow River Concerto for Piano* is a work which was composed by a committee. In such cases we are dealing with a unique creative ensemble rather than an individual artist. The question of who the real author of such a work is depends on the interactive dynamic between members of the ensemble. In the case of the *Yellow River Concerto* one assumes that genuine collective creatorship is involved. In the Rubens works, we acknowledge Rubens as the creator—unless the secondary contributions are so manifest as to warrant the qualifying description 'from the studio of Rubens' instead.

My major claim, then, is that (in contrast to all forms of technological production, and theory and discovery in other forms of knowledge) original art involves the personality of the creator (or identity of the creative ensemble) being internally related to the final product of artifice.

Earlier on I described the way in which art embodies ontological increases of being for experience itself. It is the individuality of a style—originality in its most basic sense—which facilitates this. Through being original the work attracts our attention, and we are then engaged, intuitively, by the internal relation between the identities of the artwork and its creator(s). All experience is a function of what is private to the particular embodied subject, and that subject's inherence in a shared world of things, other persons, institutions, and values. Now in the original artwork, individuality of vision is achieved through an interaction—harmonious or conflictual—with the shared world.

The reciprocity of individual self and otherness which is at the basis of all experience is here presented in the most positive terms as an enduring object of perception and/or imaginative realization. Self and other are experienced as mutually enhancing in a way that draws on the totality of the senses and imagination rather than on intellectual recognition alone.

There is a further key aspect to this. For to interact positively with one's fellow humans demands at the very least a respect for oneself and for other people. At the heart of this is a sense of mutuality—of problems, situations, and strategies shared.

Now in our interactions with other people, this mutuality is generally under pressure from, in the one direction, an excess of the abstract, and, in the other, an excess of the concrete.

The abstract dimension centres on the fact that no matter how much another person tells us how he or she thinks or feels, we can never—qua finite embodied subject—see the world from where the other sees it. The unfulfillable longing for such congruence constitutes, of course, the poignancy of human love. We need the fullness of the other's view of things, but it is not wholly available to us; it remains to some degree abstract.

At the opposite extreme there are many occasions, when, in the case of those whom we care for, or who are of interest to us, we become so preoccupied by them that this comes at great existential cost to ourselves. We feel under pressure to identify with their problems, or to offer advice, etc.

Now (in a metaphorical sense) the great *beauty* of style in original art is the way it situates us between these two extremes vis-à-vis mutuality. On the one hand we are shown a view of the world which is necessarily tied to the person who has created it, but which is not simply a factual report of how he or she happens to think or feel about such and such a subject matter. It is a sensible presentation of things which draws—through its very structure—on thought, the senses, and feeling. We touch the creator in real and concrete rather than abstract terms.

On the other hand, this is a work—a physical object that has become causally discontinuous from the physical existence of its creator, through being finished. This means that the other's vision which is embodied in the work is one which we can enjoy on our own terms to some degree.

We can recognize common interests and strategies, etc. without feeling that compulsion or pressure to recognize which is part and parcel of our direct social and emotional interactions with other people. We can also participate in those increases of being described in the previous section. The upshot of all this is a unique *aesthetic* mode of empathy, one where mutuality—in the sense of respect for the other and respect for self—is at a premium. It is a way of understanding—*a distinctive cognitive structure*—which cannot be derived from any other source other than art.

This experience can be characterized in terms of disinterested enjoyment in an interesting way. For whilst our enjoyment of the work logically presupposes that we believe it to have been created by some other person, it is not necessary that we have any knowledge of exactly who created it, or any knowledge about their lives or personal circumstances.

Factual knowledge of this kind may enhance our 'sharing' of the work's stylistic presentation of things, but we do not have to have such empirical knowledge of the artist's 'real existence' in order to appreciate it in such terms. And whilst such appreciation may have practical benefits, believing it to have such effects is not a necessary condition of it being pleasurable to us. In logical terms our enjoyment is—like so many other varieties of aesthetic experience—relatively disinterested.

Let me now summarize and comment on the scope of the artistic image. My basic point is that artistic originality of style is *sui generis*. Whereas in all other forms of production—be it technology or knowledge in the human and physical sciences—the personality of the producer is only contingently related to process and production, in art it plays a necessary role. This necessity enables the artwork to engage the distinctive aesthetic form of empathy just described.

It is crucial to understand the scope of this claim. The world of human choices and actions cannot be determined with the clarity of a mechanical system of slots and grooves. Human praxis has its opaque boundary zones; and art is no exception to this.

Here are some examples. First, as I noted earlier, much art is of the kitsch or mass culture variety. This means that it is derived closely from models already laid down, on the basis of formulae bound up with functional efficiency vis-à-vis entertainment value. In other cultures, images are often produced according to models laid down by tradition for very specific ritual purposes. In these cases, the work is generally consumed purely in terms of its ostensible function.

However, it may be that in comparison with other such functional artefacts, the work appears *original* in the senses which I described earlier. If this is so, the work will stand out in normative terms. It will bring about those increases of being and aesthetic empathy which are distinctive to the making and experience of art. Originality of style, as it were, energizes such potential.

This is also true of the applied arts, in a complex way. If some functional artefact such as a building, or a piece of cutlery or furniture, is created in an original way (in respect of its appearance or the way it fulfils its function), then it takes on a symbolic as well as sensible presence. It declares itself as a distinctive way of fulfilling that function. It becomes a self-representational manifold.

The most important boundary zone of all occurs within what is generally accepted within western or western-influenced culture as art practice. Hundreds of thousands of works are produced by students, amateurs, and aspiring artists. Many of these simply involve a coming to terms with motifs and idioms already established. Some will go beyond this in the direction of genuine originality but the bulk will not.

In this sort of case, matters can only be decided by debate concerning the specific example. One must decide such things as to what degree the artist's touch or choice in the articulation of particular details within the fabric of the whole is important. If key elements in the work's phenomenal fabric are left undetermined by the artist (i.e. basic instructions are issued but it is left to others to decide the exact nature of their realization), then the mode of creativity moves away from that involved in the making of original art.

The whole issue addressed by this chapter comes down to this. Human beings have the capacity to make images. Within this class of artefacts, there are paradigm cases which are original in a distinctive way that cannot be explained in terms which characterize techniques of production in other spheres of artifice, or in the formulation of knowledge. We need a word to pick out this unique and irreducible human practice. And, of course, we have one—*art*.

As a concept, art has evolved historically in concert with the decline of overt social function in favour of the making of images for their own sake. Practices concerned with overt social function alone can be used with a small 'a' in a very general sense to encompass image-making per se. However, Art with a capital 'A' is that mode of image-making whose originality is internally related to the existence of its creator or creative ensemble.

This dimension of originality changes our relation to the image. Rather than see it as mere decoration or as an object of functional or escapist significance, deeper levels of awareness are engaged. In enjoying the various aspects of its original formal structures, we find the exemplification of fundamental structures in self-consciousness itself. The world of otherness echoes our own being; its foreignness is overcome.

Now, of course there is no clear convention whereby we 'read' art explicitly in these terms. Rather the exemplification of self-consciousness is grasped *intuitively* along the lines set out in the Introduction to this book. Intuitive articulation occurs when understanding or recognition is achieved not through intellectual cognition alone, but through a complex coordination of concepts and sensibilia. We will pick up cognitive cues and avenues of perceptual and imaginative exploration, whose fullness resists adequate paraphrase. This fullness of meaning can be 'cashed out' in very basic conceptual terms (as in the present analysis, and the tradition from which it stems) but to do so is to denude the sensory and cognitive richness of the experience.

4.6

Having set out my general theory of the artistic image, some specific key issues concerning the evaluation of art need to be clarified.

For example, in using the two normative axes to explain the distinction between 'art' in the sense of mundane images, and 'Art' in the sense of original works, this might seem to entail that all examples of the former must be bad (or at least limited) in artistic terms whilst all examples of Art 'proper' must be good—by virtue of their individuality. But this would be counter-intuitive. On occasion, even the most minor works can be in some sense 'good' and some examples of Art 'proper' can be manifestly bad or mediocre. The proposed theory of the canon seems unable, therefore, to encompass a very basic evaluative truth.

This is an important point. The view which I am proposing, however, can accommodate it, and avoid the foregoing difficulty.

First, within the image-products of mass culture we do, indeed, make distinctions of value. Sometimes this will be in terms of mere functional efficiency, i.e. in relation to how well an artefact fulfils the purpose for which it was made. But within the frame of functional artifice further, more complex, evaluations can occur.

In terms of cartoons and TV comedies, for example, persons who attend closely to these idioms might enjoy idiosyncrasies in how the image is constructed in terms of design, colouring, scripting, or acting (as appropriate). On the basis of this, it will be possible to distinguish between images which are genuinely formulaic, and ones which also make us attentive to phenomenal details in how the format is developed in this particular case.

Sometimes such idiosyncrasies will actually enhance the entertainment function, but on other occasions they may restrict it to a narrow audience. In the latter case, over time, however, the work or series may develop the proverbial 'cult status'.

What I am describing here are ways in which, even in common mass-culture idioms, there is room for individuality, and thence artistic merit. Whether this merit is such as to make the work into Art with a capital 'A' depends entirely on the particular case. There is no reason at all why a work in a mass-culture format cannot, under the right circumstances, be good Art in the highest sense—a masterpiece, even (a point which is, of course, especially pertinent to film).

It is also worth noting that, even in functional contexts, it is probably useful for images which are intended to entertain or be decorative to have some kind of formal interest and transcend wooden plots, and monotonous repetitive characterization and the like. Likewise, if an image has expressive properties as part of its structure, it will be advantageous for them, usually, to be organized, and not stilted or simply stereotyped.

Formal or expressive merit may incline a work in either of the directions just mentioned. It might enhance entertainment or decorative function, but equally, it could become a source of interest in its own right. In the latter case, a work's artistic potential begins to be significantly realized.

Given these points, the nature of formal and expressive satisfaction in this context should be addressed. It is surely the case that formal unity—to be interesting—must involve some kind of relation between unity and diversity, and expressive qualities must be controlled but without falling into cliché or sentimentality and the like. However, the ways in which these criteria of merit actually apply is a function of the individual case, and, in particular, how the work compares with others of the same broad kind.

I am arguing, then, that even in products of mass culture, loosely canonic criteria can be involved in terms of both originality, and formal and expressive values.

However, whilst the products of mass culture can transcend themselves towards full artistic meaning, this is the exception rather than the rule. Such artefacts exist to inform, entertain, persuade, or to decorate. If their individuality stands out—for whatever reason—then they begin to play a very different kind of cultural role. They now move within the sphere of new ways of sensibly articulating experience and the world—an activity which, as we have seen, is of distinctive aesthetic significance. The focus of meaning in the image in such cases is qualitatively transformed from that of function to that of individual style. This is the realm of art.

The question arises then as to judgements of merit within art. Given the normative basis of Art, it might seem that even a poor quality work must be better than any example of mass culture.

But this does not follow. Those images which exceed their mass culture formats (in the ways described) can be of greater artistic worth than works in characteristic 'high' formats which turn out to be mediocre. Individuality of style is a necessary condition of artistic meaning, but not in an absolute sense. One cannot demand, for example, that *every* work by an artist establishes a new individual style. Rather we expect such style to be achieved and maintained through a sustained body of creative work. There are also several qualifying factors involved in this maintenance. They enable us to make distinctions of 'good', 'bad', 'middling' and the like in relation to art.

In this respect, it is vital to emphasize that originality in art involves negotiating formal and expressive qualities. These are inescapable. Qua phenomenal or imaginatively intended whole, the artwork is, by nature, a bearer of formal values. As a stylistic characterization of its subject matter from a specific human viewpoint it also has intrinsic expressive significance. We look, accordingly, for individuality of style which negotiates these dimensions in a satisfying way.

This being said, formal and expressive criteria have very little explanatory value beyond these general considerations. For whilst formalists spend much time spelling out the importance of such things as unity in diversity, or the avoidance of stereotype and cliché, what actually counts *as* unity and diversity or whatever, is no more than an empty formula, unless related to concrete examples. One's understanding of formal and expressive values depends on how they are applied through *comparison and contrast based on specific cases.*

For a long time in western art, it was possible to use exemplars in this context. In painting, for example, Raphael was taken to be a great combiner of all the excellences. However, subsequent developments in high art have challenged our very understanding of what formal and expressive values actually amount to.

This is especially the case with modern and some postmodern idioms where tendencies such as Expressionism and Dadaism seem to make a mockery of formal and expressive values *in any traditional sense.* However, the qualifying clause is crucial here. For even with painters such as de Kooning, Pollock, and Baselitz, careful comparison will show that their seemingly unstructured compositions can be argued to be, in key respects, actually well balanced, and, whilst extending beyond traditional criteria of formal or expressive harmony, etc., are still amenable to some analysis in terms of these notions.

Indeed, given a work, or any artistic *oeuvre* in any medium, it is possible to point out the ways in which—in comparison with other works by the same or other artists—the work stands out in formal or expressive terms, or, in contrast, simply follows a familiar format. If the latter, we are invited to consider whether it merely counts as a 'potboiler' or even a descent into unintended self-caricature.

The question arises as to whether there could be a work that was extremely original, but formally or expressively bad. Again this is a complex issue which depends fundamentally on the particular case. It is possible that, for example, when a work is first created, it seems to be wholly bad in formal terms, but that it is, nevertheless, taken up subsequently, as a way of doing things by other artists. *New criteria of formal and expressive unity can be created.* This would suggest that if a work's originality is artistically meaningful, it will establish a new form of unity, however at odds this may be with previous criteria.

What is not possible is for an artwork to have no relevant formal or expressive qualities whatsoever. For if it lacked these, then its originality would be entirely empty. Originality would be a property of the work, but not one which actually did anything to determine its aesthetic structure.

There are of course, some putative 'artworks' which are like this— namely Duchamp's unassisted ready-mades. These are items that do not stake any claim (through their medium or format) to formal or expressive significance. This means that we can only interpret them as bearers of some sort of theory. However, as I showed in my first chapter, this makes the work's meaning systematically indeterminate, and, at best, no more than an exemplar of theory.

I am arguing, then, that formal and expressive values regulate judgements of quality within art. They enable distinctions of good, bad, or whatever. One cannot make them into sufficient criteria of artistic merit, however, because of their dependence on comparative contexts. This is why my account of the canon has stressed originality. Formal and expressive quality are not the same thing as originality, but their application involves reference to the same kind of comparative context.

Our major interest in them concerns their *complex aesthetic significance* in constituting a style rather than their *simple* aesthetic appeal as formal or expressive qualities per se.[14] Indeed, if *that* significance were the major consideration, then natural beauty, copies, and forgeries should satisfy us just as much as original artworks.

But they cannot. For as I have shown at length, originality of style and an internal connection to the creator's identity are decisive factors in art's distinctive variety of the aesthetic. Even in judgements concerning a work's formal or expressive qualities, questions of merit are necessarily comparative and thence involve issues of originality.

Some formalists, of course, have offered an entirely different approach to all these issues. They have argued that aesthetic judgements are 'unanalysable' and 'intuitive' and based on the sensitivity of the observer.[15] I shall now consider this approach.

First, because such judgements concern the structure of sensible or imaginatively intended individuals, their aesthetic unity can never be paraphrased adequately. No judgement of aesthetic value can be made without the observer having had direct perceptual or imaginative acquaintance with the object.

However, whilst this imports an unanalysable element into aesthetic appreciation, it does entail that this element is absolute. One can give reasons why such and such a work is aesthetically meritorious, and support these by reference to comparative material. The decisive factor is that debate about this material should constellate around the sensible or imaginative particularity of the work itself—rather than, say, its mere conformity to established criteria of value.

In fact, if a person could not justify his or her assessments of artistic merit by reference to comparative material, we would have no reason for accepting them. To counter this, one might claim the logical possibility of a

---

[14] The contrast here is more or less the same one explored in Chapter 3 between beauty as such, and the more complex notions of artistic beauty and aesthetic ideas—which are mediated by knowledge of the form's artifactual origins.

[15] The most thoughtful example of this variety of formalism in recent years is Clement Greenberg's *Homemade Esthetics: Observations on Art and Taste* (New York and Oxford: Oxford University Press, 1999). It should be emphasized that whilst Greenberg is famed as a critic of the visual arts, his approach in this collection encompasses literature also. His basic position, however, is contradictory. This is because whilst he wants to hold that judgements of taste have objective validity, and involve comparative factors, he seems to reduce these to merely intuitive considerations. My point, however, is that the comparative dimension involved here, must of necessity have a diachronic historical character. The ultimate problem for Greenberg is that he emphasizes form rather than style, and thus lacks the key concept which would connect the artwork's phenomenal structure to its place in tradition.

kind of aesthetic *idiot savant*. Such a person has no knowledge of any history of the arts whatsoever, yet his or her artistic judgements always happen to pick out works which—independently of his or her verdicts—are generally accepted as high-quality art.

But in such a case, we can just as well insist on the chance element. Statistically there might be an *idiot savant* without comparative knowledge who always 'gets it right' about good art. However, the very fact that such a person cannot explain his or her judgements at all in comparative terms is *definitively* indicative of their chance character, and thence the fact that they are not authentic judgements of artistic merit.

This is because without reference to comparative criteria, what the *idiot savant* is judging is merely the aesthetic quality of formal appearance rather than that of stylistic interpretation. The former has a bearing on judgements of artistic merit, but it is not a sufficient criterion. To judge a work's merit qua art, the dimension of originality is necessarily involved, and recognition of this is *conceptually* connected to comparative historical knowledge of the medium.

The formalist claim that judgements of aesthetic or artistic merit are 'intuitive' is again partially true. In psychological terms we are rarely aware of all the complex cognitive and comparative factors which are at work in them. But it would make no sense to talk of a 'judgement' unless something was related to something else through the act of cognition. No matter how psychologically intuitive a judgement may be, in logical terms it must have some determinate cognitive content.

Now the vital point is that whilst such 'intuitive' judgements are not experienced through direct awareness of the logical factors involved, we can, in principle, become aware of these factors. Through introspection or by attending to the context of judgement, we can explain the salient features involved.

This is a case of what in the Introduction to this book, I called 'explicable intuition'. Such judgements are psychologically intuitive, but logically presuppose knowledge which can be explicitly comprehended. Judgements of artistic merit are like this. In psychological terms they may be intuitive, but they are logically enabled by familiarity with the history of the relevant medium.

Finally, let us consider the possibility of sensitivity as the basis of artistic judgement. Much hangs, of course, on the definition of 'sensitivity'. In

Chapter 1, I argued that a basic sensitivity to the aesthetic is a factor in the development of self-consciousness itself. But sensitivity in the present context is surely meant to be 'above average' or 'out of the ordinary'.

Now this is surely not a necessary or sufficient condition of judging artistic merit per se. In this respect, the example of the aesthetic *idiot savant*, noted earlier, is instructive. He or she may have an enhanced innate sensitivity to aesthetic form, but this cannot encompass judgements of artistic value for reasons already noted. Sensitivity is only relevant to such judgements in so far as it is grounded in the appropriate comparative knowledge of the medium. It is this comparative dimension which provides *evidential weight* for judgements of artistic merit.

It should be emphasized, however, that such knowledge is not a sufficient condition of such judgements. There may well be people with prodigious factual knowledge of history of the arts but with no ability to apply these in judgements of artistic merit. But that being said, the degree of sensitivity which is required to make such judgements does not entail sensitivity in any out-of-the-ordinary sense. Heightened sensitivity can facilitate judgements of artistic merit, but is in no sense constitutive of them.

Having outlined the distinctive scope and value of the artistic image in general terms, I will now address some cognitive structures which are distinctive to specific media and which give a special character to the making and aesthetic experience of them. This will also allow the identification of further factors which are *canonic* for the media in question.

PART III
Distinctive Modes of Imaging

5
Twofoldness: Pictorial Art and the Imagination

Introduction

To understand the fundamentals of pictorial art and its broader significance, I shall focus, in the first instance, on a key perceptual relationship. In *Art and its Objects*, Richard Wollheim observes that 'the seeing appropriate to representations permits simultaneous attention to what is represented and to the representation, to the object and to the medium'.[1] This is the fundamental issue which needs to be explored.

Interestingly, Wollheim's provisional characterization of 'twofoldness' or 'seeing-in' is then hardened by him. Twofoldness is not only permitted in our perception of pictorial art, it is actually demanded.

The most significant and important justification of this consists in Wollheim's claim that 'seeing-in derives from a special perceptual capacity, which presupposes, but is something over and above, straightforward perception. This special capacity is something which some animals may share with us but almost certainly most do not, and it allows us to have perceptual experiences of things not present to the senses: that is to say, both of things that are absent and also of things that are not existent.'[2]

In this chapter, I will qualify and develop this position so as to bring out some logically distinctive features of pictorial art. Wollheim himself tentatively links the 'special capacity' noted above, to phenomena such as dreams, daydreams, and hallucinations. This may be an apt linkage,

---

[1] R. Wollheim, *Art and its Objects* (Cambridge: Cambridge University Press, 1980), 213.
[2] Ibid. 217.

but it is by no means the decisive one. For the phenomena which Wollheim mentions are specific instances of a more general and fundamental capacity—namely imagination. Surprisingly, Wollheim himself does not interpret them in such terms, but it is an approach which allows the understanding of pictorial art's most decisive features.

As we have seen in previous chapters, imagination's central meaning is that of the capacity to generate images—mental states which refer to sensible phenomena, through (in part) resembling or being iconic with them in specifiable respects. The great benefit of this capacity is that, as Kant puts it, it constitutes 'the faculty of representing in intuition an object that is *not itself present*'.[3] Indeed, Kant also characterizes imagination as 'a blind but indispensable function of the soul, without which we should have no knowledge whatsoever, but of which we are scarcely ever conscious'.[4] In the main body of this chapter, I will argue that the twofoldness of pictorial art enables us to become conscious not only of imagination per se, but also of the specific characteristics which allow it to function as a necessary condition of experience. To show this I shall, in Section 5.1, outline a general theory of the transcendental significance of imagination.

Section 5.2, will use this account to develop and qualify some of the important ramifications of Wollheim's notion of twofoldness. It should be emphasized, however, that, in contrast to Wollheim, my approach throughout will focus on the making and appreciation of the artistic image rather than the simple perception of what it is of.

5.1

I begin by applying and further developing the Kantian approach to imagination which I outlined in Chapter 3. All animals have at least the

---

[3] Kant, *Critique of Pure Reason*, trans. N. Kemp-Smith (London: Macmillan and Co., 1973), 165. An alternative approach to the imagination and its relation to visual art can be found in Robert Hopkins's *Picture, Image and Experience: A Philosophical Inquiry* (Cambridge: Cambridge University Press, 1998). For a useful collection addressing the link between art and imagination in more general terms see M. Kieran and D. M. Lopes (eds.), *Imagination, Philosophy, and the Arts* (London: Routledge, 2003). A classic approach to the general problem remains Roger Scruton's *Art and Imagination* (London: Methuen, 1974). What separates my approach from all these, is its Kantian insistence on imagination in its *transcendental* function, as a necessary condition of experience.

[4] Kant, *Critique of Pure Reason*, 112.

capacity to attend to stimuli, to recognize prey and predator, to distinguish between possible mates and rivals amongst their own kind, and to distinguish between those creatures which are of their own kind and those which are not. They also have the capacity to follow familiar routes and tracks, and anticipate possible dangers.

These factors suggest that animals possess what Bergson calls 'habit-memory'[5] and the ability to apply what I shall call 'protoconcepts'. Let me elaborate these two notions in turn. First, habit-memory. Since the animal can attend to phenomena through successive moments of time, and is able to find its way back to the burrow or nest, or whatever, we must assume it has basic retentional capacities. This assumption is also compelled by the fact that the animal can anticipate possible danger and modify its behaviour accordingly.

Now this capacity to draw on past experience does not entail that the animal can recall specific facts from its own individual history. Rather it has a habit-memory analogous to that of human experience. For example, in learning to ride a bicycle, or to tie one's shoelaces, it is the accumulating of experience rather than being able to recall individual events in the process of learning which are decisive in giving us the skill. One might, of course, recall spectacular disasters which were involved—and these may have salutary instructive effects in the present, but these are not necessary in the acquisition and continuing exercise of the skill.

In the case of animals this is even more emphatic. One presumes that they have no capacity to recall specific facts about their past. Rather experience is retained in a way which allows the formation of behavioural habits which enable the animal to negotiate its present environment and anticipate possible dangers.

The question arises, then, as to whether animal habit-memory involves imagination in the sense outlined in the introduction to this chapter. Now it might be that the link between habit-memory and imagination in both animals and humans is, in fact, a very deep-seated one. For present purposes, however, I shall not develop this possibility. I shall be content, rather, to suggest that in animals, there is a power of imagination, which can, on occasion, intrude on its recognitional acts.

[5] See e.g. Bergson's *Matter and Memory*, trans. N. M. Paul and W. S. Palmer (London: Harvester, 1978), 89–105.

To support this claim, one must note first that some animals, in sleeping, exhibit involuntary behavioural traits akin to those manifested by sleeping humans. This suggests that they might dream, and, if this is the case, we must assume that they have the capacity to generate imagery. If this is so, we would also be justified in assuming that this generative power served some cognitive purpose over and above providing the fabric of dreams; but the question is, *what* purpose?

I would suggest the following. Earlier on, I noted how images of specific past learning-events can intrude in a salutary way on our present exercise of some skill. If animals can generate imagery, this may occur on similar lines. A locale where a predator was encountered in the past, may provoke images of a creature of that type each time it is entered. Again, if an infant has gone missing, familiar features of the nest or burrow may stimulate the animal to generate images of infant creatures of its own kind. In these cases, the environment prompts the animal towards special care or urgency in its present orientation. The image gives an emphasis to factors which have a vital bearing on the creature's life situation.

It is important to note that if this account is right, we must interpret animal imagination as *ostensively rigid*, i.e. something which is provoked only by encounters with appropriate stimuli, rather than being summonable at will. This ostensively rigid non-volitional character also marks the second key term which I introduced at the start of this section, namely the 'protoconcept'. In so far as the animal can make the cognitive discrimination noted earlier, it has a capacity with limited kinship to human concept application. However in contrast to humans, there is no evidence which would allow us to assume that this capacity can be employed in anything other than an ostensively rigid manner, i.e. non-volitionally and in the presence of the relevant stimuli.

Indeed this embodies a deeper contrast with human powers of concept application. If an animal recognizes a prey or its mate, one presumes that the act of recognition is not one which distinguishes between this specific prey and prey per se, or between its mate and other past or possible mates.

In human concept application, in contrast, the use of a concept is reciprocally structured. That is to say, an individual is recognized as an instance of a kind or class or whatever, and the kind or class or whatever is understood as a function of individual instances which are spread out across different times and places.

Given these points we are now in a position to consider the conditions of specifically human cognition. How is it possible for us to apply reciprocally structured concepts in an ostensively non-rigid and volitional way?

The immediate answer, of course, is through the acquisition of language and the use of signs. Through symbolic articulation our concepts are given a communicable and stable character which allows them to be used at will, and across many different situations and contexts including, most notably, those in which the objects articulated by the concept are not immediately present. But we must ask again, how this is possible.

It is instructive here to consider the following observations by Ernst Cassirer.

Only when we succeed, as it were, in compressing a total phenomenon into one of its factors, in concentrating it symbolically, in 'having' it in a state of 'pregnance' in the particular factor—only then do we raise it out of the stream of temporal change ... Everything that we call the identity of concepts and significations, or the constancy of things and attributes, is rooted in this fundamental act of finding-again. This is a common function which makes possible on the one hand language and on the other hand the specific articulation of the intuitive world.[6]

This pre-linguistic comprehension of the total phenomenon in one of its aspects is only intelligible as a function of imagination. Imagination is gradually released from its ostensively rigid animal form as the infant, through coordinating its bodily activities, is able to compose its environment into an arena of things amenable to volitionally repeatable inspections and manipulations.

In playing with and exploring its environment, the infant gathers things together and takes things apart; it learns that a repeated action can bring the same results each time; it learns that some things can be done and some cannot; and if something cannot be done now, it might become possible if continued efforts are made. All in all, the infant learns crude practical rules through regularizing its activity to achieve desired effects.

This explorative establishing of order may initially engage imagination in a crude associative way. Moments of accomplishment or gratification provoke associated images from the past or fragmented imagery of possibilities

---

[6] Ernst Cassirer, *The Philosophy of Symbolic Forms*, iii. *The Phenomenology of Knowledge*, trans. R. Manheim (New Haven and London: Yale University Press, 1966), 114.

(without, of course, being explicitly recognized in these terms). Such illuminations would enhance the child's coordinative activity.

However, the more important point is that as the probings of and responses from its environment are repeated and become familiar, the capacity to generate images of items or situations becomes volitional rather than associational. The fruits of the infant's repeatable achievements vis-à-vis sight, dexterity, and bipedal mobility provide rules or skills wherein it can, at will, project the hidden or latent aspects of a thing or situation in imagination.

The more, indeed, that the infant can generate such images, the more it is able to compose its environment into a field of means and ends. One might even go so far as to say that it learns a kind of crude categorical composition of the world. Notions such as unity, plurality, totality, reality, negation, limitation, and cause and effect, are not learned initially as concepts, but rather as constraints and possibilities which, through repeated encounters, guide the infant's activities and projections.

Imagination, then, fleshes out and enables the infant to negotiate that which is not immediately given in perception. This not only massively enhances its practical hold on the world, but also facilitates its cognitive grasp, by introducing the rudiments of symbolic articulation. It is this, of course, which the acquisition of language both refines and extends.

Given these points, one might reasonably conclude that the formation and application of concepts and the volitional exercise of imagination are reciprocally correlated—one cannot have the one without also having the other. If a being is to apply concepts in anything other than the ostensively rigid animal mode, it must be able, in imagination, to project different possible places, times, and contexts in which such applications might occur.

When imagination is directed by concepts or descriptions its volitional character is, in turn, augmented. The conceptual or descriptive core enables it to project, and make concrete, very diverse possibilities of experience as alternatives to our present perceptual position and existential situation. Freedom and choice in any positive practical sense are informed by, and motivate, such projections.

I am arguing, then, along the Kantian lines that imagination gathers up possibilities of perception, in a way that makes non-ostensively rigid concept application possible. The acquisition of such concepts reciprocally facilitates the exercise of imagination allowing it to become fully volitional.

This is a first transcendental aspect of imagination. The second can also be derived from Kantian insights. For in so far as the cooperation of understanding and imagination organizes the stream of sensations into a unified field of things, events, and possibilities, it also serves to give structure to our experience of time. In composing the phenomenal field the human subject must be attentive to the continuous succession of moments, to variations of size, shape, and intensity, to causal transformations, and to the modal characteristics of possibility, actuality, necessity (and their opposites) vis-à-vis an item or event's position in time.

Through our practical and cognitive activity, in other words, imagination is simultaneously organized in a comprehensible framework of present, past, future, and counterfactual possibility. If our capacity for projecting what is not immediately present were not organizable in these terms, we would not rise above crude ostensively rigid cognition.

Now it is vital to note that this is not just a case of imagination being a necessary condition of our objective understanding of the world. For, qua understanding, this involves the activity of a cognizing subject. Indeed, as we saw earlier, to master the reciprocal structure of concepts entails that we comprehend their applicability in times, places, and contexts other than those which we might be presently inhabiting.

This comprehension of other times and places of possible inhabitation opens out a sense of our own present, past, and future, and alternative routes which might have led to our present. Acts of objective cognition, in other words, and the unity of the cognizing subject are reciprocally correlated. Through applying concepts we simultaneously make the world intelligible in objective terms, and achieve consciousness of self. Imagination's directed organization of the temporal flow is at the heart of both dimensions. This is therefore, the second transcendental aspect of the imagination.

There is also a third. To understand it, we must first consider a feature of the image which has not been emphasized in the discussion so far. This consists in the fact that the image schematizes, that is to say interprets, that which it is an image of in terms of some of its sensory qualities, but not others.

Now the importance of this consists in a relation with memory. It is all too easy to think of memory in terms of faded pictures, or decayed sensory impressions, which are retrieved by present consciousness. The relation between our present context and memory images is, in fact, much more complex and creative. For the intentionally complex states which memories are of, cannot simply be replayed in the present. They do not come ready-made in exactly defined frames. Indeed, if there were not an element of schematization involved—if memories could return with all the power of an immediately present perception—it is difficult to see how the present perception could be sustained in an intelligible continuous way.

Given the schematic core of memory-images, we might regard such imagery as a specific use of the imagination. *Remembering*, as opposed to simply recalling, facts about our past, involves the generation of images which satisfy descriptions about events or situations which we have experienced.

The vital point to emphasize is that such images are generated in the present and not simply retrieved. How we remember a past situation, and to some degree, what we remember, is given a specific character by the specific interests of our present circumstances. The factual basis of memory—even when it is veracious—allows for considerable stylistic and creative licence, in its generation of an answering image.

Each time we remember the past, we do so from a new existential position. This means that in remembering the same fact from our past on different occasions, our iconic projection of how that fact occurred can vary. Each new present reconfigures our orientation towards the past, a point which is, of course, accentuated by the fallibility of even factual recall.

These considerations yield a quite specific notion of the self. It is a holistic structure which changes from situation to situation, even moment to moment. Determining how and what we are involves a continuing narrative, rather than mere description, of chronologically successive experiences.[7] It involves selective interpretation and valuation of past, future, and counterfactual possibility from the vantage point of the present. The imagination, with its schematizing and stylizing structure, is at the heart of this—let us term it—*fabric* of the self. This is the third transcendental aspect of imagination.

---

[7] The importance of narrative structures in personal identity has been widely recognized since Alasdair MacIntyre's *After Virtue: A Study in Moral Theory* (London: Duckworth, 1980). For a good example of how the approach has been developed in more specific terms since then, see Peter Goldie's paper 'One's Remembered Past: Narrative Thinking, Emotion, and the External Perspective', *Philosophical Papers*, 32/3 (2003), 301–19. One of the interesting things about this paper is that as well as addressing the importance of emotion for narrative thinking, it also considers its role in those situations (involving tragedy or trauma or the like) which bring about a gap in such thought.

5.2

To see how these transcendental aspects figure in relation to pictorial art let us return again to Wollheim's notion of twofoldness, and, in particular, a disagreement which he has with Gombrich over its perceptual scope.

Gombrich's claim[8] is that it is not possible to perceive what is represented and the medium of representation simultaneously. What is involved, rather, is an alternation of perceived aspects as exemplified in the perceptual switches which take place in seeing the duck/rabbit figure of gestalt psychology. Wollheim's position, in contrast, is that the elements of twofoldness do, indeed must, permit simultaneous perception.[9] Now it is important to note how the question of varieties of pictorial representation has a bearing on this issue. To show why this is the case, I shall again develop a tripartite distinction made by Kant which was first raised in Chapter 3.[10]

The distinction is between mechanical, agreeable, and fine art. In the broadest terms, mechanical art is that which seeks to convey information in visual terms, or to use such information as part of a strategy of persuasion aimed at a specific viewing audience. It is the stuff of such things as instruction manuals, or advertising. Agreeable art is that which aims simply to please or amuse. We are dealing here with kitsch representations, or ones whose functions are purely escapist.

Both these modes of representation share a common characteristic. If we are to perceive them as pictorial representations as opposed to mistaking them for realities, it is logically presupposed that we believe them to be pictures—that they have a 'made' character.

However, in these cases the belief functions primarily in a dispositional sense. We know that they are representations, but their nature is such that our belief to that effect plays no significant occurrent role in the process of perception. We engage with them, rather, simply in terms of what they represent. If, indeed, we do attend to the medium, this to some degree inhibits the representation's intended function. For we are meant to be informed, persuaded, entertained, etc. by the represented subject matter per se, rather than the way in which it is rendered.

---

[8] See, e.g. Ernst Gombrich, *Art and Illusion* (London: Phaidon, 1978), 170–203.

[9] See Wollheim, *Art and its Objects*, 213

[10] This is outlined in §§43–8 of Bk. I of his *Critique of Judgement,* trans. W. Pluhar (Indianapolis: Hackett and Co., 1987).

This, however, brings us to artistically significant representation. For Kant—questions of aesthetic form aside for the moment—this has the characteristic of originality and exemplariness. Originality here should be taken to mean a work's capacity to engage our attention through its refinement or innovations in relation to the traditions of making in that medium. And exemplariness should be taken to mean the work's embodiment of patterns and practices of production and composition which can be fruitfully developed by other artists.

By affirming the importance of originality and exemplariness, Kant shows how our readings of aesthetic form and representation are actively mediated by fundamentally historical considerations. If a representation is aesthetically significant or original, this means that it differs in a positive way from other representations. It stands out from the norm established through our experience of other works.

Interest here, accordingly, focuses on the way in which subject matter is rendered—on compositional strategies, treatments of light and colour, conceptions of pictorial space, and the handling of light and paint. The work may stand out in these terms, of course, simply on the basis of its contrast with our previous personal experiences and preferences. If, however, our perception is historically informed by a deep familiarity with the medium and its traditions, then the work may be all the more striking by virtue of its objective claim to originality.

In the case of the pictorial fine artwork, then, the belief that the picture is a picture—that it has been brought forth through human artifice—is forcefully occurrent. It is not a mere disposition or even an inhibition to our seeing of that which is represented (as in mechanical or agreeable art), rather it permeates our perception. Our orientation is primarily towards the twofoldness of the work.

What this means in practice is that we perceive the work of fine art *as an image*. Its dual aspects are simultaneously joined only qua image. And whilst we might merely remark upon its image-status in a descriptive sense, its historical distinctiveness makes us much more attentive to aesthetic being.

Wollheim is, therefore, right to affirm that the elements of twofoldness are simultaneously perceived, but it is also vital to emphasize how this is made possible. Our awareness of the medium as a rendering of what is represented involves not simply perception, but perception *of* the work *as image* informed and situated in quite specific, ultimately historical terms.

Wollheim, unfortunately, underplays both the significance of image-status, and its historical embeddedness.

I am arguing, therefore, that in relation to mechanical and agreeable art, twofoldness is not to the fore. Gombrich's account of alternative perceptions of the two aspects may be loosely appropriate to these, bearing in mind that one of them—the subject matter which is represented—is of primary significance. In the case of artistic representation, in contrast, twofoldness is the very basis of our perception.

Rather than taking this mild critique of Wollheim any further, I will be content to go beyond it, by making some connections between twofoldness and the transcendental significance of imagination. In what follows, I focus on our recognition of these functions as exemplified in the artist's *making* of the work.

Let us begin with the image's function in the holistic core of experience. A first point to note, is that in affirming twofoldness, we are recognizing that the representation has been made and composed. It is an image which has been volitionally generated by physical means, so as to satisfy the artist's intention to represent such and such a kind of subject matter.

Whereas this intention-directed volitional generation of imagery is meant to be overlooked in mechanical and agreeable representation, in artistic representation it is to the fore. This means that the making of pictorial art exemplifies the ostensively non-rigid structure which enables the imagination to serve those transcendental functions outlined in Section 5.1.

It also manifests another aspect of this structure—the one which marks imagination's decisive role in the narrative fabric of experience. For whilst the pictorial artwork is iconic with the kind of thing which it presents, it does not—no matter how 'naturalistic' the style—simply duplicate or clone that thing in visual terms. Rather the image is manifestly stylized.

We see it as a schematization or visual interpretation of its subject matter. As we have already seen at length, the term style is of paramount importance, for to engage with a work's style in the fullest sense, goes beyond formal considerations alone. It is to attend to how that, which the picture is of, is *made manifest*. In perceiving style, in other words, we are perceiving twofoldness.

Let us take this further. In perceiving the work's style—as a volitionally generated, physically realized, intentionally directed image—we know that it was made. However, it was not made *ex nihilo*. In recognizing the work's stylistic distinctiveness we, at least unconsciously, link it to precedents or the lack of them, in other works (by the artist or by others). We may also note the way in which some of the artist's stylistic traits—such as a hard edged articulation of form—are ones which characterize a more general school or movement, or even the sensibility of an entire historical era.

With this in mind, we can look back on the function of the mental image in the ongoing narrative of experience. Such an image—deployed in memory, or as a projection of the future or counterfactual possibility—interprets and stylizes its objects on the basis of the self's present existential interests but reciprocally, the interests of the present are a function of its inherited past experiences, its futural or counterfactual projections; and, indeed, a broader context of contemporary social attitudes, sometimes negotiated reflectively, but more often absorbed without awareness that the absorption has taken place.

All these factors inform the generation of a present mental image. The pictorial artwork exemplifies their intersection through a publically accessible idiom. Indeed, it is precisely because we here focus on how the work stylizes, and its historical conditions and consequences, that we are situated in the heart of the holistic experiential nexus, which shapes and is sustained by the generation of imagery per se.

I shall now link artistic representation to the other two transcendental functions of imagination, namely its role in gathering up and giving temporal stability to the perceptual manifold.

In order to make this connection we must first recall what is at issue in Gombrich and Wollheim's disagreement over twofoldness. Gombrich holds that the perception of twofoldness is a kind of gestalt switch—from material base to representational content or vice versa. Wollheim in contrast holds that such properties can be seen simultaneously. Representation per se can form the object of a single perception.

Now in my foregoing arguments I have lent support to Wollheim by linking the singular perception of twofoldness to specifically artistic representation. This support, however, must now be significantly qualified on two grounds. First, whilst the singular perception of twofoldness is appropriate to art, there are circumstances where twofoldness in Gombrich's dual perceptual sense can also be loosely appropriate. I say 'loosely' here, because what I am talking about is not simply a radical switch from one perceptual emphasis to another, but rather something much more subtle and dynamic.

It is the recognition of this which demands the second qualification to Wollheim's position. His notion of twofoldness is a useful working concept, but is logically more complex than his customary employments of it would suggest. In fact, it might be better to talk in this respect of *fourfoldness*.

This is because pictorial representation's structure can be analysed in terms of four logically distinct aspects—(1) the physical or material base; (2) the work's formal properties (e.g. line, shape, texture, mass, volume, light, and colour); (3) physiognomic properties, i.e. ones with specific ranges of emotional or psychological association; (4) representational content.

For present purposes, the specific relation of twofoldness which holds between (2) and (4)—formal qualities and representational content—is of most interest. To enjoy formal qualities for their own sake is to enjoy complex relations of unity, diversity, reality, limitation, negation, and, overall, balance between these relations. The perception of them is enormously complex and, in a positive sense, highly unstable.

In an artist such as Jackson Pollock, for example, shape and form is often animated within a shallow optical space in a way that sets up strong formal rhythms. This invites the view to imaginatively continue the rhythms either backwards into the plane, or outwards to break its surface.

Again, in artists such as Barnett Newman or Mark Rothko extended bands of colour set up ambiguous figure/ground relations, and complex suggestions of presence, absence, and void. To perceive all these qualities in relation to one another, involves strong changes of perceptual emphasis even at the purely formal level. In particular there is systematic ambiguity as to which formal properties are to be seen as closely tied to the physical reality of the painted surface, and which are to be linked to those specific conditions of optical illusion which the work creates.

This ambiguity of reality and illusion at the formal level also extends to figurative works. One might, for example, distinguish between infrastructural formal qualities (line, shape, texture, mass, etc.) and superstructural formal qualities[11] which are a function of the work's representational content.

---

[11] For more on the infrastructural/superstructural relation see my *Art and Embodiment: From Aesthetics to Self-Consciousness* (Oxford: Clarendon Press, 1993), 18–20.

Consider Manet's *Déjeuner sur l'Herbe* (1863). This work can be appreciated in formal terms not only for its qualities of light and colour and the like, but also for the way in which the particular disposition of human figures tends to compress the relation of foreground and background. Manet's use of representational content here serves a specific formal function which is loaded with psychological associations. A nominal outdoor 'natural' scene is rendered claustrophobic and aggressively artificial. The manifest artifice of this formal strategy, indeed, is also rendered more insistent by the incongruity of a 'picnic' scene where the male figures are attired in contemporary garb, whilst one of the female figures is naked.

Now if a picture is of artistic merit, we are rarely content to negotiate its twofoldness just in terms of a singular perception of it (although this, as I have agreed with Wollheim, is fundamental to our appreciation of it). Rather, we are also taken by the way in which representational content is *achieved* from the artist's handling of formal qualities, and the way in which such representational content functions, superstructurally within the formal structure. What all this involves is a close, more dualistic, perceptual attentiveness to the *emergence* of content from form, and their conditions of reciprocal dependence within the work.

Such attentiveness involves a perceptual toing and froing from a shifting and unstable level, to one which is, in a decisive sense, spatially and temporally fixed and fully articulate. This latter level is that of representational content per se. A picture is only a picture in so far as it individuates recognizable kinds of two- and three-dimensional visual items within a notional plane.[12]

The basis of this is natural—based on resemblance—but it is also conventionally mediated to a high degree. Strong or fully realized perspectival accents are especially significant in such a context. For whilst they do not 'correspond' to the actual process of visual perception, they form a convention which enables virtual relations in a two-dimensional plane to be projected in a way which is maximally consistent with the systematic relation of visual items in the real spatio-temporal continuum.

The spatio-temporal coherence of such pictorial representation cannot be emphasized enough. In so far as a picture represents recognizable kinds of

---

[12] For examples of different ways at arriving at this same conclusion see Robert Hopkins, *Picture, Image and Experience: A Philosophical Inquiry* (Cambridge: Cambridge University Press, 1998) and Flint Schier, *Deeper into Pictures* (Cambridge: Cambridge University Press, 1986).

things and relations in a perspectivally accentuated space, it simultaneously articulates an implicit temporal horizon. The space can be notionally entered, and the viewer can take up different virtual positions—both spatial and temporal—within it.

On entering such a virtual system and moving continuously through it, near objects would be reached before more distantly located objects. Indeed, the fact that, from an external viewing position, one thing blocks our view of another or has hidden aspects is, in neither case, taken as evidence that the hidden things or aspects do not exist. Rather the situatedness of the visually accessible aspects within a system of perspectival accents—however informal—offers cues whereby we can imagine ourselves moving through this virtual space to occupy positions where what is hidden in relation to the external viewing position would become visually accessible internally. (I shall return to this issue at length in Chapter 8.)

Now, in Section 5.1, I identified the way in which imagination enables us to project the hidden aspects of things, or of states of affairs which are not immediately given in perception. This projective capacity is essential for concept formation in so far as to have a concept in the fullest sense entails that we can envisage its possible applications in times and places other than that of its immediate employment.

In exercising imagination in this context we, at the same time, unify consciousness of self. For to project other times and places where a concept might apply, is to project ourselves there as possible users of the concept. (Consciousness becomes consciousness of self when it can conceive occupying times and places other than the one presently occupied.)

Through stabilizing, and (in concert with concept-application) giving spatio-temporal unity to the perceptual manifold, therefore, imagination also gives unity to the self. These transcendental functions enable experience to be achieved. They allow the phenomenal flux of scattered perceptions to be gathered up and systematized. Experience's achieved character is not something which is much remarked upon in adult life. However, it is, in symbolic terms, paramount in the dualistic version of twofoldness which I am currently considering.

We will recall that to create and/or appreciate an artistic representation involves attending to the emergence of representational content from formal qualities, and to the function of the former in relation to the latter. This means that we appreciate how the image achieves a virtual spatially and temporally unified system of relations, from a more shifting and unstable zone. In such an image we are presented not just with the immediately visible aspects of the kind of subject matter which is being represented, but also a system of visual cues which enable the projection of hidden aspects and states of affairs—or, to put it another way, a system of possible viewing positions within the represented space.

Such an image exemplifies transcendental imagination's stabilization of the perceptual manifold and the unity of the self. If, accordingly, our perception shifts from this level to formal qualities and back again, we symbolically trace the emergence of a stable experiential world from a more unstable realm of phenomenal qualities. In one sense, time goes backwards in a symbolic replay of how experience itself emerges through the powers of imagination.

In another sense, the toing and froing, from representational content to formal qualities, serves to disclose what the passage of time hides, namely the fact that experience—even in its crudest sense—is achieved. And this is the supreme significance of twofoldness in the sense of perceptual dualism. It offers a kind of eternalization of the dynamic origins of experience. In each life, experience emerges only once. In artistic representation it emerges always—or at least for as long as the representation survives and is appreciated.

Of course, in a philosophical analysis such as this the phenomenon of experiential emergence can be described and analysed. Artistic representation, however, exemplifies the process at the ontological level of its occurrence, namely the sensible. It is shown rather than said.

Our criterion of showing here is perhaps best illustrated by reference to the *intuitive* illuminatory power of events and relations at the sensible level. When a person falls in love or forms friendships, for example, one can offer a reflective analysis of the reasons why this has happened. But such an explanation will be by no means the whole truth. The situations in life which provoke us to action or to emotional responses, involve complex matters of appraisal which draw on different modalities of sense operating as a unified field.

These appraisals themselves are not simply registered by consciousness, but draw on the subject's awareness of present, past, and possible physical and existential positioning. Reflective thought's explanation of such responses can only operate with very general reasons. Its abstractness cannot fully articulate the depths of our immediate sensibly grounded appraisals of the world. Yet, nevertheless, we are able to act on the basis of such appraisals. They give direction to experience. They are cognitive acts which embody an intuitive knowledge which draws on the depths of perception and experience.

The link between transcendental imagination and twofoldness in its dualistic perceptual sense, is of this intuitive order. It is one element in a complex network of responses which comprise different ways of aesthetically appreciating pictorial art. Pictures are intimately familiar to us. We are at home with them. They are a friendly part of our total rationalization of the world.

But if we try to analyse why this is so, the answer is elusive. Very general notions such as 'expression' seem applicable, without even quite illuminating what is involved. For what is involved here is a complex nexus of intuitive knowledge embodied in the artistic image. Some of it focuses on Wollheim's singular notion of twofoldness; other aspects focus on the dualistic version's relation to the transcendental imagination.

In the latter part of this discussion I have presented this relation in a schematic analytic form. Its affective power, however, consists in the capacity to resonate intuitively with experience at its point of origin, and to make that resonation available indefinitely. This capacity is the province of artistic representation as a mode of *image-making*.

Conclusion

I have argued, then, that Wollheim's notion of twofoldness is of great utility in directing us towards some of the profoundest aspects of pictorial art. I have also indicated how Wollheim's approach requires some qualification if it is to fully encompass these aspects.

In one respect it is rather surprising that he himself did not develop the notion of twofoldness in such directions. I say this because, whilst Wollheim did not use transcendental imagination as an overt working concept, he did explore cognate themes in *The Thread of Life*—most notably that of 'experiential memory'.[13] It is precisely themes of this sort which can and must be linked to artistic representation, if its full significance in human experience is to be properly understood.

Having explored a fundamental cognitive structure in pictorial art, I turn now to a similar feature in literature.

[13] See esp. *The Thread of Life* (Cambridge: Cambridge University Press, 1980), 104–21.

6

Between Language and Perception: Literary Metaphor[1]

Introduction

To understand the cognitive structure of metaphor, and its distinctive role in literary art, we must start from *experience*. To 'experience' in the most minimal sense, is to follow rules in relation to language, perception, and action. It is difficult to see how such a capacity could be formed and exercised in the absence of constants in the human condition. Such constants can be most easily identified at the level of perception and embodiment.

They are, however, deeply entwined with our existence as rational and self-conscious beings. As Merleau-Ponty observes, 'it is no mere coincidence that the rational being is also the one that holds himself upright or has a thumb which can be brought opposite to the fingers: the same manner of existing is evident in both aspects'.[2]

This chapter will focus on the role of metaphor as a kind of junction between rational articulation and perception. Its general argument will be twofold. First that the tensional structure of metaphor embodies a constant in human experience, which is capable of being expressed in different ways under different historical conditions; and, second, that literary metaphor[3] is the clearest exemplar of this.

---

[1] This chapter is a revised and extended version of a paper presented to the Classics seminar at Corpus Christi College, Oxford, in Hilary Term 1997. I am especially indebted to James Urmson, C. C. W. Taylor, and George Boys-Stones, for their critical comments.

[2] Maurice Merleau-Ponty, *Phenomenology of Perception*, trans. Colin Smith, rev. Forrest Williams (London: Routledge & Kegan Paul, 1974), 170.

[3] In this analysis I shall focus primarily on metaphor in poetry.

To establish these general points, I shall, in Section 6.1, analyse the logical characteristics of metaphor, and the way in which they link predication and perception. I will further suggest that whilst this linkage is not an overt focus of attention in the ordinary usage of metaphor, it is so in the literary context. (Metaphor, indeed, has a conceptual link with literary meaning that it does not have with other art forms.) In Section 6.2, I shall explore this possibility through its exemplification in the Archaic Greek poet Archilochus' use of metaphor, and will give reasons why his treatment of metaphor has canonic significance as well as artistic value.

6.1

Ricoeur offers a useful 'nominal' definition of metaphor as follows. It consists in 'giving an unaccustomed name to some other thing, which thereby is not being given its proper name'.[4] However, even if metaphor hinges on a transposition of terms, it has further logical characteristics which, in conjunction with this, give it its peculiar linguistic potency.

Foremost amongst these is the fact that since metaphor involves a kind of deliberate error, this can only be significant in so far as it occurs in a broader context of linguistic regularity—of conventional ordered usages. This is why Ricoeur, Emile Benveniste, and Max Black (among others) emphasize metaphor's discursive or sentential character. As Black puts it, metaphor involves 'a sentence or another expression in which some words are used metaphorically while the remainder are used non-metaphorically'.[5]

---

[4] Paul Ricoeur, *The Rule of Metaphor*, trans. Robert Czerny, John Costello, Kathleen McLaughlin (London: Routledge, 1994), 65.

[5] Max Black, *Models and Metaphors* (Ithaca: Cornell University Press, 1962), 27. Donald Davidson has criticized Black's view in his well-known paper 'What Metaphors Mean' (included in *Inquiries into Truth and Interpretation* (Oxford: Clarendon Press, 1984)). He argues that there is no such thing as metaphorical meaning as an intrinsic linguistic form, rather 'It is something brought off by the imaginative employment of words and sentences and depends entirely on the ordinary meanings of those words and hence on the ordinary meanings of the sentences they comprise' (p. 247). Now Davidson's emphasis on metaphor as a *use* of language is entirely justified. However, he makes no attempt to analyse the structure and vectors of this 'imaginative' use. What makes this so restrictive for his own strategy is that, without such an analysis, Davidson has no way of explaining how metaphors can be distinguished from blatant falsities or truisms per se. My own approach, in contrast, builds on metaphor's starting point in the thwarting of expectations based on the ordinary understanding of predicative conventions, and then explains the broader perceptual and imaginative context for language which makes this use cognitively significant.

(In the rest of this chapter I shall follow Black's practice in designating the metaphorical term as the 'secondary subject' and the non-metaphorical referent as the 'principal subject'.)

Now there are a number of reasons why the linking of metaphor and sentence are important. The first pertains to language itself. Following Strawson[6] we can characterize the basic structural feature of language as that which permits singular identification. There is a fundamental polarity involved, which, as Ricoeur puts it, 'on the one hand is rooted in named individuals, and on the other hand predicates qualities, classes, relations, and actions that in principle are universal. Language works on the basis of this dissymmetry between two basic functions.'[7] The significance of this vis-à-vis metaphor is that, whilst having the character of a deliberate error or bizarre truism, the secondary subject functions in the most formal terms as a feature predicated of the principal subject.

This predicative role, however, is an exceptional one. Starting from a metaphor that is not deadened by its frequent repetition Nelson Goodman claims that,

Briefly, a metaphor is an affair between a predicate with a past and an object that yields while protesting. In routine projection, habit applies a label to a case not already decided. Arbitrary application of a newly coined label is equally unobstructed by prior decision. But metaphorical application of a label to an object defies an explicit or unconscious prior denial of that label to that object. Where there is metaphor, there is conflict[8]

The point is, then, that in metaphor, the predicated label gravitates around a formal element of incongruity. The predicative 'is' characterizes the primary subject in terms of a label which is, in the most literal terms, not applicable to it, or extremely strange if it is. This is usually because the predicate is blatantly not the kind of thing which can be truthfully asserted of the primary subject; or—as in the case of 'no man is an island'—is a blatant or bizarre truism. In metaphor, expectations based on the predicative conventions of language are simultaneously and manifestly affirmed by form, but denied by our normal expectations. Metaphor is inherently tensional.

---

[6] See Peter Strawson, *Individuals* (London: Methuen & Co., 1959).

[7] Ricoeur, *Rule of Metaphor*, 71.

[8] Nelson Goodman, *Languages of Art* (Indiana: Hackett and Co., 1976), 69.

This carries a further implication. Since metaphor transgresses conventional literal usage, it is thereby conceptually tied to the notion of novelty in both an objective and subjective sense. The objective sense consists in the fact that at its point of emergence a metaphor defines itself as innovatory in relation to standard predicative practices surrounding its principal subject; the subjective (but more interesting sense) is that innovation of this sort presupposes wit or inventiveness in the one who formulates the metaphor for the first time. (I shall return to this issue.)

In logical terms, then, metaphor is a fundamentally predicative structure wherein a literally inappropriate term is applied to an item in a novel way. Kant judiciously notes the possibility of 'original nonsense',[9] so, mindful of this, one might ask, what is our criterion of a metaphor as opposed to merely nonsensical predication?

The answer is, when the act of untoward predication *works* in relation to the principal subject. But then, of course, we must ask what is our criterion of 'works' in such a context? What is the concrete function of metaphor?

In this respect, Black's theory proves instructive. He observes that: 'The metaphor selects, emphasizes, suppresses and organizes features of the principal subject by implying statements about it that normally apply to the subsidiary subject.'[10]

Indeed, the metaphorical term draws on as Black puts it a 'system of associated common-places'[11] which pertain to opinions, values, beliefs, and institutions into which a member of a linguistic community is initiated through the very act of learning to speak. Black is, I think, right about the basic function of metaphor—which is the cognitive elucidation of a principal subject—but he is somewhat misleading about how this is achieved and the significance of the achievement.

Ricoeur has suggested that what is lacking in Black's account is a sense of that key feature of metaphor which Aristotle noted, namely its capacity 'to set before the eyes'.[12] What this means, in effect, is that Black does not have an adequate theory of imagination. It could also be argued that Ricoeur's approach suffers from a similar failing.[13] However, rather than

---

[9] Kant, *Critique of Judgement*, trans. J. C. Meredith (Oxford: Clarendon Press, 1973), 168.
[10] Black, *Models and Metaphors*, 44–5.   [11] Ibid. 40.
[12] Quoted in Ricoeur, *Rule of Metaphor*, 207.
[13] Ricoeur makes much of Kant's notion of 'schematism' and its relation to the productive imagination. But whilst imagination plays a key role in metaphor it must be clearly linked to the structure of perception.

show the complex problems which beset Ricoeur's account, I shall instead address the central issue, namely how it is possible for a metaphorical term to offer cognitive elucidation of that which it is applied to.

In this respect, let us consider first how ordinary predication works. In order to articulate a proposition it is presupposed that such an articulation is consistent with the grammatical rules which govern the language of which it is a part. These rules constitute a kind of logical field in relation to which the sense of the proposition can be recognized. If the proposition is used to achieve singular identification in relation to the user's present perceptual field (and this ostensive function does seem to be the logically basic one) matters get rather more complex. For when propositions articulate perception, this perceptual discursiveness involves a latent field in addition to the rules of language.

To show this let us consider a simple example. I judge that the woman outside is wearing a red dress. This act of perceptual predication has what can be described as a perceptual sense as well as a linguistic one. The complex factors involved in perceptual sense have been powerfully illuminated by Merleau-Ponty. In relation to the example of perceiving a red dress, he describes how it is positioned:

A punctuation in the field of red things, which includes the tiles of roof tops, the Flags of gatekeepers and of the revolution, certain terrains near Aix or in Madagascar, it is also a punctuation in the field of red garments which includes, along with the dresses of women, robes of professors, bishops, and advocate generals.[14]

Any judgement concerning the red dress, therefore, is not *simply* an act of recognition. It is situated and defined in a broader perceptual and associational field. Hence, as Merleau-Ponty concludes,

If we took all these participations into account, we would recognize that a naked colour, and in general a visible, is not a chunk of absolutely hard, indivisible being, offered all naked to a vision which could be only total or null, but is rather a sort of straits between exterior horizons and interior horizons ever gaping open, something that comes to touch lightly and makes diverse regions of the colored or visible world resound at the distances[15]

---

[14] Maurice Merleau-Ponty, *The Visible and the Invisible,* trans. Alphonse Lingis (Evanston: North-western University Press, 1968), 132.
[15] Ibid.

The point is, then, that predication in its most logically basic func-tion—the articulation of perception—engages with the dimension of perceptual sense. Given a specific perceptual object, it is in principle possible to apply an infinite number of predicates to it. But in concrete perception this infinite stock is not in practical terms available to us. What we predicate of the object—the perceptual sense which we assign to it—is dependent upon both its position and our own position within an organized field of items and relations whose presence is not immediately manifest in the act of perception itself.

This latent field is composed of hidden or peripheral items in perception, the body's actual and possible positionings, the percipient's objective knowledge of the world, and, equally importantly, the percipient's personal history, values, and social experience.

It must be emphasized that this personal dimension is by no means a wholly private matter. This is why Merleau-Ponty's foregoing character-ization of perception as 'a sort of straits between exterior horizons and interior horizons' is so appropriate. The common perceptual and physical basis of human embodiment means that the personal and experiences of individual subjects will gravitate around shared or shareable patterns of interpretation and response. Hence, whilst my latent perceptual field and yours can never be exactly congruent, they will, nevertheless, have a deep structural continuity by virtue of our shared embodied condition, and our immersion in a world of mind-independent items.

Now, of course, the point about a latent field of this sort is that it *is* latent. Our acts of perceptual predication are defined by their position in such a field, but only exceptionally will we have an explicit understanding of the structure of such positioning. If this were not the case our cognitive activity would be overwhelmed by an excess of sensory and imaginative data.

Given this point, however, we must ask if there is any linguistic strategy wherein the relation between perceptual predication and its latent field, is exemplified The answer is yes—metaphor. Metaphor hinges on a literally inappropriate predicate being applied to a principal subject. If, however, such a linkage makes sense, there must be some logical connection between the secondary and principal subject.

This connection is provided by what I have called the 'latent field'. One of the key structural elements in the latent perceptual field is a space of imaginative association and projection. I would suggest that when language is used metaphorically it engages this imaginative space. The fact that the secondary term is able to achieve a cognitive elucidation of the principal subject, is because it posits some relation or quality or whatever, which is a feature of the latent imaginative field surrounding that subject.

In recognizing the relation between secondary or principal subject as metaphorical we discern an analogy. If the metaphor is living and forceful, we can imaginatively traverse elements in the latent field which connects the principal subject and its analogical predicate. In this way the principal subject is elucidated by virtue of our deepened experience of the field of relations in which that subject is positioned, and given its full definition.

Of course, many metaphors—like many acts of predication per se—are applied without the referents of the terms involved being immediately present. This, however, is the power of metaphor. For, by virtue of its linguistic form—and the imaginative traversal which this invites—it involves a key feature of that latent field which is also implicated in language's most basic function, namely the articulation of perception.

In this way, it is at least an echo of this function; and if the principle and secondary terms themselves refer to perceptible items (as is most often the case in metaphorical relations) then the effect of the metaphor will be to exemplify language's articulation of the perceptual world and the embodied subject's mode of inhering in it.

To further illustrate my position, let us consider an example. 'Falling in love' is one of the most common of all metaphors. It has, indeed, become deadened by repetition. However, the deadening of a metaphor is, ironically enough, a sign of its power. It is so effective as to be taken up by all sides and in all locations, thus becoming, in time, a commonplace. Let us ask then, what it is about the metaphor of 'falling' which makes it so effective as an elucidation of love. Love, of course, is an emotional state rather than a position in space, hence one cannot literally 'fall into' it. However, falling as opposed to jumping into or taking possession of something is fundamentally a non-volitional act. And this is one of the most basic and poignant facts about love. One might wish to enter into such a state, but one cannot achieve it by choice alone.

This is because of the latent field which situates all our emotional engagements. One can give a reason why, in emotional terms, one feels as one does. But the relation, event, or quality (or chain of such factors) which constitutes the reason does not simply 'register' in an individual's experience. It engages—in terms of harmony, tension, and conflict—with the totality of a life (i.e. with that holistic structure of experience discussed in previous chapters).

The 'reason' why one feels as one does is merely the salient feature which emerges from a multitude of latent factors and relations. This is the existential context for the metaphor 'falling' in love. 'Falling' signifies both the complexity of the field from which the emotion of love emerges, and the fact that we cannot control it in a volitional sense. The terms involved play off against our actual experiences and description of falling, and our own experiences of, and knowledge by description, of, love as an emotion.

In the most immediate terms, 'falling' is literally incongruous. However, the very incongruity of the juxtaposition provokes us to project avenues of imaginative association which, in ranging across publicly accessible and private experience, allow love and 'falling in' to be logically connected. The secondary term elevates a specific 'player' in the latent field surrounding the principal subject, into an explicit role. If the metaphor is a living one, the unexpectedness of this elevation stimulates the imagination into filling out the space between the two terms. It is in the actual or potential traversal of this space that the principal subject achieves its cognitive elucidation.

Again it is important to reiterate that such imaginative traversal involves a reciprocity of objective and subjective factors. For whilst, to return to our specific example, 'falling in' and 'love' are objective phenomena, and are informed by a common cultural stock of knowledge, our particular experiences of them also have a specific private character.

Hence, how one imaginatively traverses the space between them will vary from individual to individual. This is why a metaphor cannot be paraphrased in literal terms. To be a metaphor is to posit an objectively significant connection, but in a way which provokes the connection to be made via avenues of imaginative and thence, in part, personal association, rather than immediate logical relation.

On these terms, then, the phenomenon of metaphor is of the profoundest philosophical significance. It is the form of language wherein the dependence of the recognition of presence upon items and relations which are not immediately present, is the active basis of signification. More specifically it affirms predication's primary function as an articulation of the perceptible. Metaphor thus exemplifies key structural features in cognition.

However, as Goodman has noted,[16] exemplification involves not only possession, but also reference. Now the tensional character of metaphor—the predication of a literally inappropriate term—is, by virtue of its immediately incongruous nature, something which can provoke some awareness, however, vague, of the relational complexity which situates all our cognitive acts.

There are, nevertheless, two restrictions on the achievement of such awareness. First, a metaphor (for example 'falling in love') may be a dead one. This means that an awareness of its broader significance itself requires a philosophical analysis of the sort offered in this discussion. Second, since the function of metaphor is to achieve cognitive elucidation of the principal subject, the achievement of such elucidation may amount to no more than that. We comprehend the principal subject in a deeper way, but do not sense the more general significance of such elucidation vis-à-vis the structure of human experience.

To overcome these restrictions, metaphor needs a framing device. This would allow the metaphor to illumine its principal subject, whilst, at the same time, being distanced from this function. The literary artwork and aesthetic object embodies such a framing device. It demands that as well as attending to what a given linguistic strategy is accomplishing, we are equally attentive to how this is achieved. Personal style in the articulation of literary form offers a context where in the philosophical significance of metaphor is strikingly manifest.

Now it might be asked why the literary artwork should be singled out in this context. Do not visual artworks, or even musical ones, have the capacity to disclose the philosophical significance of metaphor?

The answer to this question is somewhat complex. As we saw in the previous chapter, pictorial and sculptural representation have the character of twofoldness, i.e. we are able to see them both 'as' that which they represent and as physical objects or events. Now in order to recognize that something is, say, a picture of an x, we must know that it is not in fact an x; that it is only a configuration of material which shares certain visual qualities with the x. This gently tensional relation between the two

---

[16] See Goodman, *Languages of Art*, 52.

elements of twofoldness gives pictorial representation a general affinity with metaphor.

There are also other connections. For something to be a picture of an x, that x must be represented in relation to a surrounding field. This might be constituted by background elements, or even, in the most minimal sense, the picture plane as such. We have, in other words, a basic exemplar of the relation between a perceived form and what I have earlier described as a latent field.

Rather more significant still, is the fact that because the representation is not identical with that which is represented, points of sameness and difference in the relation enable us to see the kind of thing which is represented in a new light. The artist's style illuminates and projects avenues of significant association around the subject matter. It gives it a kind of cognitive elucidation.

Now if these points are correct, pictorial representation might be interpreted as a visual mode of metaphor. However, there are a number of surprising factors involved. First the metaphorical status is well concealed. In order to make a picture of x one simply follows certain rules governing the appropriate implements and media. One 'intends' to make a picture rather than construct a metaphor. The metaphorical character of pictorial reference is absorbed into the broader conventions which govern such representation, and thence loses its overt metaphorical character.

Even more surprising is that it is not possible (within the framework of normal pictorial representation) to construct a *particular* metaphor. Caspar David Friedrich, for example, seems to have intended pictorial devices such as crescent moons as metaphors for the Resurrection and other aspects of Christian doctrine. However, particular visual metaphors of this kind cannot be recognized within the internal resources of the work itself. To determine whether a specific pictorial motif or relation is being used metaphorically requires collateral iconographic evidence drawn from the cultural context in which the work is produced and received.

The only possible exceptions to this are in idioms where the normal conventions of pictorial representation are disrupted. Surrealist works are an example. In this context, however, whether a juxtaposition of items is intended as a metaphorical link, is extremely difficult to determine in purely visual terms. It may be, for example, that the juxtaposition has been brought about purely to baffle or disturb the viewer.

Literary works relate to metaphor in a very different way. There is a twofold aspect to such works to the degree that we can distinguish the literal sense of the descriptions or narratives or whatever which constitute the work, and the stylized articulations of language in terms of which these are expressed.

However, this twofoldness is much less clearly defined than in pictorial art, and it is not founded on physical or associational analogy between the referent(s) and the referring term(s). Meaning in literary language—indeed language itself—does not have an intrinsically metaphorical structure. Rather, metaphorical expression is one use to which language can be put—in a literary context or otherwise.

It is this narrower scope of application which allows particular metaphors—rather than the globally metaphorical structures of pictorial art—to be constructed. In language and literature, indeed, a particular connection can be recognized as metaphorical purely on the basis of the internal resources of the text or utterance itself in the broader context of general language-use.

If, therefore, the philosophical significance of metaphor is to be disclosed in the most direct terms, it is to literary idioms that we must look. For present purposes, the case of Archilochus the Archaic Greek poet is especially useful. His choice and deployment of metaphor is massively shaped by the specific societal and historical circumstances of his time, and, of course, his own existence as a mercenary. However, it is precisely these historically specific factors, and their personalized expression in poetic form, which disclose the philosophical significance of metaphor in a heightened way. In Archilochus we can clearly recognize universal structure embodied in the particular.

6.2

Archilochus addresses recurrent themes of war, love, sex, friendship, revenge (both human and divinely sanctioned), civic propriety and impropriety, and political happenstances. His metaphors draw on all these themes, sometimes in a closely interwoven way. A useful starting point for analysis is one of the most extended fragments, *Encounter in a Meadow*.

The poem is a narrative description of an amorous episode. It is seemingly addressed to a friend, but the bulk of the text involves a recounting of what the woman involved said to Archilochus, and what he said to her. The woman deflects an initial overture. Archilochus then makes his key move:

> the love-goddess offers young men
> a range of joys besides
> the sacrament, and one of them will serve.[17]

By characterizing sexual intercourse in terms of the 'sacrament' metaphor, Archilochus launches a twofold strategy of persuasion. On the one hand, he makes it clear that he reveres the act of physical love (and, thence, by implication, the woman who is the object of that act); on the other hand he is able to indicate a space of possibilities which do not demand such a serious step. The strategy appears to work. For whilst there is an omission in the fragment, it becomes clear that a rendezvous has been agreed. Indeed, Archilochus promises that 'I'll do it all just as you say.'[18] After another omission we encounter the following ambiguous passage:

> But please, my dear, don't grudge it if I go
> under the arch, through the gates;
> I'll dock at the grass borders,
> be sure of that.[19]

Is this an indication that whilst not compromising the woman by calling at her house, the poet will nevertheless install himself close by? Such a reading is viable. It is, however, interwoven with a secondary meaning, arising from the fact that the whole sentence also functions as a kind of extended metaphorical reassurance that when they meet, the poet will be satisfied with an onanistic alternative to copulation.

Now it might be thought that the sentence in question is better described as allegorical than as metaphorical. However, it is somewhere between the two. Allegorical meaning is normally a form of linguistic disguise. We recognize it only through knowledge of a context external to the text itself. But Archilochus' progress 'under the arch, through the gate' to 'dock at the grass borders' serves to develop the *already established* theme

---

[17] Included in *Greek Lyric Poetry*, trans. M. L. West (Oxford: Oxford University Press, 1994), 3.
[18] Ibid.   [19] Ibid.

of alternatives to the 'sacrament'. The nature of this progress, indeed, is
further contextualized in the climax of the poem.

> and laying her down in the flowers,
> with my soft textured cloak
> I covered her; my arm cradled her neck, while she in her
> fear like a fawn
> gave up the attempt to run.
> Gently I touched her breasts,
> where the young flesh
> peeped from the edge of her dress,
> her ripeness newly come,
> and then, caressing all her lovely form,
> I shot my hot energy off,
> just brushing golden hairs.[20]

Given this onanistic outcome, Archilochus' earlier progress 'under the
arch, through the gates' to 'dock at the grass borders' can be seen as a
loosely metaphorical anticipation of it. The stealthy and cautious securing
of place functions as an analogue to the qualified sexual fulfilment which
later ensues. Indeed, it is also *a reconnoitre*—a simultaneous testing of the
ground and act of reassurance vis-à-vis the woman. By preparing the
way in advance through hinting at a limited rather than total sexual goal
Archilochus 'softens up' the opposition.

This metaphorically based strategy exemplifies Archilochus' more general
tendency to assimilate sexual goals to the securing of position. For it involves
a stealthy arrival and safe installation in a potentially hostile or resistant
place. In other fragments the metaphorical linkage of sexual goals and
occupation of place is even more explicit. In exultant terms, for example,
Archilochus declares that

> I used to explore your rugged glens in my
> full-blooded youth.[21]

More significantly, in a fairly extensive fragment, Archilochus again
addresses reassuring words—this time to a woman who has already respon-
ded positively to his overtures. Consider this passage:

[20] Ibid. 4.   [21] Ibid. 3.

This citadel that you are walking in
was never sacked by any man, but now
your spear has conquered it, yours is the glory.[22]

Here the metaphor of secured place is used as the illumination of a generally concealed (or at least understated) power relation. Woman-as-object-of-desire-for-man is a notion which is often understood simply in terms of sexual gratification provided by the latter for the former (and elsewhere, of course, Archilochus fully embraces this possibility).

However, in the last quoted passage the poet foregrounds a different dynamic. His desire itself is the citadel which the woman has taken. Note how the intensity of this conquest is underlined by the reversal of customary metaphorical associations even as they are juxtaposed with a rather forced analogy. For it is the woman who has entered the man. She has symbolically appropriated and used the phallic spear. In so doing (and this is the rather forced analogy) she has effected an emotional conquest which finds no parallel in the agonistics of the poet's physical combat with rivals in battle.

Archilochus' use of martial metaphor extends, of course, far beyond the sexual realm. In the following fragment, such metaphor is used to illuminate a more general existential crisis, and, through clarifying it, to provide a more secure vantage point from whence to survey the travails of existence.

Heart, my heart, with helpless, sightless troubles now confounded,
up, withstand the enemy, opposing breast to breast.
All around they lie in wait, but stand you firmly grounded,
not over-proud in victory, nor in defeat oppressed.
In your rejoicing let your joy, in hardship your despairs
be tempered: understand the pattern shaping men's affairs.[23]

This extended congruence of martial metaphor and existential position finds its most concentrated and forceful statement in the following lines:

On my spear's my daily bread,
on my spear my wine
from Ismaros; and drinking it,
it's on my spear I recline.[24]

[22] Included in *Greek Lyric Poetry*, trans. M. L. West (Oxford: Oxford University Press, 1994), 5.
[23] Ibid. 11.   [24] Ibid. 13.

This fragment is fraught with ambiguity. However, one viable reading of it is as follows. Archilochus metaphorically links the flesh-and-blood-spattered spear—the stuff of life and death in combat—to the means of material subsistence and gratification. The fruits of combat earn him the basics of life. Interestingly, however, the poet—in reclining on his spear and drinking highly reputable wine—introduces a complex metaphor which both energizes and distances itself from the notion of battle as his means of material subsistence and gratification.

The energizing dimension hinges on a metaphorical drinking of blood which depends on the support of the spear; the distancing element consists of the simultaneous reading of this as an image of luxurious consumption and repose. It is through his life as a warrior that Archilochus finds the means and motive to reflect and savour. Little wonder, then, that in the preceding fragment Archilochus declares that

> I am a servant of the lord god of war
> and one versed in the Muses' lovely gifts.[25]

Let us now consider this analysis in relation to the theory of metaphor outlined in Section 6.1. Any act of cognition or judgement is given its character by the relation between the immediate object of such an act, and a broader latent field composed of the object's hidden aspects, its relation to other perceptible items, and its position within the personal experience and values of the cognizing subject. The power of metaphor consists in its capacity to elucidate a given term by evoking aspects of its latent field.

In the case of Archilochus both the subjective and objective dimensions of this field are manifestly evoked. His treatments of love, sex, and existential situations are, as we have seen, not just narratives but ones whose metaphorical content and development are formed by factors which are not immediately present, namely his life and particular experiences as a travelling warrior. This experiential field strikingly defines the way in which he addresses themes which are not themselves intrinsically martial.

In Archilochus, therefore, metaphor and its positioning within the specific poem, discloses a more general truth about how individual moments of experience are created at the intersection between that which is immediately addressed, and a personal sense of past, future, and counterfactual

---

[25] Ibid.

alternatives, which surround it as a latent field. The personality of the creator here discloses the creation of personality itself.

It is this creative subjective dimension which also energizes the objective aspect of the latent field. In human and animal communities, coexistence and the pursuit of mates are fraught with rivalries, competition, conflict, and stratagems. They also involve the traversal and inhabiting of specific places and regions. All these factors (and many others besides) weave in and out of all coexistence and courtship.

However, in our ordinary linguistic descriptions it is hard to evoke the complexity of this objective field of interactions and locations. Archilochus' metaphors, however, situate us coherently within it. His experience as a warrior, and gifts as a poet, enable him to link love and courtship, for example, to those martial or strategic elements which surround their pursuit and enjoyment.

The particular metaphors chosen are ones which link a given situation to an element or elements in the encompassing social or physical field, thus enabling the reader imaginatively to traverse the space between them. Poetic form and format means that the metaphor is not simply absorbed into the world of immediate verbal interactions, thence to be lost, or end up as a dead metaphor. Rather it is given renewed life through its position within the poem, through the poem's position within the artist's *oeuvre*, and through that *oeuvre*'s role in the synchronic and diachronic development of the traditions of poetic form. And these factors all play off, of course, within a general sense of the species' ongoing historical development.

I am arguing, then, that Archilochus' particular *style* of metaphor discloses fundamental philosophical insights concerning constants in both the ontological structure and the content of human experience. This possibility is inherent in, and distinctive to, all literary metaphor; Archilochus' style enables us to discern it in a particularly heightened way.

These considerations in themselves, are indicative of the fact that his treatment of metaphor—one of the most distinctive and fundamental literary devices—is both innovatory and a model for others. The artistic value of his work has, thereby, a broader canonic significance. There is also a further level of such significance to his work. It pertains to a constant in poetic form, rather than one in experience per se.

To explain. The origins of poetry probably lie in a formalization of language (vis-à-vis such features as trope and meter) for objective social purposes bound up with ritual and religious belief. Here, the articulation of metaphor would be closely tied to such purposes, and attention would focus, accordingly, on issues of the metaphor's use, more than the poetics of its articulation. Such ritual functions mark out the objective pole of the poetic idiom—the point where it touches or is absorbed by its societal contexts.

Archilochus use of metaphor, in contrast, is an element within a poetic style which helps define the opposite logical extreme. In strictly historical terms he inaugurates a recurrent tendency towards an aggressive and worldly subjectivism which finds an echo in figures such as Omar Khayyam (if we read the *Rubaiyat* in non-allegorical terms), François Villon, and the John Donne of the Sonnets. Archilochus thus creates a defining *logical* moment in the development of poetry as a symbolic form. His style of imagery, and its patterns of development and deployment, fully articulate poetic form's capacity for expressing constant elements in the subjective dimension of experience. More specifically, his metaphors are the most concentrated achievement of this.

Conclusion

In this discussion then, I have argued that the form of metaphor discloses key structural features which are involved in all cognition. For this disclosure to occur effectively, metaphor must be articulated in a mode wherein we are invited to attend to how it achieves its effects. The literary artwork offers the most basic instance of this. In such a work, attention focuses on the stylistic means whereby the creator articulates his or her subject matter.

Archilochus exemplifies these points in a particularly illuminating way. His metaphors elucidate their principal subjects through reference to a latent field which gravitates around both recurrent factors in human experience, and the poet's own highly distinctive personal perspective on them. Indeed, his personal perspective is so emphatic as to define the subjective logical extreme of poetic form itself. His style opens out a space of meaning which establishes itself as a possible idiom for others. This is the *canonic* significance of his work.

Now in an analysis such as the present one, the function of metaphor is described. In Archilochus and, indeed, *all* literary discourse, metaphor is *realized* as part of the fabric of a created aesthetic object. In recognizing the metaphorical connection between principal and secondary subject, we are invited—by the tensional gap between the two—to traverse it in imaginative terms. The latent field which is a precondition of language's articulation of perception, is here brought directly into play. We are also invited to enjoy the novelty of this connection, or its place in the structure of the poem as a whole.

What results is not so much full-blown philosophical understanding, as an empathic enjoyment of the relation between individual creative awareness and the structure and possibilities of being human as such. We enjoy aesthetically grounded philosophical insight. This is the supreme achievement of metaphor in its artistic context.

In this chapter, then, I have sought to show the ways in which literary metaphor per se engages with deep factors in human self-consciousness and perception. I turn now to factors which are distinctive to musical meaning.

7

Musical Meaning and Value

Introduction

In the present consumerist age nothing seems to be much valued unless it can be bought or sold or has some kind of use-value. On these terms, the arts risk being treated as entertainment, with any sense of their having a higher significance dismissed as 'elitist'.

Despite this contemporary prejudice, the preceding chapters have shown that art has vital involvement with our understanding of both self and world. Indeed, its aesthetic structure has a deeper significance still. The unique ontologies of different media make their own special contribution to stylistic interpretation. We have encountered aspects of this *metaphysical depth* (as I shall now call it) in relation to pictures and literature. I shall now explore it in the context of music. Here the vital aspect is music's capacity to be meaningful without having to refer to any specific individual (be it person, animal, object, event, singular or plural).

Recent metaphysical approaches to music have centred mainly on its type/token ontology, i.e. the individual work's status as a type which is instantiated through the different copies of its score, and its different performances, but which cannot be sufficiently identified with any one of these 'tokens'. This has involved some very worthwhile analyses.[1] But unless the possibility of metaphysical depth is also addressed, music—like all the arts—risks being counted as a mere luxury which can, with impunity, be relegated to secondary status in terms of educational priorities.

---

[1] See e.g. Julian Dodd, 'Musical Works as Eternal Types', *British Journal of Aesthetics,* 40 (2000), 424–40.

In this chapter, accordingly, I shall address musical meaning and value, with a view to clarifying their metaphysical and aesthetic significance. The investigation will show that music has a logically distinctive character that cannot be reduced to other forms of meaning, and that this is a function of both intrinsic qualities and the way in which they are mediated by refinement or innovation in relation to existing musical idioms. Metaphysical depth pertains, in other words, to both aspects of music's axes of normativity.

There are two approaches which are useful in clarifying these issues. The first is the claim that, in some sense, musical meaning is bound up with the presentation of emotion. Peter Kivy[2] notes that there has been something of a convergence of opinion amongst analytic philosophers as to what this involves vis-à-vis music's expressive aspects, but it might also be claimed that the resulting discussions have tended to focus somewhat on the relations between these aspects and their capacity to arouse kindred emotions in the listener.[3]

The result is that the structure and scope of expressive properties, and, in particular their more exact connection with the emotions per se, have not been clarified in the requisite detail. In this chapter, I will hope to rectify this by following up recent analytic philosophy of the emotions and by developing some clues from Suzanne Langer (though not in directions she would necessarily have approved of).

[2] In his *New Essays on Musical Understanding* (Oxford: Clarendon Press, 2001), 71. Apart from Kivy himself, the two most influential thinkers whose views converge on this issue are Jerrold Levinson and Stephen Davies. See e.g. the relevant essays in Levinson's impressive collection *The Pleasures of Aesthetics: Philosophical Essays* (Ithaca and London: Cornell University Press, 1996); and Davies's crucial *Musical Meaning and Expression* (Ithaca and London: Cornell University Press, 1994). My own approach is particularly close to Davies. He notes, for example, that 'Music presents emotion characteristics. Just as a willow can be sad-looking or a person's face happy-looking, music can present an expressive appearance in its sound (without regard to anyone's felt emotions). This is because we experience the dynamic character of music as like the actions of a person; movement is heard in music, and that movement is heard as purposive and as rationally organized' (Davies, *Musical Meaning*, 277). These remarks also summarize my own general approach. However, I develop that approach in a *very* different way from Davies. In particular, I stress the importance of musical form as a *stylistic interpretation* of emotion and its narrative context. This leads to an analysis of our response to music which stresses aesthetic factors, rather than the naturalistic grounds favoured by Davies. It should also be emphasized that the overall conception of art which shapes my account of musical meaning, is very different from Davies's.

[3] For a particularly searching approach to this see Derek Matravers, *Art and Emotion* (Oxford: Clarendon Press, 1998). Kivy in chs. 5, 6, and 7 of *New Essays on Musical Understanding* develops a viable 'cognitivist' response to the question including a sustained and (in my mind) convincing rejoinder to Matravers.

This approach connects in complex ways with a second useful inspiration. I refer to Schopenhauer's analysis of music as an expression of the World Will. The problematics of this connection have been well described by others.[4] But even if we do not subscribe to Schopenhauer's philosophy, it is possible to follow him loosely in seeing important connections between musical form and metaphysics in terms of specific aspects of human being-in-the-world, as well as the narrative structure of finitude.

Indeed, it will be a fundamental contention of this chapter that the distinctiveness of musical meaning hinges on an expanded notion of expressive properties, comprising music's virtual embodiment of the gestural aspects of possible emotions *and* less specific narrative elements which condition the emergence and development of such possibilities. This allows music to embody the relation between subject and object of experience, and intersubjective communication, in unique ways.

To clarify this metaphysical depth, I shall proceed as follows. Section 7.1 will address an area which is not often considered in this context, namely the distinctiveness of our auditory experience of the world. It will be suggested that the key factors in this experience have significance for musical meaning. Section 7.2 will take some first steps to show this through arguments based on recent general theories of the emotions. Special emphasis will be given to the emotions' cognitive structure and their necessary relation to bodily gesture.

In Section 7.3 it will be shown that music connects with emotion through, in the first instance, emotional aspects of the vocal gesture, and then the formalization of this (via pitch) through musical instrumentation. Special emphasis will be given to the way in which these developments invest music with the character of virtual expression. In Section 7.4 the logical distinctiveness of musical meaning will be spelt out on the basis of its metaphysical depth, and, in particular, the unique way in which it diminishes the boundaries between subject and object of experience, and subject and subject. A secondary level of distinctive musical meaning will be identified on the basis of metaphysical issues raised in Section 7.1. A number of important qualifications to my general position will also be made.

---

[4] See e.g. the chapter on Schopenhauer in Malcolm Budd's *Music and the Emotions: The Philosophical Theories* (London: Routledge, 1985). See also Kivy, *New Essays on Musical Understanding*, ch. 2.

Section 7.5 will go on to consider the metaphysical aspects of musical value, and, in particular, the conditions whereby we can make a transition from music per se to music as an art form. It will be argued that this is made possible not only by questions of form, but also by the way in which the particular work or *oeuvre* offers a new existential perspective through its creative historical difference from other works. This dimension, as it were, activates the individual work's metaphysical depth.

In Section 7.6, I will develop this claim through elaborating four categories of value, and in Section 7.7, will defend my approach against some objections through a consideration of canonic music in the postmodern era. I will finally draw some general conclusions concerning metaphysical depth and music's experiential value.

7.1

The ontological structure of auditory experience centres on a number of key factors. The first is *temporal necessity*. All sense perception is in time but to understand the unity of spatial objects one does not have to scan the relation of part to part, and to the whole, in any exact temporal sequence. One can look at each element after another in any order that one wishes.

In contrast to this, to perceive the unity of a sound involves understanding it as an auditory event or sequence of events. It is necessary, accordingly, that the specific auditory elements must be perceived in an exactly successive temporal order. In the absence of such a temporally necessary order the sound is no more than unintelligible noise.

A further significant implication follows from this. For since our very sense of 'things happening' is constituted by the temporal necessity of continuous events, the sound-event and its sequences will tend to exemplify this fundamental metaphysical character in a way that spatial events do not. This is because our practical lives are immersed in our spatial surroundings and all the many distractions and dangers which these surroundings present.

Sound is much less burdened in this respect. It can, of course, alert us to practically significant space-occupying phenomena, but it is usually those phenomena rather than sound in its own right which we have to respond to. Indeed, it is only exceptionally that sound amounts to anything like a threat on its own. It is better fitted, therefore, to exemplify the metaphysical structure of events without distraction, at the immediate sensory level.

A second (and more unfamiliar) dimension of auditory experience is its *indexicality*. In the case of vision, touch, and taste, there is not such a gap between the object and our experience of it. True we can distinguish between the object which we see, or touch, and taste, and our experience of it, but we do not usually take the experience to be *so* distinct from its object, as to be a mere *sign* of its presence. When we see, touch, and taste, the object of these senses seems so proximal as to be almost identical with the experience of it, even though in the strict physical terms our experience is only an effect of it.

With smell and sound, however, matters are rather different. Here the olfactory or acoustic experience often arises when the object which gives rise to it is concealed or distant from the body (or, of course, both). We take the experience to be an indexical sign, i.e. one which is causally produced by, and is thence taken to be indicative of, the presence or proximity of some person, creature, or state of affairs.

A capacity to recognize signs of this sort is surely common to all animal modes of consciousness, and is of especial importance in tracking or avoiding prey and predator respectively. It is also probably one of the key factors involved in the transition from consciousness to self-consciousness.

In the case of olfactory indexicals, the signifying element is rather indeterminate. One can distinguish between strong and weak smells, but it is not easy to quantify their intensive magnitude in such a way that this can express the proximity (or otherwise) of the producer in exact terms. Sound, in contrast (with human beings at least), has more indexical scope and precision. It can register the presence of that which is causing it at distances much greater than that found in the relation of smell and its producer.

More significantly, it can also register the imminent presence of its producer with dramatic vividness and exactness through intensity of volume and the precision and order of auditory reports. It deeply anticipates and emphasizes the presence of its producer, whilst—qua indexical sign—being no more than an effect of that producer.

Sound, then, exemplifies one of signification's most primal modes with particular lucidity. It can return us, in a sense, to the origins of signification. Indeed, the auditory indexical has an interesting broader significance through exemplifying what I shall call *qualitative enigma*. This centres on the fact that sounds are, for the most part, of a radically different ontological order from the things which produce them whilst, of course, being no more than expressions of the presence or proximity of those things.

Such enigmatic difference from, and expression of, its cause, gives the auditory indexical a striking symbolic potential. It can exemplify the enigma of qualitative change in our experience of the universe per se. At an objective level we can explain why one kind of thing can produce the familiar effects that it does, in terms of physical properties and natural laws. But how and why physical properties and natural laws produce just these effects is, in ultimate terms, a mystery. We can describe with increasing comprehensiveness and detail how things change, but *why* these changes take place is not explicable in unconditional terms.

Our immediate perceptual lives, of course, are full of dramatic qualitative transformations of one kind of thing into another, but because these are so much a part of everyday experience we lose sight of the wonder and ultimate enigma of how and why one kind of thing changes into another.

This is especially the case when the qualitative changes in question involve spatial factors—factors which are at the heart of our most immediate practical dealings with the world. In the case of smell and sound, these practical distractions are less manifest. Sound in particular (as an indexical sign which vividly and precisely anticipates or emphasizes the presence or proximity of its cause whilst being of a different ontological order from it) will always have something of the character of surprise, unexpectedness, or uncertainty, even whilst being entirely familiar. The enigma of sound is, in other words, a potentially powerful exemplification of the generally enigmatic character of our experience of qualitative change.

I have, then, shown how the ontology of auditory experience has a distinctive and complex character. It is founded on the temporal necessity of the acoustic event but, through this event being an indexical sign of that which produces it, sound has an intrinsic capacity to evoke the enigma of qualitative transformation at a direct experiential level.

To make the transition to music two further factors must now be evoked. The first concerns the role of volition. In the case of sight, touch, and taste, we do not in any literal sense, produce visible, tactile, and gustatory experiences at will. We have to align our bodies in relation to the objects of those senses. This means either changing our position so that we encounter the appropriate external stimuli, or—as in the case of making a doodle or eating food—physically acting on material which is external to the body.

In the case of olfactory experience, in contrast, smells can be both encountered and produced. However, the capacity for such production is only partially volitional in so far as it is necessarily mediated by the presence of chemical processes over which we cannot exert control.

With auditory experience, in contrast, the volitional element is paramount (though not, of course, absolute). We can encounter sounds produced by other things, but equally, we can produce a complex range of sounds at will, through vocal articulation. These sounds are the purest indexical signs of the body's capacity for volitional activity. The enigma referred to earlier, indeed, is all the more powerful in so far as it is here engendered through the body's free expression. Something universal—qualitative change—is experienced not just as the site and the surround of human activity, but as something which is in part constitutive of such activity.

And this volitional dimension also mediates the temporal necessity of acoustic events. If a sound is intelligible it must follow a necessary order in time. Likewise, if sound is to be used for communication, it must follow a volitionally directed necessary order. The basis of this is repetition. Through its capacity to be repeated at will, sound can be formalized as a basis for communication. A key feature in the ontology of sound is here restructured as a fundamental element in consciousness of self and other.

We have, then, the world of sound—temporally necessary events, indexicality, qualitative enigma, and the volitional appropriation of these factors in the human production and repetition of sound. The auditory world both envelops us and answers to some of our most basic cognitive needs. Indeed, it is of the profoundest metaphysical depth, in so far as the relation between the temporal necessity of events, qualitative change, and volitional control, exemplifies the most fundamental factors in the free embodied subject's interactions with the world.

If this account is correct, then sound has *intrinsic expressive significance*. By articulating sound we make ourselves at home with the world in terms other than that of physical safety and familial and social bonding. Sound's metaphysical depth relates us positively to the world's rhythms of change. It offers a special kind of emotional security.

Expressive factors are, of course, profoundly involved in all our vocal activity—and in language especially. But the immediate practical relevance of such activity means that we are readily distracted from what is distinctive and vital in our auditory involvement in the world.

This metaphysical depth can, of course, be articulated in abstract terms through philosophical analyses such as the present one. However, our sense of it is much more striking and has deeper ramifications, when it occurs at the immediate sensory level itself, i.e. when auditory experience is able to *exemplify* its expressive significance through figuring in an aesthetic whole.

What is needed, therefore, is a special idiom wherein the voluntary repetition of sound can be generated in a way which transcends mundane activity and factual vocal communication so as to engage aesthetic attention. The idiom in question, is, of course, music.

Given this general outline of the intrinsic expressiveness of auditory experience, it must now be shown how this finds more specific embodiment and development in the form of musical meaning. It is to this task that I now turn.

7.2

A useful starting point is to follow up and then go far beyond some points made by Suzanne K. Langer. She observes, for example, that 'The great office of music is to organize our conception of feeling into more than occasional awareness of emotional storm, i.e. give us an insight into what might truly be called the "life of feeling" or subjective unity of experience.'[5] This observation is correct in so far as it highlights the organizational and elucidatory function of music in relation to the emotions. Unfortunately, Langer's broader approach focuses much too heavily on feeling's 'felt' and visceral dimensions. More recent literature on the emotions has emphasized a complex network of factors in addition to this. And it is this overall complexity which must be negotiated before emotion can be effectively applied in the musical context. The remainder of this section will perform such a negotiation.

[5] Suzanne K. Langer, *Feeling and Form* (London: Routledge & Kegan Paul, 1953), 126.

Perhaps the most generally important factor in emotion is its cognitive core as a *mode of appraisal*. Traditionally in western philosophy the emotions have been seen as disruptive factors in our rational comprehension of the world. However, since the 1970s an opposite emphasis has arisen. It centres on the emotions' status as potent cognitive and organizational factors in experience.[6] For in order for us to be motivated to action, some person, item, or state of affairs must be judged in terms of its positive or negative significance for our lives. And such a judgement will provide, in turn, a powerful motive for further activity based on attraction or aversion to the item or state of affairs in question.

This leads to a second (and closely related) factor in the life of emotion, namely, its *narrative context*. Any emotional appraisal judges its object as positive or negative in terms of its relation to one's personal interests. But, as Alasdair Macntyre and others have argued, one's personal interests and sense of self are not simply nodes of isolated desire or awareness.[7] They involve a *narrative* structure based on a person's present situation *interpreted* in relation to his or her individual history and the broader societal values which contextualize it. The positive or negative factors at issue in emotional appraisals hinge upon this relation. They are shaped by it just as their outcomes, in turn, influence the developing narrative of a personal history. Active relation to a narrative, in other words, is, in part, constitutive of emotional responses.

The third key factor in the life of emotion is of the most decisive significance for musical meaning (as I will show in more detail later on) and must, accordingly, be given an especially sustained analysis now. It consists of the primacy of the *gestural* aspect in providing criteria for the ascription of, and for reference to, emotional states. Unfortunately there are some significant misunderstandings of this issue. Consider, for example, these remarks by David Pitt:

---

[6] The approach which I will follow is broadly consistent with that proposed by William Lyons in his *Emotion* (Cambridge: Cambridge University Press, 1980). For a much wider ranging account see Robert Solomon, *The Passions: Emotion and the Meaning of Life* (Indianapolis: Hackett, 1993); and Peter Goldie's *The Emotions: A Philosophical Explanation* (Oxford: Clarendon Press, 2000).

[7] See Alaisdair MacIntyre, *After Virtue: A Study in Moral Theory* (London: Duckworth, 1980), ch. 15. The importance of narrative structure and context for the emotions is an important theme in Martha Nussbaum's work, notably *Love's Knowledge: Essays on Philosophy and Literature* (Oxford: Clarendon Press, 1990). More recently, Peter Goldie has emphasized the importance of the emotions for narrative structure in his paper 'One's Remembered Past: Narrative Thinking, Emotion, and the External Perspective', *Philosophical Papers*, 32/3 (2003), 301–19.

We do not perceive each other's emotions directly, in spite of how things might appear to us. Emotions are internal psychological states, and as such are not directly perceivable. Our perception of each other's emotions is indirect, proceeding via recognition of characteristic behaviours. We may say that we see or hear that someone is sad or happy, or whatever, but such seeing or hearing is no more direct than it is in the case of seeing that something is heavy or hearing that it is hollow.[8]

These remarks present a somewhat old-fashioned (but still very common) misconception of the emotions. The idea is that behavioural manifestations of emotion are signs from which we infer the existence of some internal state which is (as it were) the emotion proper. However, whilst we might separate behaviour and internal state for analytic purposes, they are, logically and phenomenologically speaking, unintelligible without reference to each other. They are aspects of the same complex phenomenon.

Of course, it is possible to feel emotions whilst hiding or suppressing their gestural aspect, but this is a special case where cultural considerations override their more natural embodiment. Indeed, as we saw earlier, emotions involve a necessary *social* dimension in so far as their cognitive and narrative aspects hinge on the relation between a person and his or her social environment. One could not make sense of this aspect unless there was an ontogenetically necessary connection between internal states and behaviour which allowed emotion to exist as much in the public domain as in the private. This is the role played by the gestural aspect.

In this context the analogies offered by Pitt in the foregoing quotation are rather misleading. Determining how heavy something is, or whether it is hollow or not, does not depend on how the item looks in these respects. Appearance is not a criterion for ascribing such properties. Physical inspection is required. In the case of emotion, however, matters are very different. How someone appears in a behavioural sense is not only logically relevant to the ascription of emotion, *it is the most reliable criterion we have.*

Of course, a person may—as we saw earlier—feign gestures of emotion or may suppress them; but this can also be the case with the only other candidate for ascribing emotions, namely the subject's verbal reports. Indeed, the only way one can test the veracity of such reports is by

---

[8] David Pitt, review of Kivy, *New Essays on Musical Understanding*, in the *Times Literary Supplement*, 23 Apr. 2003, 23.

observation of the subject's behaviour—a task which will focus heavily on his or her gestures.

The gestural aspect of emotion, then, provides us with the best public criteria for the identification of emotions. It is logically correlated with the 'inner' aspect. Given the necessity of this connection, it would be in defiance of Occam's Razor to take the two factors as separate from one another—a case of symptoms, and actual state. We must see them, rather, as respective public and subjective aspects of the same complex bodily phenomenon. On these terms, it makes perfectly good sense to say that, through beholding the appropriate forms of gesture, we can, under normal circumstances, directly perceive emotion.

This being said, it must also be admitted that the 'internal' or (better) *visceral* aspect is a necessary fourth aspect of emotion. It is necessary, because without such a factor coming into play at least sometimes it would not be *generally* possible to separate emotional responses from appraisals per se, and from merely feigned gestures. The 'felt' aspect is *involuntary* and thence—for the subject at least—an indicator that one is fully in the grip of an emotion. However, this visceral dimension should be seen, at best, as one aspect of the emotional whole—and one which (as suggested above) is the 'internal' correlate of other factors involved.

I have argued then, that emotion is a complex state with four different aspects. Given this analysis it is clear that if music is to be linked to the embodiment of emotion in any significant way the emphasis needs to be on emotion's gestural, narrative, and appraisal-embodying dimension rather more than on their visceral character (though a place will have to be found for this). Indeed it is through linking music to the aforementioned factors that we will also be able to relate it (in Section 7.4) to the metaphysics of auditory experience, discussed in Section 7.1.

7.3

I turn, then, to the connection between music and the emotions. A first key point concerns the cultural mediation of gestural aspects. It may be that some such features—such as tears and crying in relation to grief—have a natural basis. It is equally clear, however, that these and other gestural aspects can be influenced by social contexts and values, and issue in codified behavioural expression. Such codification accentuates the dimension of communication and control.[9]

Both nature and codification are important for music by virtue, in the first instance, of *the voice*. We saw in Section 7.1 how the voluntary character of vocalization is, in metaphysical terms, of key significance in our active orientation towards the world. Given this, it is natural that the voice is a decisive means for realizing the gestural aspect of emotion. The extraordinary range of intonation and auditory volume available to it, allows it to manifest and qualify an extensive range of emotional responses. It is *the* major organ of emotion's gestural dimension—even though one does not customarily think of the larynx's activities as a form of gesture. In fact, the emotionally significant vocal gesture is more complex still. In this respect we will recall that sound has an indexical relation to its producer. It follows, therefore, that since the voice is an indexical sign of the vocal gesture, the actual emotional meaning resides not in the activity of the larynx as such, but in the indexical auditory sound/signs which it produces. In a decisive sense the auditory indexical is the *completion* of the vocal emotional gesture through being both its physical and intended culminating effect.

Other gestures (most notably facial expressions) can, of course, embody emotion, and also be *used*—through manifest display, or exaggeration, or whatever—to *deliberately* communicate the fact of our being in the grips of such a state. In the case of the vocal gesture, however, an indexical signifying element is partially constitutive of the emotional state *as such* through completing it (in the sense just noted). Indeed its intrinsic communicative scope is significantly broader than that of other communicating gestures in so far as it can be registered by the recipient even when the vocalizer is not in his or her immediate proximity. The vocal gesture, in other words, is by nature suited for communication and socialization in a way that other emotionally significant gestures are not.

Now a decisive transition must be made. The acquisition of language enables the codification of the vocal gesture in a way which allows it to be used for precise communication. This involves not only reporting facts but

---

[9] Interestingly, Ronald de Sousa has proposed a theory where the narrative context for emotion is deeply permeated by sociocultural factors. On his terms, socialization is the decisive factor in patterns of emotional response. See his 'The Rationality of Emotions' in Amelie O. Rorty (ed.), *Explaining the Emotions* (Berkeley and Los Angeles: University of California Press, 1980).

also the *style* of their utterance. As well as *what* is said, *how* it is said (in terms of vocal intonation) can be an integral part of the meaning which is to be communicated. It is indeed, possible, to recognize the emotional tones of an utterance or conversation (e.g. angry voices in the distance) even if one is not in a position to recognize what the angry exchange is about.

The acquisition of language also dramatically extends the range of emotional inflections in the voice, in so far as the codification of the vocal utterance allows it to be controlled and directed. Often we talk of being in the grip of an emotion but in so far as the emotion finds embodiment through linguistic vocalization, the involuntary dimension is brought under some degree of control, however slight.

Vocalization, then, is the most important way of exemplifying and qualifying emotion's gestural aspect. Even without reference to language, it is partially constitutive of the emotional state which it exemplifies. When such vocalization is structured by language, the way in which the utterance is pronounced can both further shape its emotional meaning, and also extend the range of such meaning by virtue of language's controlling and directing force.

Music is a continuation of these factors. As Suzanne Langer observes: 'Music begins only when some formal factor—rhythm or melody—is recognized as a framework within which accent and intonation are elements in their own right, not chance attributes of individual speech.'[10]

This formalization carries further import. As we have already noted, it is possible for a person to feign the gestural aspects of an emotion so as to illustrate a point, or to deceive, or, in some contexts, amuse other people. This means that *the gestural aspects here exemplify a possible emotional response rather than an actual one.* Of course, it may be that an actual emotional response occurs, but the formalization involved means that *we do not have to* interpret it in such occurent terms. It locates the emotion in the domain of possibility, rather than that of actuality. I shall henceforth use the term *virtual emotion*, accordingly, in relation to this.[11]

In ordinary usage, the term 'virtual' means 'almost' or 'amounting to'. Indeed, because of the discourses of digital media, the usage is now especially tied to the level of sensory appearance. This is why 'virtual' is especially

---

[10] Langer, *Feeling and Form*, 142.
[11] Langer also uses the term 'virtual' but my usage should be understood strictly on the lines indicated in the main body of my text.

appropriate for the relation between vocal music and the emotions. When such music is described as virtual emotion, it means that we are dealing with sensible aspects which exemplify the gestural dimension of emotion, but whose form does not demand that we take the agent or bearer of the aspect to be actually 'in the grips' of the *full* emotion in question (i.e. experiencing its visceral aspects).

The formalization in rhythm or melody which Langer describes builds on this. For when a person sings or hums a melody it may follow a gestural format which communicates a particular emotion or range of emotions. However, the person may just be performing the music, rather than undergoing its full emotional content. The formalization of vocal gestures through rhythm and melody serves to present them as wholly voluntary virtual embodiments of emotion. They have a recognizable character as this or that emotion or range of emotions, but without us having to regard them as states of any actual person.

Of equal importance is their immediate sensory character. For vocal gestures of a virtual kind do not simply indicate or abstractly describe some emotional possibility, they characterize it in a quite specific way through the style of the formalization and its vocal expression. *They present emotion at the same ontological level where fully realized states of emotion are manifest.*

I am arguing, then, that vocal music marks a point of transition from emotional responses per se, to virtual embodiments of emotion. The question arises, then, as to whether instrumental music can be seen as a further development of this tendency. And the answer is 'yes'.

To see why, it is worth considering another remark by Langer: 'Vocal music can only approximate to the flexibility, the distinctiveness, the tonal and rhythmic accuracy of instruments.'[12]

The mediating term between voice and instrument is the fixation and use of *pitch*. Langer suggests that this probably owes its existence in large part

to the discovery of inanimate physical sources from which sounds of definite pitch may be obtained by plucking, striking, rubbing, or blowing. By means of pitched instruments, intonation is at once objectified, instruments furnish a standard to which vocal pitch may be held.[13]

[12] Langer, *Feeling and Form*, 143.
[13] Ibid.

On these terms, then, the use of instruments allows an objectification of the vocal gesture, such that musical pitch becomes more controllable. That means, of course, that formalization of rhythm and melody can also be extended and stabilized.

Clearly, through instrumentation, music is extended even more in the direction of virtuality. For whilst an instrument requires a person to play it, the music which is played is manifestly not an actual emotional state of any person.

That being said, it still has a logical bearing on the ascription of such states. On the one hand, as we have seen, instrumentation is a continuation of the vocal gesture's emotional intonation; on the other hand, since the emotional import of gestures can be characterized by their effects on other things as well as by their intrinsic features, we can read certain kinds of sound as evidence of gestural character. If they are intentionally produced by human artifice and are describable as elated, tranquil, or agitated, or whatever, then we will tend to read them *as* virtual exemplifications of the appropriate kind of emotionally significant gesture. All in all, instrumental music preserves its origins in vocal intonation but extends this to a higher level of virtuality.

We find, then, that through the voice and instrumentation, music virtually exemplifies emotion under its gestural aspects. Let us now address a second key connection between music and the structure of emotion. As ever, Langer is instructive as a starting point.

Rhythm is the setting up of new tensions by the resolution of former ones. They need not be of equal duration at all; but the situation that begets the new crisis must be inherent in the denouement of its forerunners.[14]

And one can generalize this insight. The character and the meaning of individual musical units are determined by their unfolding role in the piece of which they are a part. They anticipate what is to come, just as they recontextualize the meaning of the parts which have gone before them. The musical work thus has the character of narrative development.

An interesting angle on this is provided by the following remark from Schopenhauer:

---

[14] Ibid. 127.

Melody is always a deviation from the keynote through a thousand crotchety wanderings up to the most painful discord. After this, it at last finds the keynote again, which expresses the satisfaction and composure of the will, but with which nothing more can be done, and the continuation of which would only be a wearisome and meaningless monotony.[15]

This remark is fanciful in its exactness but not in its overall sense. The tonal scale-system allows the relation between music (be it vocal or instrumental) to be formalized to such a degree that the narrative structure inherent in rhythm becomes much more complex. The development of themes, rhythms, and harmonies is formally describable in terms which can also exemplify the emergence of emotional states in relation to personal and group narratives.

To see the importance of this, consider the following. One might describe a piece as 'cheerful' or 'sad' but if there was no more to be said of it than that, it would not be a piece of much significance. The real substance of music lies in the way that one stage of recognizable possible emotional import is transformed into another—often in an extended way through the use of melodic, rhythmic, and harmonic factors that bear some analogy to the progressing tones of a conversation.

As it develops, the tone of the protagonists' vocal gestures will change, sometimes having a mere matter-of-fact character, sometimes a sense of urgency, or sometimes merely a sense of accumulating meaning (the possibilities are, of course, endless). But whatever the case, by simply listening to the tone of a conversation, and without bringing in its factual content, we can follow its cumulative narrative development to definite emotional 'conclusions'.

On these terms, then, recognizable and sustained emotional characteristics will often only emerge from a broader tonal matrix as passages of climax or resolution. This means that if we wish to characterize musical meaning *as it is distributed in a work as a whole*, then it is as the virtual embodiment of expressive properties *in a sense which includes factors other than specific emotions*. The term *virtual expression* should be understood to comprise both

---

[15] Arthur Schopenhauer, *The World as Will and Representation*, trans. E. Payne (New York: Dover, 1980), 321. It is worth noting, in passing, that my linking of musical meaning to the voice and its instrumental formalization would have been vehemently resisted by Schopenhauer.

recognizable emotional gestures and the tonal narrative progressions which build up to these and/or move them along.

There is a further interesting link between these musical factors and experiential form. The analogy here is based on the relation of *figure and ground*. There can be no perception or knowledge of any kind unless some 'intentional object' is specified. Logically, such an object can only be specified in so far as it stands out against, or emerges from, a background of factors other than itself. The intended object, therefore, is a *figure* defined in relation to a *ground*.

This is the most basic structure in both immediate spatial perception, and in the way memory and imagination find their bearings through an individual's present self-definition in relation to a ground of events, relations, and places, which form the setting or context for his or her activities, and, in particular, for emotional states.

Music offers a parallel to this, in terms, of the relation between, on the one hand, dominant melodic and/or salient rhythmic and harmonic factors, and, on the other hand, the broader harmonic and rhythmic background which contextualizes these and facilitates their emergence. In conjunction, these formal devices form a kind of developing network of *temporal* figure/ground relations, wherein individual 'present' dominant characteristics emerge from a less well-defined temporal background of events and situations.

The fact that this analogy rests on a cognitive structure which is fundamental to our existence in space and time means, accordingly, that music will tend to carry associational meanings suggestive of experience in a fuller sense, i.e. not just the character of emotions and their tonal narratives, but also of the kinds of real action and situations (involving persons and events) in which such emotions might be generated.

That being said, it is important to emphasize that the specific nature of such *existential associations* (as I shall call them) is mainly a function of the personal experience of the listener, rather than the objectively describable tonal character of the music. This character prompts and guides our patterns of association, but their individual content is provided by the way in which the music engages our personal experiential perspective. Hence, whilst virtual expression can involve existential associations as a subjective (and extraordinarily vital) aspect of musical meaning, they cannot bear the burden of its objective definition.

Having linked music to virtual expression, a vital question must be addressed before proceeding any further. It is that of whether the link between music and virtual expression *must* be made. Is it not possible, for example, to give a purely formal description of the interplay of themes, harmonies, and the like without even having to mention the analogies noted above?[16]

The answer to this is complex. Formal appreciation is an important aspect of our engagement with music. But it is not *the* most fundamental. In fact, at the conceptual level, formal appreciation of music qua art cannot be entirely separated from expressive factors. There are three arguments to show this.

First (in order to distinguish music from the mere enjoyment of beautiful natural or decorative forms), musical art must be taken to involve the creation of distinctive and individual aesthetic forms. But if this is so, then the notion of artistic originality is involved and this entails *expressive* factors in so far as a work's superiority to other created forms is, of necessity, a constitutive element in our appreciation. To enjoy form in this context is (at least in part) to be moved by, or to admire, the artist's treatment of it.

Expressive factors also arise in a second 'formal' context. In Chapter 3, I developed a concept of artistic beauty, but, following Kant, showed that this is not the most distinctive aspect of art. Traditionally, formalists have tended to treat formal relations and representational content as though they were two very different aspects of the artwork. But elements of content can also have formal significance. We talk for example, of how a balance of characterization between two individuals in a narrative gives it a sustained dramatic tension, or the way in which a passage of evenly distributed brushstrokes in a landscape painting makes the clouds seem heavy with foreboding.

The point is here, that artistic form can embody *aesthetic ideas*, i.e. *forms which interpret subject matter*. Hence if music *can* be related to the presumption of virtuality without contradiction (and I have shown in detail how this is possible), then its formal relations must be meaningful in an expanded sense. They must encompass virtual expression.

---

[16] The classic formalist account remains Edward Hanslick's *On the Musically Beautiful*, trans. Geoffrey Payzant (Indianapolis: Hackett, 1986).

To restrict the significance of musical form to narrow 'formalist' considerations, in contrast, would exclude music from art's most distinctive dimension of meaning through arbitrary stipulation. Virtual expression is *musical form in its most artistically developed sense.*

A third argument can be offered. In the formal appreciation of music expressive factors are inevitably involved. In immediate terms, for example, one talks of 'violent' passages and the like. Indeed, even such 'pure' formal notions as 'harmonious', 'clumsy', and 'elegant' entail some kind of expressive association, by virtue of being analogical derivations from broader aspects of human interaction and gesture.

This applies even to so neutral a term as 'balance'. Sounds—even in scale systems—are not the kinds of entities which can be 'balanced' literally other than in quantitative terms (such as loudness or duration). If we wish to talk of balance in some qualitative 'formal' sense, this can only be through analogy.

But analogy with what? We might invoke quantitative relations with qualitative outcomes, e.g. when too much salt spoils the taste of something. However, the question then arises of *why* such quantitatively based analogies should make the experience of sound significant. There must be something important about the phenomenon which is activated by the analogy. My account of the metaphysical significance of sound in Section 7.1 and my linkage of it to intrinsic expressive significance (bound up with vocal gesture) clarify what is at issue here.

I would argue then that the only feasible explanation of formal appreciation's analogical base is gesture. Musical forms—such as fugues, first subjects, recapitulations, sonatas, and the like—describe formal structures. But formal appreciation goes beyond this, and invokes virtual expression (however, subtly disguised).

Formalism in music, therefore, cannot stand on its own. It is conceptually connected to expression in three different ways, two of which involve the all-important presumption of virtuality.

It should also be emphasized that there are good historical reasons for seeing formal appreciation as actually secondary to, and emergent from, virtual expression. The formalist approach is a specialist product of modern western culture, whilst music per se is a transhistorical, transcultural practice reaching back for millennia. It would follow, therefore, that musical meaning must be grounded in something of non-specialist import which, at a certain stage of its development, is able to generate an additional culture of formal appreciation.

This, of course, is the significance of virtual expression. We care about the beauty of musical forms *because* they are already significant for us as virtual expression. If one is highly cultivated in the understanding of musical form, one may be overwhelmed by formal issues—but only because such forms have already been established as having broader existential import. Through our broader culture they are transmitted to us as representations of virtual expression. And even if our formal appreciation does not take this factor into account explicitly, it is, nevertheless, one of the conditions which makes such appreciation possible.

If a formalist rejects this account, it is incumbent on him or her to offer an alternative which can explain the genesis and transcultural ubiquity of music. In this chapter, I have provided such an account, and will develop it much further. Music constellates around the emotional resonance of the voice and the progressive formalization of such resonance through language, and the use of musical instruments. The musical work, qua vocal gesture or the instrumental extension of such gesture, is codified across many cultures in terms of a presumption of virtuality. To hear it, is to hear it *as* virtual expression.

Hopefully, this approach is consistent, has explanatory scope, and also finds a place for formalism—albeit in a secondary role.

Let us, then, continue the account of the relation between music and the emotions. First (as we saw in Section 7.2), actual emotions arise when something is appraised on the basis of its significance for one's life. This means that the gestural aspects are enabled by a narrative complex encompassing one's previous experiences and actions. Given this, the very fact that music converges on the virtual embodiment of emotion's gestural aspects, means that the formal connections from which these aspects emerge *must* also be read as virtual embodiments of narrative movement and relationships.

They provide a sense of actions and decisions and the like which make the emergence of more specific emotional characteristics intelligible. Without this, we would have to read the salient emotional content as if it formed discrete (as it were) ready-made elements for which the other melodic and harmonic material were a mere setting. However, whilst the principle of unity in such a work would be formal, the idea of such ready-made emotional musical units is unintelligible.

In overall terms, therefore, the musical work must have the character of virtual expression—of possible emotional characteristics *generated in a narrative context*.

We are thus led to the third connection between musical meaning and the emotions. We will recall that emotions are a form of *appraisal* in so far as they involve judging some factor in terms of its positive or negative significance for our lives. In the case of music, matters are different because of its character as a virtual embodiment of emotion. This involves a dimension of appraisal—but shifted from the personal to the public domain.

The key point here is that by offering up such gestures in a public context, the audience is invited to appraise whether or not this music is a worthwhile virtual presentation of the kind of expression which it is addressing. We are implicitly invited to judge whether or not this virtual expression 'rings true', in artistic terms. The full ramifications of this will be developed later (in Sections 7.5 to 7.7) when I address the nature of musical merit.

Before considering the fourth connection between music and the emotions, we must take stock of some matters arising from the connections already made. In particular, it must be emphasized that, whilst virtual expression relates to the narrative and appraisal structure of emotion, *it also changes these structures*.

In the case of appraisal, neither the observer nor subject of an occurent emotional response is always explicitly aware of the nature of the appraisal which is involved. With virtual expression, in contrast (as we have just seen), the way in which the gestural emotional possibility is presented, becomes the object of appraisal itself.

The transformation of the narrative dimension in virtual expression is just as radical. In the case of occurent emotional states it is impossible for the observer and subject of such states to have anything other than a partial and unstable comprehension of the full narrative factors which determine the nature of the appraisal. Even in the subject's case, his or her enabling narrative is not some factual open book of easily recognized causes and conditions of present conscious states. It is a shifting interpretative matrix.

Music qua virtual expression, in contrast, *objectively* exemplifies this interpretative narrative structure in the form of part/whole tonal and/or auditory relations—where the whole is not just the sum of its parts, but where, nevertheless, the whole and its parts are given complete in such a way that the nature of their relation is clarified. In this context, to be 'clarified' does not mean sufficiently analysed in factual terms, but rather made communicable through sensible/imaginative modelling or exemplification. Through this aesthetic embodiment it can be explored and learned from in renewable ways as one's own experience changes.

Given this, we might expect that the relation between music and the other two aspects of the emotions will also be significantly affected. In the case of the all-important gestural connection, the gestural aspect is genuinely shared. Virtual and occurent emotions cannot be distinguished at this level in isolation. However, the context in which this aspect is exemplified is that of virtual expression—the musical work as a whole, where the appraisal and narrative aspects are different (in the senses noted above) from occurrent states. This means that through being manifestly emergent from virtual expression, the meaning of the gestural aspects is also changed. It is recognized *as* virtual rather than occurrent, and is judged in relation to the mode of its emergence rather than in its own right. It exists, in other words, as an *aesthetic* configuration.

These considerations allow us to (at last) make the fourth and final link between music and the emotions, and to place it in a proper philosophical perspective. As we have already seen, the visceral aspect of emotion is often seen as what the emotions are really about. I, however, have argued that it is only one in a complex of factors.

Now given the differences between virtual expression and occurent emotion, it is clear that the visceral aspect of the former will be different from that of the latter. In particular, the nature of its correlation with the other aspects will be relatively open. This is because the gestural aspect of virtual expression is *manifestly* virtual in the way just described. Hence, whilst it may have a quite strong emotional character of a specific kind, this will at best incline us to respond to it in similar terms *on occasion*. The greater likelihood is that our response will be different—perhaps sympathetic, surprised, fascinated, or whatever, by virtue of the way in which the virtual emotion is *made* to emerge from this particular formal/narrative configuration.

On these terms, it is virtual expression—the emergence of emotional possibility from its narrative matrix—which is logically decisive. The *kind* of visceral aspect aroused is a wholly secondary matter. Such arousal will be guided by the virtual emotional character of the music, but determined, ultimately, by the listener's sense of (or indifference to) the conditions of its virtual emergence.

7.4

I shall now summarize my main arguments so far and draw some major conclusions concerning what makes musical meaning distinctive. Some important qualifications to my position will also be considered.

My first major points addressed the metaphysics of auditory experience, emphasizing its temporal necessity, indexicality, qualitative enigma, and the significance of repetition as a means of harmonizing these contrary ontological factors on a volitional basis. I then formulated a theory of the emotions based on the importance of appraisal, narrative, gestural aspects, and (to a much lesser extent) visceral feeling as criteria for emotional states.

A special emphasis was assigned to gestural features, since vocal intonation is one of the most important manifestations of this. It is indeed, through vocal intonation and its formalization and development through language and musical instruments that we can regard music as the virtual embodiment of emotion. In so far as such embodiment involves a specific characterization of emotions (rather than a mere report of them) it involves unconscious self-appraisal as a worthwhile way of communicating the emotion in question.

It was further argued that music was a virtual embodiment not just of emotion but also of the narrative matrix from which they emerge. This meant that, in more general terms, music should be understood as *the embodiment of virtual expression*.

The upshot of this is that we encounter music through a presumption of virtuality, i.e. we take it to be 'about' possible emotional gestures and narrative avenues of transformation between them. What distinguishes this virtual 'aboutness' from, on the one hand, mere reports of emotional states and narratives, and, on the other hand actual ones, is the fact that music presents gestural and related narrative criteria of emotions at the same sensible level as that of fully realized emotion but without the performer, composer, or listener *necessarily* having to experience the complete emotion in question at the time of performance or composition.

We now reach the decisive point. As I have argued in previous chapters, it is a characteristic of all art forms to represent the world in a *relatively disinterested* way. By this, I mean one can enjoy what a poem or a play is about or what a painting or a sculpture represents, without having to believe that such content actually exists or has existed. Even with such things as historical novels, we are engaged by the richness of possibility in terms of which the author represents his or her subject matter rather than how well it conveys information about its historical reality. (If that was what we needed, it would be better to read a factual history book.)

There is, of course, a very familiar problem about how it is possible to fear or pity fictions. But that is precisely what is solved here. We do not fear or pity fictions as such, unless we mistake them for realities or factual reports. The fact that literary and visual formats are images of possible states of affairs (interpreted and organized from the artist's stylistic viewpoint) altogether changes our relation to them. *We identify with a vision of tragedy, rather than tragedy per se. Our response is an aesthetic one.* Its disinterested character means that we can read what happens as if it were happening, but because the work is an image, we are also distanced from it. This is not a negative factor; for it means that we can identify with or 'play' with what is represented, in part, *on our own terms.*

However, whilst all art operates primarily at the level of sensible possibility, the literary and figurative arts are constrained in a key respect. Even though we do not demand references to individual persons or states of affairs which actually existed, yet we can nevertheless recognize possible specific individuals and states of affairs as content within the sensible or imaginative possibility which the work projects.

With music matters are very different. For whilst there are core characterizations of specific kinds of emotions and connecting narratives, these are not linked to any recognizable individual bearer of them. The projected auditory gestures may have been intended to be about the composer's experience, or that of an imaginary person, even that of a nation, but the work is significant without it *having to be* understood in relation to any such factor. Qua virtual expression, *music presents a form of experiential possibility; one, as it were, without any definitive owner.*

This approach has some broad affinity with several contemporary analyses of our response to music, most notably Jerrold Levinson's. Levinson points out that

Since a listener is standardly made sad by apprehending and then identifying with sadness in the music, naturally the thought of that emotion is present to the mind concurrent with whatever is felt. In the second place, identifying with the music involves initially the cognitive act of imagining that the music is either *itself* a sad individual or else the audible expression of somebody's sadness. In the third place, such identification involves subsequently a cognitive act of imagining that one, too, is sad—that it is *one's own* sadness the music expresses—and thus, however, amorphously, that one has something to be sad about.[17]

All these factors can, indeed, be involved in our characterization of music. Unfortunately, Levinson does not explain why emotion expressed through these means has a distinctive and valuable status. In particular, he overlooks the image-character of music and our correlated awareness of it as a stylistic interpretation of the relevant range of expressive qualities. Furthermore, by failing to negotiate the disinterestedness of aesthetic emotion, Levinson leaves no reason for regarding our responses to music as anything other than quasi-emotional.

This incompleteness invites distracting objections of the sort proposed by Peter Kivy. Kivy holds that when identifying with people, we do so on the basis of appropriate sets of beliefs concerning the identity of the specific person or persons in question. But on Levinson's approach to music (and, of course, mine as well) there is no specific person with whom we are identifying. There is only an abstract persona who is supposed to occupy the music. Kivy then observes, in sarcastic vein, that 'One is being asked to identify with an "indefinite agent". One might just as well try to form a personal attachment to Spinoza's God, or cosy up to a barber's pole.'[18]

---

[17] Jerrold Levinson, 'Music and the Negative Emotions', in his *Music, Art, and Metaphysics: Essays in Philosophical Aesthetics* (Ithaca: Cornell University Press, 1990), 306–35, at 321–2. In the chapter on 'Musical Expressiveness' in his book *The Pleasures of Aesthetics* (Ithaca and London: Cornell University Press, 1996) Levinson observes that 'When music is expressive it disposes us to construe it as if it is or harbours an individual externalizing its inner life, through novel and unprecedentedly powerful means' (p. 115). My point is that without an adequate set of criteria for the 'novel and unprecedentedly powerful means' we have no real basis for understanding the positive difference between emotion in music and the expression of emotion per se. In my terms, the relevant criteria are founded on relations between the ontology of music qua virtual expression, the significance of disinterestedness, and issues of stylistic difference which I will address in the next section.

[18] The key arguments are found in Kivy's *New Essays on Musical Understanding*, 92–118, at 110.

Kivy's sarcasm is entirely misplaced. For it could just as well be applied to his own central doctrine, namely music's possession of expressive properties. In a piece of music qua sound or score, there is no specific person who is the bearer of such properties. Since we lack the appropriate beliefs to ascribe them specifically, therefore, it follows that they are assignable only to an 'indefinite agent'.

The way round this problem is to stress music's image-character as virtual expression. As I have already explained in great detail, this character involves a sensibly presented *possibility* of expression, achieved through the artist's stylistic interpretation. This twofold level of significance at the level of the work-as-artefact enables those possibilities of identification described by Levinson, and their more accurate understanding in the aesthetic empathy which I have emphasized.

In fact, this latter notion can now be further developed. Virtual expression offers a kind of *aesthetic education* of the emotions through sensibly exemplifying key cognitive structures of the emotions (most notably, the narrative conditions of their emergence) at a publically accessible level. But the fact that this emotional content is embodied in an aesthetic whole means that the narrative structure is much more lucid than in our introspective or observational emotional experiences. To perform and listen to music is to follow the development of emotion aesthetically rather than be pressurized and controlled by it (as in the context of everyday life situations).

This involves a significant diminution of the division between music and those who compose it, perform it, or listen to it. For since the gestural and narrative richness of the work is not observably tied to any individual then we can appropriate it, enjoy it, even live it on our own terms to a degree that is impossible with other artworks. In other artistic media, no matter how much, for example, we empathize with Hamlet's suffering, or with a particular landscape, Hamlet and the landscape are still *recognizably* other than us in the most specific ways.

Of course, it is possible to understand and appreciate a story where the characters and even places and times of occurrence are anonymous. But such anonymity is an exception in literary meaning, whereas in music it is the norm. Anonymity in literature and visual art, indeed, involves incompleteness in the way in which identified individuals are characterized. Music, in contrast, involves characterizations which are not assigned to identified individuals in the first place.

In music, therefore, the work, the performer, and listener *inhabit one another* without significant restriction. The 'otherness' of the music is diminished in so far as it is experienced as a characterization of possibility, rather than the actuality of another definite individual.

This, indeed, creates a sense that we are *in* the music rather than merely encountering it as an 'external' object of auditory experience. And whilst any artwork allows empathic identification with its producer (a point which I will return to later on), the lack of individual reference in the musical work gives this identification a phenomenological closeness and intimacy which is not available from other media. Indeed, even those existential associations described earlier (where spatio-temporal situations, or even other persons, might be suggested by music) owe their individual character to what the listener's imagination puts into them.

I am arguing, then, that musical performance and reception involves a diminution of the boundaries between subject and object of experience, and between subject and subject. Through such *phenomenological fusion* we can enjoy an enhanced state of free-belonging to the world. This metaphysical depth is the distinctive core of musical meaning in its purest sense.

Having identified the primary level of musical meaning, an important secondary dimension must now be elaborated on the basis of issues raised in Section 7.1. The immediate context for this is the fact that no human being can be fully aware of all the things that are involved in its behaviour. What we do manifests attitudes, values, relations, and physical settings all of which shape our individual identity, but of which we are rarely fully aware.

In this respect, for example, our behaviour constantly reveals our animal nature, but it is unusual for us to think of ourselves as animals in the course of our everyday dealings with the world. Again, whilst, by definition, we are material bodies constrained by physical laws concerning space-occupancy, and whilst our behaviour is regulated by this fact, it is very rare for us to think of ourselves explicitly in these terms. (Indeed, many people probably *never* actually consider themselves as material bodies.) In such cases, our behaviour *exemplifies* truths about human being and its place in the world, but without us being conscious of them—except under unusual circumstances.

A further example of this is one so simple as to rarely be remarked upon, namely that sound can exemplify important features of our relation to the world. In Section 7.1, I described the major factors involved here, namely temporal necessity, indexicality, qualitative enigma, and volitional repetition. I indicated their intrinsic expressive significance, and suggested that this emerged mainly through music. I shall now show *how* music exemplifies all these factors in its own unique way, and will argue that this should be regarded, accordingly, as a vital secondary level of musical meaning's distinctiveness.

First, then, the temporal necessity of auditory wholes. To be intelligible the specific parts of an auditory event must be comprehended in an exactly successive temporal order. This also characterizes the more general character of 'things happening'—where component events link up to form those sequential continuities which are the basis of our inherence in time.

Qua auditory phenomenon music does this with an extra dimension of significance. This is not just because it is a form of sound which attracts special attention, but because it adds its own special feature vis-à-vis the character of musical meaning. In the previous section, I devoted much effort to drawing the link between such meaning and narrative. In narrative the individual parts must follow one another in a specific and temporally exact order, and this is especially true of music. If any element of the work is relocated in terms of 'before' or 'after', then the character of the whole is changed. On these terms, narrative exemplifies the temporal necessity which holds between the order of elements in the event per se, and between continuous event-sequences in reality per se.

Now (as we shall see in more detail in the next chapter) whilst literary and filmic works are temporally extended narratives, their spatial content and reference to identifiable individuals distracts us from the temporal necessity which is at work in them. In music there is no such distraction. Its narrative structure (in compositional or performance terms) more manifestly exemplifies the temporal structure of the event and the event-sequence than other art media. Indeed, by completing and preserving these structures in a finished work which can, in principle, be performed innumerable times, it also symbolizes their recurrent role in human experience.

Music can also go further. For it not only exemplifies the necessity of the event-sequence per se, but also that of the specifically human relationship to it. We inhabit the horizon of continuous events, through interpreting it as a narrative structure where the meaningfulness of one moment is determined by its necessary relation to those which have gone before and to those futural ones whose existence it is helping to create. Each moment has *holistic potency*. Music embodies this structure with especial purity in so far as each of a work's individual parts is manifestly dependent on its relation to all the others for its meaning. This is temporal necessity, as it were, bracketed off from immediate practicalities and *humanized*.

I turn now to a second major point from Section 7.1, namely that sound is an indexical sign of the presence or proximity of that which causes it. Indexicality, indeed, is the mode of signification which seems to be basic to all animal life. And again, music has the capacity not only to exemplify this primal phenomenon, but to do so in its own distinctive way.

In this respect, I argued earlier that music embodies possible gestural aspects of emotion and its narrative connections—all in all, what I have called virtual expression. Now whereas in most indexicals the human or animal producer imprints itself and leaves a trace on inanimate material, music works, in large part, the other way round. It is sound with virtual expression produced (in the case of instrumental music at least) from inanimate material. True enough, it is human agency which manipulates the material in question so as to produce the sound, but the point is that a dimension of difference is introduced here, which enables music to exemplify indexicality in an exceptional way.

This leads to a third important and closely related point. Since music which is played on an instrument, is not in any sense an actual state of a person, this heightens the dramatic enigma of qualitative change discussed in Section 7.1. The reason why is because, whilst familiar, there is always something a little *miraculous* in the generation of emotionally significant sounds from an inanimate instrument. The spiritual character of the sound indexical gives, thereby, the qualitative enigma a most striking exemplification.

Connections can also be made with the fourth major factor from Section 7.1, namely the volitional and repetitive dimension of auditory experience. The fixing of intonation, rhythm, and melody in music allows it to be established on the basis of stabilized repetition, making it independent of the memory of the performer. This, of course, still allows a great deal of scope for interpretation, but once a work can be preserved in a score, or takes on some other fixed or relatively fixed format, it admits of a repetition which harmonizes potentially antagonistic factors. These are, on the one hand, the temporal necessity of auditory experience's event–character, and, on the other hand, the volitional flexibility of vocalization. Through codified music, a temporally necessary sequence of auditory events can be activated whenever a musician chooses to perform the piece.

I am arguing, then, that there is a secondary level of distinctiveness in musical meaning, which arises from the unique way in which it exemplifies metaphysical truths at the auditory level. There is a twofold reciprocal dynamic at work in all this. On the one hand a virtualization of meaning whereby music embodies possibilities of expression, and on the other hand, a devirtualization where music exemplifies broader metaphysical factors bound up with its reality as auditory experience.

Elements from this less familiar secondary level form a kind of penumbra of meaning which both enriches and is inseparable from the primary level. I say 'inseparable' here because *it is through the very act of embodying virtual expression that music also exemplifies the decisive structures of auditory experience* which have just been described. It discloses and enhances auditory being and our relation to it, at the sensory level rather than the purely intellectual. Through this, the divide between listener and the 'otherness' of the auditory world is significantly diminished. To fully comprehend musical meaning, therefore, we must do full justice to this key secondary metaphysical dimension.

In the literature, however, it has not been done justice to. Even as profound a philosopher as Maurice Merleau-Ponty suggests that music does no more than set out 'certain outlines of Being—its ebb and flow, its growth, its upheavals, its turbulence'.[19] Merleau-Ponty's characterization here is intended to contrast music unfavourably with painting. For him, the latter has profound metaphysical depth by virtue of its disclosure of fundamental perceptual structures.[20] My analysis, however, has shown that, as a function of its primary meaning, music can also exemplify broader metaphysical truths—and do so in a much more determinate way than is allowed for in Merleau-Ponty's remarks. Music is a medium which (like painting, sculpture, and architecture) has its own metaphysical being as a key factor of meaning.

Before moving on to the major question of musical value, some important qualifications must now be made. The foregoing analysis has focused

[19] Merleau-Ponty, 'Eye and Mind', in Harold Osborne (ed.), *Aesthetics* (Oxford: Oxford University Press, 1970), at 57.
[20] I discuss this theory in detail in ch. 6 of *Art and Embodiment*.

exclusively on music in the tonal system. But how does it relate to alternative structures? In the case of non-western scale-systems the answer is relatively easy. The formalization of vocal gesture brought about by language, and then its extension into instrumental music, can be powerfully mediated by different cultural circumstances. Hence, whilst the virtual embodiment of expression through vocal gestures and its instrumental formalizations are, in a sense, natural drives, how these operate and are codified will vary according to the different social and physical environments in which they take place.

The case of non-tonal systems in western music is slightly more complex. In the cases of atonalism and serialism, there are logics of progression but these are severely restricted in terms of expression. They are condemned to sound eerie, elusive, alienated, or destructive, even though in formal terms their unity may be highly integrated. The problem here is that western music cannot forget its own origins and history. The presumption of virtuality wherein we read it in terms of expression is founded on the tonal system and its antecedent modes. This is the context in relation to which atonalism and serialism will tend to be judged, irrespective of the composer's intentions and the formal literacy of his or her audience.

However, we ought also to consider serialism and other non-tonal forms in the context of what I earlier described as the *secondary* level of musical distinctiveness—bound up with its physical status as sound. At this level music uniquely exemplifies metaphysical factors bound up with its physicality. *There may be room to formulate a theory of meaning for non-tonal works which relates primarily to this level.* This possibility, however, is one which I do not have the space to follow up here.

Two final qualifications must now be made. The first concerns the specific case of sung music. For when music has words, this surely means that reference to specific individuals must be involved as part of the content, and that, accordingly, the sung work will not possess distinctively musical meaning. However, this would only be true if sung music were no more than music with words added to it (or vice versa). In most cases this is not true. With sung and choral works (whether accompanied by instruments or not) musical formalization will tend to harmonize the relation between the performer or listener and the cited individuals.

This is because sung music—by definition—is more than words. The musical aspect (with its positive indeterminacy vis-à-vis individuals) enhances the transindividual significance of the words, but, at the same time, they can sharpen our awareness that even musical indeterminacy ultimately constellates around the *possibility* of concrete individual experience other than our own. In vocal music we have a potential reciprocal enhancing of literary and musical meaning. Whether this potential is realized or not is a function of the particular case, and its broader relations.

The last qualification to be made is that whilst music has the distinctive characteristics which I have described, this should not be regarded as the basis of a hierarchy with music at the top. The reason why, is that each art form has its own metaphysical depth, i.e. a special way of relating subject and object of experience, which cannot be reduced to the same criteria which operate in the other forms.[21]

We are thus led to a key transitional issue. I have argued that musical meaning has a primary and secondary metaphysical depth which is the basis of its distinctiveness. As a general theory, this means, accordingly, that *How Much is that Doggy in the Window?* and Shostakovich's *Fifteenth Symphony* must be analysable on broadly the same principles. But surely we would regard the latter as having metaphysical depth to a degree that the former does not. How is this to be explained?

The answer is that whilst all music has the metaphysical structure outlined in this discussion, not all works are able to disclose it. To see why, we must now consider the ways in which some works are able to transform the scope of existing musical idioms. This is the question of musical value and the correlated issue of under what conditions music *per se* becomes musical *art*.

7.5

A great deal of popular and folk music is created in order to entertain — to enhance the sense of relaxation from labour — or for ritual purposes bound up with religious worship, mourning, courtship and marriage rituals, or general community celebration. Such *functional music* (as I shall term it) is usually much constrained by this broader context. Characteristically, it will

---

[21] As we have already seen in previous chapters, for example, the relation of literature and metaphor, and painting and the imagination have distinctive and rewarding characteristics which cannot be duplicated by the other art forms.

involve highly repetitive rhythms, the proverbial 'catchy' tune, and be of relatively short duration.

In western consumer culture, indeed, these and related factors are rendered in highly formulaic terms so as to attract a maximum audience. Many works of this kind do little more than repeat such formulae at a lowest-common-denominator level. They facilitate acquiescence and the giving up of active critical listening. Real choice is replaced by mere buying options.

However, it is useful to ask why music is able to entertain and serve such a range of ritual functions and is able to have such mass appeal. The answer is surely bound up with all the factors considered in previous sections. Music draws upon the primal disclosive power of auditory experience and the expression of this through vocal and formal structures which are virtual embodiments of expression.

It also breaks down divisions between subject and object of experience, and subject and subject. We may like a piece for its catchy tune or danceable rhythm, but the catchiness of the tune, and the danceability of its rhythms—no matter how trivial—are bound up with the deeper levels of experience outlined before. These levels of ultimate bonding with the world and other persons resonate throughout music, even though, as consumers, we are so habituated to the effects as to have no understanding of the causes.

This being said, there are clear ways in which one's response to music can transcend mere consumption. Such transcendence involves an attentiveness to how the particular work is structured in sensible terms, and to the basis of its distinctive musical character. Both these demand consideration of a work's creative difference from other works—in terms of such things as complexity of instrumentation and rhythm and melody, or sophistication of lyrics.

In this, respect, for example, many would argue that the songs of the Beatles, Bob Dylan, and many others far transcend their nominal 'pop' formats. Indeed, it is striking that jazz and popular music have acquired well-developed patterns of critical connoisseurship which insist on strong hierarchical distinctions of value. Hence, in the field of pop, there is music which is just there to dance or relax to, but there are other pieces which invite the performer or listener to think in terms of new or alternative life possibilities.

What this shows is that the distinction between lower and higher forms of music is not determined primarily by genre.[22] Indeed, just as much pop music or jazz can transcend mere entertainment, idioms such as sonatas or symphonies—whilst being structurally more suited to sustained and complex musical development—can end up as mere repetitions of established approaches, and, in consequence, be artistically inferior to the more accomplished popular idioms. But what is our criterion of value here if it is not one of genre?

As one might imagine, the answer to this is of some complexity. A familiar strategy would be to invoke formal criteria such as 'beauty' and the like—and this has some justification in so far as it directs us towards how the work coheres in sensible and imaginative terms.[23] One might then invoke complex notions of formal unity and/or more specialized aesthetic concepts such as the sublime. These, however, are of little critical use in practical terms. The real problem is that value is not only a function of a work's formal structure and the gestural elements which that formal structure organizes, but also of *its relation to other works in a horizon of historical comparisons.*

It must be emphasized that this is not just a question of the conditions under which artistic quality is recognized, but of the actual constitution of musical art. If a work simply repeats compositional or performance strategies of a kind already established then it is, in metaphysical terms, little more than repetition—mere functional music. If, however, it is creatively different from other works, then it literally adds something new to the world through recontextualizing our relationship with that which already exists, and pointing towards the future. Of course, we do not expect every work by a composer to create a new style. Rather we look for works

---

[22] Richard Shusterman arrives at a similar position through his analyses of rap music. This and related issues form important themes in his classic *Pragmatist Aesthetics: Living Beauty, Rethinking Art* (Oxford: Blackwell, 1992).

[23] Some of the problematics of beauty in relation to music are brought out through Peter Kivy's use of it in *New Essays on Musical Understanding*. As far as I can tell, he offers no sustained definition of its criteria for application in the musical context. We are told, for example, that 'to move me by its somber, stately melancholy music must be *beautifully* somber and stately and melancholy: it must embody somber stately melancholy in a musically wonderful, a musically beautiful way' (p. 113). As I read Kivy, musical beauty refers to both the phenomenal structure of the work, and also to its distinctiveness—that which makes it special. However, whilst beauty might be applied to the latter as a kind of honorific term, other factors of a relational kind are logically involved. The uniqueness or distinctiveness of a piece is, accordingly, much more than beauty in its customary sense. Reference must also be made to the second axis of normativity.

which vary or refine, and formally develop the style which a composer has already established.

These stylistic differences centre on *how* the work coheres in both formal and historical terms. To be attentive to such factors is to negotiate musical *art*. In a decisive sense, the musical artwork attracts our attention and educates our taste through stylistic traits which transform the aesthetic possibilities available to us. In particular, it enables a sense of empathy (of shared vision and value) with the composer's and/or performer's insights, as well as an enjoyment of what the music presents in more immediate terms.

It should be emphasized here, that whilst this form of empathy involves reference to the work being produced by someone other than ourselves, the focus of attention is the achieved distinctiveness of the work itself, rather than the biographical details of the composer or performer. This empathy, indeed, is the heightened form of that diminishing of barriers between subject and subject which I have already referred to. We see *with* the creator, rather than see *that* he or she is such and such a person with such and such a biography.

I am arguing, then, that artistic quality is necessarily mediated by historical difference. This is what enables us to formulate and justify canonic distinctions between music which has no more than functional significance, and music which exceeds this and *becomes art*. It also enables us to make broad distinctions of merit within the domain of musical art itself. I shall now address these possibilities in more detail in the next two sections.

7.6

The canonic basic of music can be organized in terms of four broad categories.[24] The first of these I shall call *neutral historical difference*. Every performance of, or piece of, music is, in literal terms, different from any other. But in the case of many pieces this amounts to mere difference and nothing more. Whilst such works are, literally, individual, they have no distinctively individual *musical* character. It may be possible to identify them as the products of such and such a place or historical time or to

---

[24] A detailed account of these same categories applied in relation to pictorial art, can be found in my *The Transhistorical Image: Philosophizing Art and its History* (Cambridge: Cambridge University Press, 2002), 99–109.

classify the idiom or genre which they exemplify, but the works have no significance beyond that. We enjoy them without any new life possibilities being opened up. Their historical difference from other works is entirely *neutral*. Metaphysically speaking, they leave us exactly where we are.

The transition to musical art, in contrast, is based on a *creative* historical difference which is meaningful through changing the terms in which music presents virtual expression. This involves refining existing musical styles and idioms, or innovating in relation to them. In metaphysical terms, we are dealing with works which *change* the existing musical situation, and by changing it, transform our relation to the world.

The most basic form of this I shall call *normal historical difference*. It involves a work or series of works establishing themselves as the basis of *a recognizable individual style*. If, for example, we consider music by the Byrds, Simon and Garfunkel, Hummel, Stanford, Honegger, or Krenek, we find work of distinctive individual style (to varying degrees) such that we can recognize the composer or creative ensemble on the basis of listening to the music alone. And if it is not actually by them, we will often be able to characterize it as being 'in the style of'. This means that as well as articulating their own individuality, the composer or performer has also created something which is of musical interest and use for others. We do not simply enjoy their music, we engage with it *as* music attending to how it is structured, as well as to what it is.

Within specific historical or geographical contexts, normal historical difference can have an enhanced local significance. For example, whilst in international terms the composers Ukmar and Gabrielčič have some individuality, in the Slovene national context they have somewhat more significance, in so far as they exemplify, respectively, the culmination of late Romanticism and modernism in Slovenian musical culture.

We are thus led towards an even more advanced category, where individual musical achievement takes on a decisive transcultural and trans-historical significance. Consider, for example, the Prelude to Wagner's *Tristan and Isolde*. Here the general stylistic traits of Wagner's developing style (and perhaps late Romanticism itself) are given a chromatic emphasis whose subtleties not only extend the musical scope of the tonal system, but also point in the direction of atonal possibilities. This is more than the achievement of an individual and influential style. It is one which changes the terms in which musical creativity is itself conceived. And through that, it offers new ways of addressing virtual expression. It not only expands musical tradition, it opens up a new direction for it.

A similar level of achievement can occur when a composer—as in Shostakovich's *Preludes and Fugues* for Piano—refines a traditional musical idiom to an astonishing degree. This allows the idioms possibilities to be rejuvenated and recast in a way that makes them accessible for creative reinterpretation by a new generation of composers and performers.

I shall call these powerful modes of musical innovation and refinement *effective historical difference* in so far as they not only influence other composers, but do so by opening up opportunities for change.

Again, like any canonic category, this will have significant ambiguity. An interesting case in point here is Henry Cowell's use of tone clusters and plucked piano strings. These innovations have the most radical significance for musical theory and practice, and Cowell is a pioneer of their use.

However, the way in which he employs them often turns out to be methodologically conservative. In much of his work, they amount to little more than flamboyant rhetorical devices for heightening the dramatic and/or lyrical impact of his tonal compositions. Whilst figuring in Cowell's individual style, they do not, in his work, amount to effective historical difference. It is rather, the use which other composers—such as John Cage—make of them which realizes this potential.

One final canonic category remains to be described. It is the most important of all. Earlier I mentioned how the Prelude to Wagner's *Tristan and Isolde* points towards atonalism. In respect of this possibility we might consider Liszt's short piano work *Nuages Gris* and Schoenberg's *Three Piano Pieces*, Op. 11 of 1909.

The former I again mention as an ambiguous example. It is possibly the first atonal piece, but Liszt never published it, and by the time it did enter the public domain, atonalism had already been established by the aforementioned work (and other pieces) by Schoenberg. By freeing melodic development from the hierarchical constraints of the tonal system, Schoenberg's works expressly articulate a new direction for music (and one which is as radical as that opened up for pictorial art by Picasso's *Les Demoiselles d'Avignon* of two years earlier). Indeed, as well as articulating atonalism, these works also point towards the possibilities of serialism, and even the aleatory innovations of John Cage and others.

Schoenberg and Cage mark what I shall call paradigmatic historical difference. This is when composers not only change established musical idioms but also transform the scope of music itself, through innovation or refinement. If Schoenberg and Cage are examples of the former, Bach, Mozart, and Beethoven are instances of the latter. In their case, it is not just that they rejuvenate established idioms, they also develop them to a level of excellence which henceforth acts as an ideal against which all musical achievement must be measured, and into which all must be initiated if they are to have any understanding of the scope of musical tradition and its achievement.

I am arguing, then, that what makes musical art is not just the beauty or whatever of individual works, but creative historical difference whereby such works change the scope of musicality by adding to its variety or by extending its scope. This is not just technical change, it is change with real metaphysical power in so far as through transforming musicality, it transforms our aesthetic experience of virtual expression, and, through making the auditory world anew, renews our relation to the world in more general terms.

This is why when talking about the expressive dimension of music we are not just describing its specific emotional and narrative character. We can also be moved by the composer's or performer's insight in its articulation, which, means, of course, that our response to the music's specific character will be mediated—and even transformed by our marvelling at the insight involved.

Of course, the canonic categories of musical which I have described do not apply in a rigid way. How one relates them to one composer or another will be a matter of debate and argument. However, the role of creative historical difference is such that it allows for a rational element to enter into discussions of musical value. Indeed, it offers criteria whereby claims concerning merit can be supported by pointing to evidence of innovation or stylistic refinement in a composition or performance.

7.7

I will now consider a possible objection to my general line of argument, and especially my conclusions concerning musical art.

The argument goes as follows. In the postmodern era, our sense of reality has been transformed—so much so that the very idea of metaphysics has been discredited. In the wake of poststructuralism and 'Theory' there can be no sense of foundational categories wherein cultural and other phenomena can be explained. All we have are shifting patterns of preference driven by dominant class, race, and gender relations. On these terms we cannot hope to explain the distinction between 'lower' and 'higher' forms of music except on the basis of such socially driven preferences. The importance of 'originality' and 'masterpieces' and the like, indeed, has been totally overthrown by the ubiquity of mechanically reproduced music.

The difficulties of this approach have already been dealt with in previous chapters. Such anti-foundationalism tends to treat the human subject as though it were disembodied—a mere field of unstabilized cognition and desires. It is not. And this is why the present discussion has emphasized the importance of constant factors in experience—both in terms of auditory phenomena, and in terms of gesture and expression.

I have also emphasized the importance of creative historical difference as a factor which actually overcomes the genre-based distinction between mass culture and high culture. The metaphysical approach, accordingly, is entirely warranted by the fact that the human condition is embodied and historically situated, and that both these factors inform the being of music to the profoundest degrees.

To underline this fact I shall address what might appear to be the most unlikely of possibilities, namely canonic musical art in the postmodern era. Composers such as Arvo Part and Alfred Schnittke offer an eclectic approach to composition which is striking and sophisticated in the way in which Classical, Romantic, and modern idioms are rejuvenated through being brought into critical alignment with one another. Their compositions embody significant elements of effective historical difference.

However, there is an even more potent force at work. In 1965 in Steve Reich's *It's Gonna Rain*, the phase technique (of multiple tapes played simultaneously, slightly out of synch with one another) is employed as a compositional structure. In this, the burden of musical meaning is carried by repetitions varied so as to transform and merge almost imperceptibly into new configurations. Techniques for the mechanical reproduction of sound are here redirected so as to act as a basis for *original* work.

In subsequent pieces such as *Six Pianos*, and *Variations for Strings and Wind Instruments* the phase technique shapes Reich's compositional strategy even in works which do not actually involve tapes. They *evoke*, rather, the rhythmic drive and precise layered repetitions which are enabled by the mechanical reproduction of sound and, on the basis of this, are able to redefine the scope of tonal music.

The importance of this cannot be properly understood without reference to Walter Benjamin's famous strictures concerning how the original artwork's 'aura' is destroyed by techniques of mechanical reproduction.[25] The putative critical point of Benjamin's theory actually has its significance completely *reversed* by Reich's music. In Reich's compositions, elements of repetition and the possibility of mechanical reproduction are used to create an individual style with its own striking aura as well as significant broader musical implications.

Reich's masterpiece *Different Trains* of 1989 brings all these factors into convergence. The work's compositional dynamic is one of insistent rhythmic repetition and variation, with audio tapes used to give exact elements of vocal narrative, as well as absorbed in the developing rhythmic drive.

In literal terms, the work evokes two parallel but horribly incongruent dimensions of Jewish experience from the Second World War years. One is Reich's own childhood rail travels across America, and the other is that of the rail transportation of Holocaust victims in Europe. By the vicissitudes of historical and geographical circumstances Reich was spared the horrendous destinies of his European counterparts. And this clash of chance and grim inevitability drives the work forward through extraordinary enmeshings of elation, reminiscence, horror, and redemption.

Different Trains is the most heightened statement to date of (the wretchedly misnamed) 'minimalist' tendency in postmodern music. It also has paradigmatic historical significance as the first great work to assimilate and transform techniques for the mechanical reproduction of sound.

Given all these points, it is clear that the age of the original masterpiece is hardly dead. Indeed, whilst postmodern sceptics often assert that the availability of a massive number of musical styles and information makes it impossible to legitimately privilege one work over another, this is a very misguided view.

---

[25] See his 'The Work of Art in the Age of Mechanical Reproduction', trans. Harry Zohn, in *Illuminations* (London: Fontana, 1970).

The truth of the matter is, if anything, the opposite. For the massive availability of comparative musical material made possible by new technologies means that the evidence on which judgements of value can be made has been massively expanded. The opportunity now exists for the education of musical sensibility on an enhanced transcultural and transhistorical basis. The age of the truly universal musical canon may only just be appearing.

Conclusion

I have argued, then, that a metaphysical approach can clarify the nature of musical meaning and value, and its broader significance in the human condition. Whilst consumer products are a means to the end of supposedly rewarding experiences, music is an end in itself. To be educated in music is to be initiated into factors which are fundamental to our sense of self and humanity.

At the heart of this is the fact that music embodies virtual expression at the same level at which emotion and its narrative context exists in the public domain, namely at the gestural level. This means that whilst not being tied to actual full emotional states, it is much more than a mere description of them. It is of decisive educative significance vis-à-vis the life of feeling through being a sensible *exemplar* of how emotional states emerge and are structured by narrative context.

Music has the further decisive characteristic of projecting possible expression without having to link it to any specific individual. The performer and listener are thus able to absorb the music very much on their own terms. At the same time, however, in so far as the musical work is known to be by someone other than oneself, this absorption can also gravitate around empathy with the composer's or performer's musical sensibility. Divisions between subject and object of experience, and between subject and subject, respectively, are diminished.

These factors constitute the primary level of musical meaning's distinctiveness. They also enable a secondary level, where music qua auditory phenomenon is able to exemplify key metaphysical aspects of the human condition in sensory terms. Again, this diminishes boundaries between subject and object of experience in unique ways, and heightens our sensitivity to the auditory dimension of being.

Now of themselves, these levels of distinctive meaning are intrinsically rewarding through their enhancing of our personal and species identities. For to be initiated into these levels of musical meaning is to be given experience which cannot be obtained from other sources. This not only broadens our general capacity to learn from and to approach the world, it allows us to attain a state of free-belonging to it. Indeed by empathizing with another's projection of expression, one can understand one's own position in life, the better; as well as, literally, enjoy sharing with the other. *Musical experience is amongst the potentially optimal states of personal and human being.*

It is, of course, possible for all this to become something of a consumer pleasure, if indulged in on a perpetually non-critical basis. However, I was at great pains to stress the fact that musical meaning is, in effect, *educable*. It can be taken to higher levels of value. To recognize value or the emergence of musical art from mere music is not, however, primarily, a matter of sensitivity. It is to recognize and respond to the effect of transformations wrought by refinement and innovation in relation to established musical idioms.

Through critical awareness in composition, performance, and listening, the situation of music is advanced just as the standpoint of all those involved advances in awareness likewise. Music becomes art, when, through changing its own scope, it changes the scope of virtual expression, and, through doing that, literally opens up new possibilities of being for composer, performer, and listener. In the final analysis, musical value as well as musical meaning is an embodiment of metaphysical depth.

Having elucidated key distinctive features of pictorial art, literature, music, and also their relation to the most profound aspects of human being-in-the world, I shall now explore this further in terms of factors which cross the divides between artistic media. My strategy will be to identify our sense of the momentary as a necessary factor in our cognition of time, and to then investigate contrasting ways in which the Moment functions in spatially based art forms, and in temporally realized ones.[26]

---

[26] The theory proposed in this chapter is an extended response to a conference paper on 'The Relationship between Auditory and Visual Reception in Musical Education' written by Professor Breda Oblak of the Academy of Music in Ljubljana, Slovenia. I dedicate the chapter to her, with gratitude for all her years of friendship and strong personal support.

8

Eternalizing the Moment: Artistic Projections of Time

Introduction

In Lessing's classic work *Laocoon: An Essay on the Limits of Painting and Poetry*,[1] the author identifies basic differences in the way literature and the visual arts address their subjects. Literary works can describe their subject matter through successive moments of time, whereas individual pictures and sculptures are confined to the representation of a single scene.

The limits set out in Lessing's distinction can be explored in many different ways. I will take an unusual approach. Rather than analysing the distinction in its own right (as in Lessing's work), I shall consider how it operates in terms of a poignant sub-problem. This concerns the different ways that literature, film, music, and the visual arts represent the momentary circumstance or state of awareness—hereafter referred to as *the Moment*. Art's capacity to preserve and eternalize such Moments is of the profoundest existential value, but has scarcely been addressed as an issue in its own right. By addressing it, it is also possible to clarify further the way in which the ontological structure of different media enables subject matter to be stylistically interpreted in distinctive ways.

In Section 8.1, accordingly, I say more about the phenomenology of the Moment, and introduce its links to style, image, and art. Section 8.2 develops these links in more detail by analysing the nature of temporal order in those arts where perceptual or imaginative acquaintance with the

---

[1] A good modern translation of Lessing's text can be found in J. M. Bernstein's edited collection, *German Classic and Romantic Aesthetics* (Cambridge: Cambridge University Press, 2002), 25–130.

image necessarily involves a linear temporal process. I will give particular attention to the specific ways in which such arts characterize the Moment.

In Section 8.3, I will go on to investigate the contrasting way in which arts of spatial realization—most notably pictorial representation—relate to the Moment. It will be argued that perspectival works have a privileged role here. Section 8.4 will develop the experiential implications of this in much more depth, and Section 8.5 will refine them further still through a comparison with photography's realizations of the Moment.

8.1

The Present, the Now, and the Moment, are different expressions of that which separates the past from the future. But the Moment, in particular, has extra connotations of the subjective experience of time and space and their contents. The culmination of eras and episodes in Moments of fulfilment and insight or whatever, are exactly the high points which make our lives meaningful, and which our life narratives tend to gravitate around.

But how do we preserve and understand these Moments? Their preservation is vital, since they are supreme expressions of who and what one is as a person. But during such Moments of experience it is difficult to be self-congruent with them—to be fully aware of them as they happen. It is only in retrospect that we come, as it were, to possess them, and dwell with them. In this respect, recollection in its own right, or aided by diaries, mementoes, and such things can be employed.

However, in the very recollection of key Moments another factor comes into play. For our recollections of them are *selective*; they exaggerate and omit on the basis of who we have become since they occurred.

This is not because we lack the power to do a full instant-replay of them, it is mainly because they are subjects *of* interpretation. Their significance and meaning will reconfigure—no matter how subtly—as our experience changes. In its retrospective form, the Moment has an image-character. Its recovery is stylized on the basis of present interests.

If this phenomenological analysis is correct, then both the recollection of, and communicability of the Moment to other people is vitally connected to artistic meaning. As we saw in previous chapters, art in general has an image-structure in so far as it characterizes a subject matter from the artist's viewpoint. The fact that this is embodied in a publically accessible and stable medium means that we can identify with this viewpoint aesthetically on our own terms.

This character is well suited to the representation of the Moment. Through art, the Moment is not just documented, it is further developed through the stylistic possibilities of the medium. Indeed, the artist can recast Moments from his or her own experience and reconfigure them as fictional Moments in another character's 'life', or, of course, invent entirely imaginary Moments of experience.

It should be emphasized that these activities do not involve the mere translation of what is already present in the artist's mind, into some outward form. The whole point, indeed, is that by constructing the Moment-image in a medium, the artist is able to interpret and develop it through his or her work. The medium of such exploration also brings its own distinctive structure to bear on how the Moment is represented. I shall now explore all these possibilities in more detail.

8.2

In earlier chapters of this book I have given considerable emphasis to the role of the image in self-consciousness, and have noted the way in which its *style* is paramount. This involves the image being shaped and defined by its relation to the whole of the subject's past, and anticipations of the future.

In making a specific kind of artefact, an artist draws on a relevant framework of conventions and techniques which govern work in that medium or those media. The artist's work is defined in relation to this horizon of tradition. His or her other work can simply exist within it—as an element in the continuity of tradition and nothing more. However, if a work's style perceptibly differs—if it refines, extends, or innovates in relation to a tradition—then the work changes how we see both past traditions, and its scope for the future. It may be, indeed, that a work's style marks a radical break with one tradition and the inauguration of a new one.

These points generally indicate, then, how style functions in art, on the basis of the reciprocal relation between the specific work, and the past and future of the tradition. The reciprocity of present, past, and future in subjective experience is exemplified at the level of objective, diachronic, historical unfolding. The problem which now faces us then is to move from this general significance of style in art, to the significance of the stylized Moment. An example from Kant is instructive here. The Second Analogy in the *Critique of Pure Reason*,[2] invites us to consider the difference between the objective unity of an event, and the objective unity of a spatial object per se. To understand the objective structure of an event, the elements which comprise this structure must be apprehended in strictly successive—that is to say *linear*—temporal terms. The event's objective unity qua event involves a sequence of elements which must be apprehended in a rigidly specific temporal order. This order cannot be reversed or redistributed in any other way.

However, the objective unity of a spatial object involves no such temporal order in the progression of percepts. In our perceptual scanning, say, of a house, we can start with the parts at the top and move down, or move from left to right, or vice versa. Here, the temporal order in which we apprehend the parts of the spatial manifold is not a strictly linear one. We do not *have* to perceive them in any specific temporal order in order to recognize the unity of the spatial object.

The relevance of this to art should be immediately apparent in a rough and ready way. Media such as literature, film, and music are radically temporal in character. That is to say, whatever physical characteristics they possess, the relevant constituent parts have to be realized in imagination, or projected, or performed *in a strictly linear order of temporal succession*. Their objective unity is fundamentally that of an event or inseparable sequence of events. In spatially orientated art forms such as painting, sculpture, and architecture in contrast, the objective unity of the subject does not demand that the parts should be perceived in a temporally linear order.

Now on the basis of this initial characterization alone, we would be justified in suspecting that the Moment will be rendered in radically different terms, depending on which mode of objective unity—that of the event or that of the spatial object—characterizes the medium in question. I shall therefore now address art in relation to these two modes of objective unity in rather more detail.

---

[2] See Immanuel Kant, *Critique of Pure Reason*, trans. N. Kemp-Smith (London: Macmillan and Co., 1973), 221–2.

First, literature, film, and music. In so far as literary or filmic works have an overt subject matter (i.e. 'refer' to aspects of the world other than themselves) they have their own *internal* time order. This can be unconscious or manifest. To the degree that a work describes events or states of mind unfolding in time, it necessarily has an internal time order, even though the work's creator may not give it any emphasis. To the degree, indeed, that the work can be described as a *narrative* or story, this necessary time order is made manifest. For here the pattern of unfolding pertains to causal relations—the way in which one event or state of affairs gives rise to another and so on, in a humanly meaningful sequence.

Such narrative structure has at least two interesting features vis-à-vis internal time order. First, time here is always either synoptic or (and this is *much* rarer) expansive. Most novels, for example, compress the years, days, hours, minutes, and seconds which they address. They omit, hide, emphasize, idealize, and exaggerate. They provide us not with real time, but rather a stylized image of passing time in selected human contexts. This may encompass a mere day as in Joyce's *Ulysses* or Lowry's *Under the Volcano*; or it may comprehend centuries as in Virginia Woolf's *Orlando*; it may even embody a less determinate quasi-mythic time as in Eliot's *The Waste Land*.

The opposite and much rarer strategy is when some event or events of only short duration, are made the basis of an expansive narrative whose unfurling takes much longer than the events referred to. However, whether the narrative strategy is synoptic or expansive, the point is that time is transformed into an image and stylized on the basis of the artist's particular orientation towards it.

Now against this, it might be objected that it is at least possible that some narratives may, in their exposition, be exactly congruent with the duration or 'real time' of the events or states which they are describing. In the case of literature and film, however, an exact and literal transcription of 'something which happened' is surely not, in itself, a work of art. The whole point of *narrative* as a form—even in documentary writing and film—is that we do not simply reproduce a succession of events, but rather link them in a way that is orientated primarily towards the eliciting of meaning. This implies, of course, that creative *reportage* involves some elements of manipulation—of disassociation from the exact time order of the events described.

The second interesting feature of the internal time order in narrative follows on from this. For since a narrative provides a stylized image of time, this means that it can depart from patterns of strictly linear temporal succession. The most familiar examples of this are those novels or films which begin with a denouement and then devote themselves to a presentation of the events which led to this outcome.

Cinema has exploited this device especially effectively. In John Boorman's *Point Blank*, for example, the beginning and end of the film merge into one another with such felicity as to cast some doubt on the exact narrative status of the events in between. Are these actual, or a kind of after-life retribution waged by the character who may have died at the beginning of the film?

Again, in Quentin Tarantino's *Pulp Fiction*, the highly episodic structure of the film as a whole gravitates around an opening scene which is drawn from events occurring much later on in the narrative. What is especially striking about this scene is that it is not a self-contained episode or denouement but gives the developing narrative a peculiar 'off-key' quality which constitutes, of course, one of the distinctive features of Tarantino's style.

Now whilst the internal time order of literature, film, and music need not be strictly linear, this is not true of their objective time order, i.e. their unity as temporally realized events. The verses of a poem, chapters of a novel, reels of a film, or bars of a musical work, must be temporally realized in the exact order of succession which the artist has presented them in. The objective unity of the work is a function of this order. If we ignore this and temporally realize the work's elements in a random way, or on the basis of our own preferences, we get at best a fragmentary or partial realization, and at worst (and, indeed, much more likely) a chaotic distortion.

This is equally true of those works whose internal time order follows a non-linear narrative pattern. If our imaginative realization does not follow the exact order in which the episodes are presented in the finished work, then we will not recognize the full narrative significance of the creator's 'rearrangements' of time. A non-linear internal time order demands a strictly linear one in terms of its temporal realization.

At this point, a query may be raised; namely what is the relation between the objective unity of literature, film, and music, and their aesthetic status? In this respect, it should be noted that whilst there are many varieties of aesthetic experience these all take as their starting point the relation between part and whole in a particular sensible or imaginatively realized object. In those arts which demand temporal realization, we cannot form an adequate sense of the whole without having—at least once—apprehended the parts in terms of the strict linear succession prescribed by the work's format. Our appreciation of its aesthetic significance will gravitate around the reciprocal relations (of harmony, disharmony, etc.) which hold between this temporal whole and its specific elements.

We are not, in other words, simply interested in recognizing the work's objective temporal unity, we are concerned rather with *how* this is achieved through the artist's style. The objective unity of the work must be recognized in the terms I have described in order to elicit an aesthetic response, but this is not a sufficient condition of such a response.

Given this analysis of those arts which require temporal realization, the question now arises of how they render the Moment. In all such arts, of course, one can talk of specific moments of insight, as can be found, for example, in the piano's first recapitulation of the opening orchestral theme from Prokofiev's *Third Piano Concerto*.

In literature and film, the Moment itself can figure as the subject of such moments of insight. Baudelaire's poem *A une Passante* is a beautiful example of this, centred on a fleeting exchange of glances between the poet and a women in a crowd. Another fine evocation is the moment when the replicant Roy Batty dies at the end of Nicholas Ridley Scott's film *Bladerunner*. (Here, indeed, this evocation is made all the more poignant by Batty's final words—'All these moments will be lost in time, like tears in rain ... Time to die.)'

Now these renderings of the Moment always occur in the context of strict temporal succession. Given the work as a whole, the rendered Moment is always in a strictly defined position. We are presented with the events—or other moments—which lead up to it, and those, indeed, which are consequent upon it.

Of course, the Moment itself may have its own, as it were, *vertical fabric*—a dimension of associations or visualizations wherein we fill it out in imagination (a point which I will return to). But its major force is derived from its *horizonal* depth, i.e. its poignant position within that field of moments occurring before it, and those occurring after it, which in their linear cohesion form the objective unity of the work as a whole.

If the rendered Moment occurs at the very beginning or at the very end of a work, we are not presented with those events which led up to it, or which flow out of it (respectively). However, the Moment's character is still substantially defined by its position. For, if we can only form a sense of the work's unity by apprehending its elements in an order of strict linear temporal succession, then beginning and end Moments carry the burden of the work as a whole, as a condition of their full intelligibility.

One might say, then, that the rendered Moment in temporally realized arts, has a distinctive illuminatory potential. Through it, *the structure of the Moment as a position within a narrative field of meanings stands revealed.* In psychological terms, Moments usually seem discrete—they appear as unique points of insight. But as we saw in the preceding chapter, they are not so in logical terms. The definition of a Moment presupposes a sequence of preceding moments, and a sequence of subsequent ones, which it both connects and separates.

This is, of course, a philosophical point. In the temporally realized artwork, however, it is given a living form. By this, I do not simply mean exemplified in a particular concrete instance, rather than stated (as in this discussion) as an abstract truth. There is a decisive additional element, namely that in such an artwork the Moment is *stylized.*

Whatever its objective factual or semantic core, this is given a specific quality through the particular way in which it is artistically realized, and the relationship between this and other ways of making or realizing. A philosopher can tell us that the Moment involves a subject being positioned in relation to a field of other moments. But only the artwork can show the ramifications of this at a sensible level. As a symbolic expression within some established medium and code, it has an objective element.

The public embodiment of this content, however, involves the creative generation of an image or other sensible form. In generating the appropriate form, the artist stylizes it. Meaning in the work emerges on the same basis as meaning in perception and self-consciousness itself. The rendered Moment is not imposed or merely analysed. Rather it is explicitly generated in relation to other moments, through the interaction between the individual artist, the medium, and his or her position within tradition.

This completeness of rendering is lacking in philosophical analyses of the Moment (in so far as philosophers ever trouble to address it). More significantly, it is lacking in our concrete experience of the Moment itself. The route to a given Moment in life never follows an exactly recognizable track, even though it is necessarily an at least partial outcome of preceding events and anticipations of the future.

But in art, it follows such a track: whatever the dimension of chance circumstances and alternative possibilities which the artist might hint at, the progression of Moments follows an inevitable course within the objective unity of the specific work. Each one bespeaks the whole. The temporal and causal depth of the artistically situated Moment locks it into place. This is a place of security and constant re-encounterability. The transience of moments in ordinary experience gives way to the possibility of symbolic eternal recurrence through art.

On these terms, then, the arts of temporal realization can achieve an eternalization of the Moment. Whether this is a positive or negative achievement depends entirely on the particular work involved. In the foregoing remarks I have indicated the positive aspects. The negative dimension consists primarily of the ease in which realizations of the Moment can degenerate into the merely nostalgic, the abjectly sentimental, or the melodramatic.

There is another key factor which must also be considered. For, as we have just seen, in eternalizing the Moment, temporally realized arts fix it in place. This positive consequence involves the suppression of a key aspect of the Moment as lived. For (as noted above) whilst, in a lived situation, we have some sense of the Moment's origins and some anticipation of its outcomes, these are by no means absolutely determinate. As finite beings we simply cannot exhaustively specify the origins and destination of a given Moment. We can form an image of them, but no more.

The origins and destinations which situate the Moment are relatively open. They function as horizons rather than exact paths into, or out from, the present. However, whilst the temporal arts suppress this to positive effect, it may be that other art media can affirm them—thus achieving a positive effect of a different kind.

Before considering this possibility, it is worth considering some interesting marginal cases. The first concerns those temporally realized works which allow an aleatory element—a dimension of chance in their realization. The extreme case of this is John Cage's 4'33". During this time sequence the pianist sits at the piano, but does not play. The content of the piece is provided by the ambience of sound generated by the particular surroundings in which the piece is 'performed'.

At first sight, it would be easy to say that such a work has no objective unity—simply a start and a finish. But the constraint of the 4′33″ time span means that whatever sounds emerge during that time are—for the audience—defined and hence characterized by their relation to these parameters. We find a play of sound which is *free*—rather than purely random—precisely because it is situated within these exact temporal borders.

To enjoy such sounds is to enjoy what Kant describes as 'chosen forms of possible intuitions'.[3] By virtue of the 'framing' context the sounds from the performance hall or spaces outside, become disassociated from their bearers and coalesce in new and arbitrary configurations. Different and developing possibilities of unity—part and whole relations—are generated within the objective constraints of the temporal frame. This extreme case is of some conceptual significance. For the linking of the acoustic elements will be heavily determined by subjective imaginative associations, and even partial visualizations. We will be dealing with a variant of that pure aesthetic response described most effectively by Kant.

This, it should be emphasized, involves a pleasure in the structure or, better, possibilities of structure, in phenomenal configurations per se. It can be had from art, but does not take account of specifically artistic qualities. And this is the point. The more a temporally realized art brings in aleatory elements the more our enjoyment of it shifts towards this more basic form of aesthetic response.

The status of the Momentary element is accordingly much more inde-terminate. If it involves acute states of insight, these derive from the sensitivity of the particular listener rather than from the work itself. They have, in other words, a chance or random character that the Moment in the non-aleatory temporal work does not.

It would, of course, be tempting to link the aleatory Moment to that relative openness of horizons which (as we saw above) characterizes the Moment's lived character. But the problem here is that the aleatory work is perhaps *too* open in this respect. For whilst the origins and destinations of a given Moment in experience are never completely open to comprehension, they are not, however, absolutely random in their generation and effects.

A rather more complex marginal case is still 'in the making' but needs to be at least noted now. The possibility exists for 'interfacing' with computer texts or graphics in such a way that the development of a narrative can be actively developed by the work's recipient. This can simply be a crude case of choosing between different resolutions to the plot, or different key events in its unfolding. The more this latter form is developed, the more the status of the rendered Moment will become ambiguous.

It is difficult to spell out the philosophical implications of this at present because so much depends on the particular kind of computer text and mode of 'interfacing' which we are dealing with. The question also arises of whether—even allowing for all the 'hype'—computer technology will ever establish itself as a major art format. (I shall return to this question in about twenty years' time.)

The more pressing and final marginal case which I shall consider is a familiar one. Often in our intercourse with the temporally realized arts, we remember little more than a schematic sense of the work as a whole, and some memorable passages and Moments. Now in this case, we often orientated towards such Moments simply because they are memorable.

But again there are other such—let us call them 'snatched'—Moments, whose insights are of such import as to seem detachable from the works which contain them. Here the fixed horizontal depth position of the Moment breaks down, precisely because we fill out the vertical fabric so much in imagination. This may be because the insight is of particular personal significance to us, or because, at the same time it perfectly encapsulates something more universal.[4]

---

[4] One of the few thinkers to have taken the relation between art and the Moment at all seriously is Jerrold Levinson in his *Music in the Moment* (Ithaca and London: Cornell University Press, 1997). The emphasis of his account falls on what I am here calling the 'vertical fabric' of the Moment. As I understand him, this is the basic idiom of non-specialist musical understanding. This may be so. But the problem is that the narrative context which enables this understanding is a logical precondition for recognizing the character of the Moment, irrespective of our psychological grasp of it. On p. 165 Levinson suggests that we make do with the vertical fabric in music in a way that would be nonsensical in abstract art. This is not true. Details of such works (and figurative ones also) are often used on book covers and the like. And it would make perfect sense to have a book devoted solely to 'telling details' from visual works. These would have value, but they would remain no more than pleasurable cuts from the works of which they were parts. And this is exactly the case with music as well. The problem here, is that Levinson's analysis is very much listener- rather than composer- or performer-orientated.

Shakespeare, of course, is a goldmine of such possibilities. Think, for example, of the life lived by the phrase 'A tale told by an idiot full of sound and fury, signifying nothing'. This characterization of the individual's life narrative and rationale, has, of course, application far beyond the particular life narrative from which it is taken. Here we begin to find a rendering of the Moment, which seems almost autonomous. It is in the static spatial arts that this possibility is most fully developed. I shall now address them.

8.3

The minimum condition for something to be a picture is that it presents configurations within a two-dimensional plane which individuate specific other kinds of visual item or relation given in three-dimensional space.[5] In this basic sense, the picture has no necessary relationship to the Moment. By virtue of representing spatial objects, the work presents them as 'in' time, but not as any *specific* Moment.

More exact reference to the Moment is secured in two ways, one of which is philosophically uninteresting, and the other of which is of key philosophical significance. The philosophically uninteresting mode of reference is that of *iconography*. An image may in itself provide no clues as to what, if any, Moment of time it is rendering. If, however, we know an appropriate text of the circumstances of a work's production and reception, we may be able to identify, say, a schematic representation of a pair of male and female figures, as depicting the moment of joining in a marriage ceremony. Iconographic evidence external to the work itself, in other words, can secure exact identification of the depicted Moment.

The philosophically interesting depiction of the Moment, in contrast, focuses exclusively on information contained in the work itself. Let us suppose in this respect that an image represents two human beings fighting. Even though the picture might be highly schematic, it may, nevertheless, contain enough relational elements for us to recognize that the figures are linked in the depiction of an *event*.

But if we are to form an exact understanding of the nature of music per se, our account must surely be orientated towards the latter in at least equal measure to the former.

[5] For a formal definition and analysis of pictorial representation see the appendix to my *The Transhistorical Image: Philosophizing Art and its History* (Cambridge: Cambridge University Press, 2002).

However, whilst an event is an occurrence in time, this does not in itself allow us to say that the picture renders a Moment. The most we can say—without recourse to iconographic evidence—is that the image depicts a particular kind of event, rather than a specific Moment of enactment. For this Moment of enactment to be rendered determinately, the image must have other properties. Characteristically these will involve greater particularization in terms of foreshortening, colour, texture, and light-effects, and more significantly still, *a coherent visual syntax* for linking individual figures and their surroundings.

The achievement of this syntax is profoundly linked to the development of perspective. In Greek and Roman times an at least rudimentary, and, in some cases, quite advanced, perspective existed. In a work such as the Pompeian mosaic *Alexander's Battle* (second century BC), perspectival problems are resolved with a stunning virtuosity that anticipates the achievements of the Italian Renaissance. This is not some generalized battle scene, but rather a depiction of the key Moment of confrontation between the two major contestants.

And this is the point. Perspectival structure—be it mathematically exact, or more informal (as in most western art during and after the Renaissance)—offers rigorous criteria for linking objects in space and time.[6] It provides a pictorial convention whereby we can characterize the relations between spatial items in terms of specific kinds of *event*, rather than mere narrative juxtaposition.

Consider, for example, Fra Angelico's *Madonna and Child with Saints* (1440). In an iconographical sense, this gathering of largely supernatural entities is not a real space. It is a symbolic narrative of theological origin. However, the figures have human form, and are disposed in relation to both their surroundings and to one another so as to present a specific moment of interactions.

The significance of this consists in its links with our actual perceptual situation. As embodied beings, the spatio-temporal world which we inhabit is not an arbitrary one. If we move, the structure of the perceptual field reconfigures in strict coordination with our movements. Space and time form a unified and potentially infinite continuum of actual and possible

---

[6] The philosophical basics of perspective are outlined ibid., ch. 3.

perceptual positions. Any given Moment of a human subject's experience embodies one such position.

Perspectivally structured works are consistent with this. For if—within the parameters of a visual medium—we wish to project a virtual space which is logically consistent with the unified spatio-temporal continuum which we inhabit, then the objects and relations in that space must recede from the viewer in a calibrated and proportionate way.

In this respect it is important to distinguish between an external and an internal viewer. The former is an observer in the real spatio-temporal continuum who looks *at* the picture. The latter is a notional viewer who can occupy positions within the perspectival space itself. The coherence of this space in relation to such an internal viewer is of great significance in orientating the external observer.

Suppose, for example, that in Fra Angelico's painting the internal observer starts from the frontal viewpoint but then changes position and walks towards the ecclesiastical figures to the right of the Madonna. The perspectival cues clearly indicate that what would be frontal for such a viewer now, would not be some arbitrary configuration of visual appearances. Rather, spatial items and relations would be reconfigured in strict *coordination* with the internal viewer's movements and change of position. In the present case, his or her view would be dominated by the enthroned Madonna at an oblique angle.

One should also note the way in which continuity of the figures and their surroundings in this scene indicate that the space available to the internal viewer does not stop where it does for the external observer, i.e. at the edge of the picture. The visual cues suggest, rather, that this particular pictorial space presents just one region of a much broader space which an internal observer could explore, in principle, to infinity.

We now reach the major point. When the external observer decodes perspectival cues which articulate the depicted scene, he or she is, in effect, *placed* in that scene *as* the notional internal viewer. The mode of this placing is decisive. Given any picture, one can, in principle, imagine what it would be like to be 'in' the depicted space.

But one should draw a clear distinction between simply projecting *into* a space, and being placed in it. A work with little or no perspectival structure allows us to project into it quite freely. Given, say, a Byzantine mosaic depicting an assemblage of Saints, one might, through imagination, take one's place amongst them in the image. However, the kind of virtual space one is occupying here is *systematically ambiguous*. We may be in a room; in heavenly ether; or simply hovering in mid-air. In the absence of more exact iconographical information, how we understand this space is left primarily to our own imaginations. We project into it on our terms. It is *volitionally characterized*.

The perspectival work is in complete contrast to this. It presents a clear and systematic spatial structure which could be explored by an internal viewer on the lines noted earlier. This space is objectively laid out in so far as it presents *a possible viewing position within a unified virtual space-time continuum*. In imaginative terms, there are all sorts of ways one might occupy such a space, but these are directed by the systematic nature of the space itself. It is one which we are placed in, rather than one whose structure is characterized in primarily volitional terms.

We have, then, a crucial contrast. If the nature of virtual space is primarily a case of how we choose to characterize it, then this has little or no consistency with the actual way we inhabit the world. An embodied subject negotiates the world within the constraints of his or her body's relation to space and time as objective realities. One cannot negotiate these factors by imaginative projections alone. Space, time, and embodiment are more than simply what we wish them to be.

Perspectival space, in contrast, is consistent with our actual perceptual situation. If we were placed in such a space, it would be traversable on the same terms as those in which we negotiate the actual space-time continuum. Irrespective of how we imagined them, spatial appearances and relations would reconfigure in strict coordination with changes of viewing position, and would offer a potentially infinite continuum of such possible positionings.

The 'question' of perspective, therefore, is not resolved by notions of correspondence with how we 'see' in optical terms. Rather, it hinges on logical consistency between perspectival space and the body's relation to the real space-time continuum.

Addressing perspective on these terms allows us to comprehend the nature of pictorial representation's most developed relation to the Moment. I say 'most developed' here because whilst non-perspectival works can render the Momentary by depicting events, it is the perspectival image which renders the Moment in the most *logically exact* terms.

The reason for this is the relation between perspective and the medium of its embodiment. The convention of perspective, as we have seen, involves the projection of a possible viewing position within a virtual space-time continuum. Any notional internal viewer who occupied such a position might attend to the scene presented for just a Moment or through a succession of them.

Since, however, the individual perspectival image can only project this viewing position in terms of a *single* plane, this means that the external observer is, *of necessity*, placed in only *one* of the viewing Moments available to his or her internal counterpart. In logical terms, therefore, as well as depicting a spatial configuration, the perspectival image also renders a single Moment in time.

Now, of course, there are some putative counter-examples to this argument. Donatello's *Feast of the Herod* (1425) from the Bapistry doors at Siena, is one good example of this. It depicts three episodes from the biblical narrative of John the Baptist, in a single perspectivally organized image. Iconographically speaking, this quite clearly involves three different Moments of action in the same overall perspectival space.

However, in purely descriptive terms what is significant is the way they are *integrated* in the unity of that space. The mode of integration is such that the episodes are not presented in strictly pictorial terms as temporally separate. Rather, they are rendered as different events happening *simultaneously* in three separate open rooms in the same building. The internal viewer's position is one which allows these events to be seen simultaneously in a single Moment of viewing. (I shall return to this example a little further on.)

In terms of challenging my argument, a rather more formidable problem is presented by Van Dyck's multiple *Portrait of Charles I* (1636). Here the work contains three different views of the monarch within the same perspectival space. The problem is, of course, that if such a space is held to render a single Moment in time bound up with a single internal viewing position, then we have a logical impossibility—the same material body occupying three separate positions in space at the same time.

Again, however, this problem only arises at an iconographical level. In the most general and purely descriptive terms, the work simply presents three different human forms of identical appearance in three separate spatial locations, simultaneously. The contradiction only arises if we view the work iconographically, i.e. if we have evidence (external to the work itself) which shows that the three identical appearances are meant to be appearances of the same person. Here, in other words, the contradiction is not intrinsic to the image, but arises from the fact that it is being *used* to denote three different appearances of the same person *as if* they were perceptually accessible at the same time from the same viewing position.

The oddness of this painting is, in fact, highly instructive. For whilst the general structure of perspective is as I have described it, it can also be *used* for purposes which render it, as it were, fragile, or which even subvert it. One way for this to happen is if—as Van Dyck does—the artist begins to play games with the specific kinds of item which he or she is relating together in a perspectival space. Things, literally, start to look odd.

In much of Dalí or Tanguy's work, for example, a basically perspectival structure is populated by items of such extreme oddness that we feel displaced into a realm of dream or hallucination—even though it remains formally consistent with the basic structure of the actual space-time continuum. In an artist such as Magritte, indeed, relations between particular visual items and relations are set up in such a way as to subvert (as in *The Human Condition*, 1934) or utterly disrupt the unity of perspective. (This is manifestly the case in, for example, his *Carte Blanche*, 1934). Here, of course, we move into the realm of hybrid pictorial spaces. This can also happen when multiple perspectival viewpoints are deliberately combined (as in the work of M. E. Escher) so as to present a visual paradox.

These hoverings at the periphery of perspective invite the following critical observation. My arguments have based great emphasis on the logical structure of perspectival images—on the most general descriptive level in terms of which we can engage with such works. This centres specifically on their rendering of a possible Moment of viewing.

But, surely (it might be retorted) what gives the perspectival image its interest is the iconographical dimension—the particular referential strategies which inform the constitution, use, and historical reception of such images. For example, whilst in purely descriptive terms, Donatello's *Feast of Herod* renders a single Moment, this surely amounts to little, except, perhaps, as a kind of formal counterpoint to the sophisticated episodic narrative which the artist intended to convey.

Now admittedly, this critical point is a useful reminder of the semantic and historical richness of the image, but it needs to be measured against another consideration. Pictorial representation's rendering of the Moment has been much neglected by art historians and philosophers alike. Yet it is the basis of a uniquely and logically irreducibly *visual* form of meaning.

Every art form has its own interesting patterns of iconography, and can be analysed (as is the penchant of the present) as a configuration of signs in a field of other signs. However, *only the perspectival image can project a possible Moment of viewing in a unified space-time continuum.* This is not an arbitrary and dull fact. For in achieving this, the perspectival image draws on, and refines, structures which are essential to the cohesion of the self. I shall now clarify this.

8.4

First, by virtue of this embodied condition, no two human beings can *simultaneously* occupy the same position in the spatio-temporal continuum. We can, in principle, occupy the same position in space as another person, but not at the same time. We can be present in the same instant of time as another person, but not in their exact spatial position. This means that whilst we share a world, our perceptual perspectives on it can never be exactly congruent. Our having of a human life history is the direct and ongoing outcome of this basic asymmetry.

However, to be conscious of oneself as a self, logically presupposes that we are conscious of others. To know what and who we are involves a sense of species identity and the ability to define ourselves in relation to patterns of sameness and difference amongst other members of the species. These capacities are acquired through both initiation into a language and all the complex social interactions in which that initiation is embedded. Broadly speaking, we learn ourselves and other people reciprocally on the basis of description and empathy. We describe what we think and feel to other people, and they to us. On this basis, we are able, through imagination, to identify with the other. This does not amount to experiencing the world as they do, but it at least enables us to form a sense of what it might be like to be another person—a sense which is, indeed, rather more than mere intellectual insight.

Now I have argued at great length in earlier chapters that art is deeply implicated in these issues. It offers its audience a distinctive way of identifying with and learning from another person's style of negotiating the world. This possibility arises from art's specific aesthetic character. Perspectival representation, however, realizes it in a unique way. In this respect, we will recall that earlier on I showed how in decoding a work's perspectival cues, the external observer is *placed* in it as an internal viewer. We simultaneously occupy the time and space of our own world, and a Moment from a possible viewing position in the virtual world.

These constitute an intersection of two different space-time continua. One is able, *simultaneously*, to see what another might see, and from the same position. That which is denied us in our direct dealings with other people is here realized through artifice.

In identifying with other people this can—if we are self-indulgent— simply involve projecting into their experience (in the sense of 'projecting in' noted earlier). We form a fantasy of how they see things. If, on the other hand, imagination is guided by descriptions provided by the other, then it can be a much more disciplined activity.

Perspectival projection is of this latter order. However, what makes it absolutely compelling is its offer of an intersection with the possible visual experience of another which is achieved not just in imagination, but directly *at the level of the visible itself*. It is, in effect, vision which has become visible. In some important works, Merleau-Ponty has linked this to the phenomenon of painting per se.[7] But the perspectival image renders it in a quite specific way. For it makes manifest the fact that vision addresses its object not just in spatial terms, but temporal ones too.

The full ramifications of this can be brought out by a comparison with the way in which the Moment is rendered by other art forms. Literature and film, for example, are arts of temporal realization; that is to say that whilst they can present events unfolding in time *as* their subject matter, the means by which this subject matter is presented is itself temporal. The lines or chapters of a literary work must be read through time in exactly the order in which the author has presented them. The frames of a film must be projected in the exact order of succession which the director has finally assigned to them in the cutting room.

---

[7] See e.g. his late essay 'Eye and Mind', included in James Edie (ed.), *The Primacy of Perception* (Evanston: Northwestern University Press, 1964), 159–90.

This linear model of temporal realization has a key implication. If, in the course of such a work, we find important moments of action or insight, then these are given their character primarily in relation to those other Moments in the work which lead up to them, and those which flow out of them as consequences. The Moment is rendered through its position in a *horizontal* field of other Moments unfolding in strict linear succession, and circumscribed by the beginning and end of the work.

Now if we focus on a specific line, phrase or Momentary scene—say the death of Batty at the end of *Bladerunner*—this can have an intrinsic significance (or '*vertical fabric*') which to some degree stands on its own in ways described earlier. We project associations and meanings around it. We fill it out in imagination.

Such projection carries a corresponding risk. For the Moment may become too autonomous from the work as a whole. It then functions as if it were a small work in its own right—but without being able to *actually* become such a work. Hence it is important that such realizations of vertical fabric constantly refer back and illuminate the field that defines them.

On these terms, then, the Moment in temporally realized arts, such as literature and film, is governed by its relation to other elements in the narrative field of the individual work as a whole. This means that there are severe constraints on how its vertical fabric is rendered. In pictorial representation the situation is reversed in interesting ways. For such works articulate their images in terms of a single plane. With enough details of modelling, texture, colour, and foreshortening, we can say that a picture renders something Momentary (in the sense described earlier).

More than this, it renders it in the full richness of its vertical fabric. The narrative field of the work as a whole, indeed, just is this fabric. There is a need to fill it out in imagination, because the plane is already full of visual material. Indeed, precisely because this vertical fabric is given complete in a single plane, it can be immediately comprehended as a whole, without us *having* to relate it to a broader *given* horizontal field of temporally preceding and successive elements.

The important terms here are 'having to' and 'given'. This is especially significant in relation to the perspectival image. Here the work presents us with a single Moment from a viewing position within a unified space-time continuum. It is an enclosed *cross-section* of flowing systematic time. Hence (as noted above) in 'reading' the work as a single image, there is no given horizonal or linear field of preceding and successive Moments which we have to relate it to. These Moments are only logically implied. They are 'present' in a purely notional sense. This gives the image nevertheless a special import.

To show this, we must again advert to the temporally realized arts of literature and film. In them, the holistic nature of any individual Moment is manifest, in so far as its character is, substantially, a function of its place in relation to the narrative Moments which precede it, and the ones which come after it. This is also the case with Moments of experience in real life. They are defined and given their character by virtue of their place in the developing whole of experience.

There is one key difference, however. In the literary or filmic work, the field which defines the individual Moment is *given*. It is fixed and circumscribed by the limits of the work itself. In real life, the field is not given. What we are in any one Moment is shaped by our past intentional experience, and anticipations of the future and counterfactual possibilities, but we cannot know exactly how. In contrast with the literary and filmic work, the elements which define an individual Moment are not fixed as a definite field. They function rather as a relatively open horizon.

If this were not the case, if in inhabiting the present Moment we could not do so without having an exact sense of both how we got to this point, and of all the things which might flow out from it, then we would be utterly overwhelmed by the quantity of information involved. Perception and understanding would be paralysed by a kind of excess of history.

This is why the holistic dimension which situates the Moment is an unconscious one. The character of the present—its vertical fabric—has a specific style which is a selective condensation determined by the body's present position, its physical capacities, our experience of the past, and our sense of both the future and counterfactual possibility.

Style, in this sense, derives from both habit memory (i.e. the embodied subject's capacity to physically and cognitively negotiate the space-time continuum without always having to think *how* to do so) and also those distinctive experiences which constitute the narrative of an individual's personal history. Style is the functional principle of intelligent bodily behaviour. It allows us to adapt to changing physical and social circumstances, in an economical and flexible way.

These factors show why the perspectival work is *so* significant. An image of this kind is much closer to the actual experience of the Moment than are temporally realized works. The perspectival accents of the individual work show it to be a cross-section of a possible position in a virtual space-time continuum. When the external observer is placed in it as an internal viewer, he or she can recognize that the presented scene is continuous (in virtual terms) with events and scenes that transpired before it, and ones which will come after it. These other Moments are not literally present in the work; rather they are implied by the perspectival structure of the depicted scene. The scene is declared as a specific position in a space-time continuum. We recognize that the scene would reconfigure if the internal viewer were to change his or her position.

Now the very fact that this possibility of alternative positioning is implied in the image's vertical fabric, makes it consistent with actual Moments of experience, in a way that literary and filmic works are not. In both the living and the perspectival Moment, the unity of the space-time continuum is implied in the style of its vertical fabric. The Moment has the character of, as Cassirer might describe it, *symbolic pregnance*.[8]

There is also a further respect in which the perspectival image is uniquely consistent with the Moment as experienced. It centres on the Moment's *achieved* structure. As we saw above, any Moment has a vertical fabric which is determined by the body's present position in the perceptual field. However, this position is also informed by the body's sense of its own general capacities and its individual history. The Moment is a relatively autonomous experience which emerges from this complex holistic network of present, former, and possible bodily positions. It does not simply happen; it is achieved.

The perspectival image's special relation with this centres on the physical means through which it is realized. Again, to bring out what is at issue here we must first refer back to the example of literature and film.

Temporally realized arts (with the arguable exception of aleatory ones) are allographic, i.e. they exist as tokens of types. What is logically decisive in the realization of such works, is not the physical characteristics of

---

[8] See e.g. Ernst Cassirer, *The Philosophy of Symbolic Forms*, vol. iii, *The Phenomenology of Knowledge*, trans. R. Manheim (New Haven and London: Yale University Press, 1966), 114.

the individual tokens, but rather the type content which they embody. The physical characteristics are overlooked except to the degree that the token is faulty, and obscures or distorts its type content. (A faded reel of film, or pages missing from a novel would be examples of this). Of course, if a film is projected on a decent-sized screen (rather than, say, watched on video) or if a novel has an attractive binding or typeface, these factors can enhance our enjoyment of the type content, but these do not (under normal circumstances) figure as part of the meaning of that content.

In such allographic works, the work itself—the type content—does not directly manifest the process of the original creation. A poem, novel, or film is brought into existence through the physical manipulation of appropriate kinds of material. However, whilst the artist makes the type content, he or she does not make the individual tokens through which this content is transmitted. Even if the artist does make a prototype token (as, for example, when a poet writes a poem down on paper) the perceptual or physical characteristics of this autographic inscription is not itself a part of the type content which it renders.

Painting and drawing, however, are out and out autographic. Such works are individual items made by the artist—usually entirely, or more rarely (as in the case of Van Dyck, Reynolds, and others) at least in part. Such works cannot be tokens of a type.[9] Of course, we do find them reproduced in books or on slides, etc., but here the work is not itself the type. Rather, these reproductions are tokens of the type 'copy of' or 'reproduction of' such and such a work.

Now to recognize a painting or drawing *as* a painting or drawing entails some comprehension of its autographic origins. Even though we may have no direct knowledge of them, we must at least assume that the image is the product of bodily and perceptual positioning which occurred at specific times and in a specific place or places. On this basis, the perspectival image's link to the experienced Moment is further deepened. For as well as projecting a possible Moment in a virtual continuum, the means by which this is achieved—the artist's bodily positioning through *gesture*—is also inscribed in the particular style of the image.

---

[9] The example of woodcuts and engravings is, in logical terms, a mediate case in so far as it involves tokens of *autographic types*.

Here the realization of the depicted Moment is manifestly a function of bodily positioning. Through being painted or drawn, the bodily means whereby *any* Moment comes to be, are declared in symbolic terms.

The importance of this is that whilst a philosophical analysis such as the present one can illuminate the nature of the Moment in general terms, the perspectival image shows this at the level wherein the most of our Moments are actually experienced—namely, directly in perception itself. In such an autographic image, The Moment, as it were, comprehends itself on its own terms.

The further significance of this autographic structure can be usefully developed through a comparison with photography. It is this I now turn to.

8.5

Paul Virilio (following Rodin) has cited the autographic rendering of time as marking a key difference between pictorial representation and another form of perspectival imaging—namely photography.[10] The picture declares time in an active way through gesture, whilst the basic logical function of photography (whatever creative modifications are made to it) is to freeze a specific Moment in time by mechanical means.

What is at stake here can best be brought out by a modal distinction which Virilio and Rodin do not employ. It consists of the fact that (in its basic function), the photograph renders an *actual* Moment, whereas the perspectival image renders a *possible* one. This latter fact is emphasized by our necessary assumption that the perspectival image is made; it is brought into existence through the body's creative gestures. Even if the work depicts some existing visual state of affairs, it cannot mechanically transcribe this.

The reason why, is that in order to render this configuration in terms of a single perspectival Moment, the artist has to negotiate it over a much more sustained period of time. He or she also has to adapt for expression in terms of a single two-dimensional plane. This means that the Moment which results will be an interpretative condensation derived from many

---

[10] See Paul Virilio, *The Vision Machine*, trans. Julie Rose (Bloomington and Indianapolis: Indiana University Press, 1994), 1–2.

different Moments of study, thought, and gesture. It will be a stylization of the object depicted, and will thence present it more as a possibility of experience, than as a transcription of what actually exists.

This factor is also underlined by another consideration. In its basic function, photography presupposes an existing item or state of affairs which will constitute that which the individual photograph is 'of'. In this sense, it is logically tied to the actual. The pictorial perspectival image is not. Neither, indeed, is any picture. For whilst the learning of how to make pictures may involve copying some given item or states of affairs, it does not have to. In the most basic logical terms, a picture is *of* a specific *kind* of thing. It may be created so as to depict, or, better *denote* an actual person or whatever, but denotation is merely one use of picturing rather than its definitive function.

Given the photograph's link to actuality and the picture's link to possibility, we can draw some useful conclusions. First, in so far as the Moments preceding the photograph and those following after it, are not given, the image has a relatively open horizon of past and future. However, this horizon is haunted by a powerful sense of impending inevitability.

Roland Barthes brings this out well in a comment on Alexander Gardner's *Portrait of Lewis Payne*.[11] Payne was sentenced to death and subsequently executed for his part in the events leading to Abraham Lincoln's assassination. Barthes says 'He is dead and he is going to die.' Exactly. The photograph presents a person anticipating death but for the viewer this image is framed by the knowledge that what is anticipated here is now an actuality. It is an event long in the past. The image exemplifies a poignant tension which holds—to greater or lesser degrees—in all photographs, and which gives the medium its distinctive psychological power.

This tension derives from the relation between the photograph's rendering of a Moment of *life* and that Moment's position in a field. For even if we do not know the exact nature of the Moments which transpired before and after in relation to the scene captured in the photograph, we know that they did actually come to pass and did so in an objectively exact order, and with an exact content. We have no choice in relation to this.

---

[11] See Roland Barthes, *Camera Lucida*, trans. R. Howard (London: Jonathan Cape, 1982), 94.

In painting and drawing's perspectival images we do. Here, a series of preceding and successive events are implied in the image. But they have the character of possibility rather than actuality. Their content and pattern of unfolding is primarily a fact of how the observer imagines them to be. Of course, one can also play this game with the photograph, but here the role of imagination is always shadowed by the knowledge that, whatever we might imagine, things happened exactly as they did, irrespective of our imaginings. (I shall return to this point.)

The perspectival images of photography, and of pictorial representation, have, then, different modal structures. They are, nevertheless, both broadly consistent with the lived Moment of experience by virtue of the relative openness of their horizons. This consistency does not, however, amount to exact congruence. After all, the photograph and the picture are artefactual images, rather than actual states of a person.

This asymmetry is, in fact, extremely fruitful. In the case of the pictorial perspectival image, for example, the past and future which inform the rendered Moment can be constructed entirely volitionally through imagination. Our actual experience is in strong contrast to this. For even though we cannot comprehend the exact chains of experience which lead to the present Moment, or which figure in it as anticipations of the future, we have at least some sense of the key events involved. Our notions of past and future are constrained by the actual fact that, in a way that our sense of past and future in relation to the pictorial Moment are not.

In the picture, therefore, we have a power over the Moment. This is not just because its vertical fabric is rendered in a more stable and enduring form than the Moment of actual experience, it is also because we can stipulate, in imagination, how the Moment came to be and what will flow from it.

The broader significance of this stipulation consists in its contrast with what (in Chapter 3) I called the *discursive rigidity* of our normal experience of the world. This rigid orientation is one wherein, for example, we judge specific things in relation to other specific things, on the basis of definite concepts and well-defined practical goals and biological needs. The actualities of life are compelling. We may choose some of the ends which motivate us; we may also have room for choice in terms of the means whereby they are realized, but once the framework of ends is in place, our lives are heavily constrained by the following of *rules*.

Now, in the picture—and perspectival image in particular—we are dealing with a virtual world and not a real one. The picture may have a practical function, but it does not have to. We can enjoy its formal qualities (of shape, volume, texture, and mass, etc.) for their own sake, but more than this, we can enjoy the perspectival images of rendering the Moment for its own sake also. As a position within a unified virtual space-time continuum, the rendered Moment is consistent with our own world. It is intelligible and interesting.

The fact that it is virtual, however, means that our imagination need not be constrained by discursive rigidity in its traversals of such a space. Perspectival structure offers a clear framework for imaginative exploration, without us having to worry about practical issues. In relation to a work such as Caspar David Friedrich's *Arctic Shipwreck* (1821), for example, we can enjoy the threatening vista without fear; and can follow an imaginary route towards the horizon without worrying about cold, pollution, or the possibility of bumping into Schwarzenegger filming 'on location'. The image offers an alternative reality which compensates for the mundanity of our own.

In respect of these issues, the photographic image is rather more ambiguous. As in actual experience, the Moment rendered in a photograph is constrained by the objective chain of events in relation to which it is positioned. (This, indeed, is even more the case if the photograph is actually taken by oneself.) However, as with the picture, the photograph embodies the Moment in a more defined and enduring form, and, in the case of photographs of persons and events other than those directly experienced by us, the factual dimension does not exercise the same degree of constraint as it does in actual experience. Our imagination is relatively free to project its own interpretation of the image.

This being said, however, the factual dimension remains real. As I observed earlier, the image is haunted by a sense of impending inevitability. Its rendered Moment is one which has now taken its place in an irrevocable past. Perhaps the intrinsic fascination of photography consists, therefore, in the constant tension between this passage of the inevitable and the imaginative 'break-outs' with which the viewer surrounds it. In actual experience a tension is just that. In the tension between a photographic image and its logical context, it can be transformed.

This is because human freedom is centrally concerned with breaking out from those patterns of inevitability and discursive rigidity which constantly surround us. These patterns, indeed, can function as challenges as much as constraints. In constructing, say, imaginary biographies and 'adventures' for the unknown people in photographs, the inevitability of the factual dimension provokes us to, as it were, 'ride' it, and assimilate it on our own terms. This assimilation cannot be absolute, but at least it allows the inevitable to function as a vehicle for free activity.

There is one final point to consider vis-à-vis the significance of the perspectival image. In such an image (be it photographic or pictorial) our comprehension of it as a whole does not entail that one specific part must be apprehended after another specific part in an exact linear order of temporal succession. We could scan the image from left to right (or vice versa), up and down (or vice versa), foreground to background (or vice versa), or through some combination of these. In the case of an event in time, or a temporally realized artwork, this is not the case. If we wish to comprehend an event, or, say, a film *as* a unity, the specific component elements *must* be apprehended in an exact order of temporal succession. One cannot do this by, for example, starting in the middle, and then seeing the end, and finally the beginning.

What I am describing here, is, of course, the Kantian distinction between the objective unity of a spatial object, and the objective unity of an event which was discussed earlier. As we have seen, whilst the perspectival image is obviously a spatial object, it also renders a Moment of time in virtual terms. In reading such an image, we find, in fact, an interaction between the two different orders of time. The virtual time inscribed in the image is that of strict linear succession. Even though it is the imagination which projects 'before' and 'after' here, it does so according to the cues laid out by the perspectival structure.

However, because the Moment is rendered in a plane, it also has the unity of a spatial object. To comprehend this unity involves the alternative modes of scanning involved above. These are temporally successive, but the mode of succession—the linear pattern of perceptual exploration—is *volitionally directed*. We can choose which aspect to attend to first, and which to attend to next, and so on. This means that the strict linear time of the perspectival image's visual structure—a term whose linearity is not subject to the will—exists simultaneously with one whose linearity is, in fact, subject to the will. A virtual rendering of objective time engenders an experience of volitionally directed time.

The significance of this consists in the exact nature of the relation. It is sometimes said that our best experiences of art can involve a felt sense of time-transcendence. This is what is at stake here. Such transcendence is not, however, a communing with some ineffable 'timeless, cosmic flow'. It is, rather, something which lifts us out of the normal temporal flux by *unifying* two different modes of its unfolding.

In normal circumstances, our sense of linear time and its volitional counterpart, merely weave in and out of one another—depending on whether our perception is negotiating event-sequences or objects. Even in those cases where both are involved, we do not normally have any sense that they are equally fundamental in our experience of the world. In fact, we do not usually remark on them at all. We merely exist *in* them.

The perspectival image, however, is one where linear and volitional time are reciprocally correlated. In this context, we cannot have one without the other. Their equifundamentality in the human condition is, therefore, symbolically rendered by the mutual dependence of time and spatial object in the experience of the Moment per se.

Given all these points, one can say that the perspectival image is unique in both its structure and effects. At the heart of this uniqueness is its status as a *distinctively visual projection of time*. When time is rendered virtually in a single spatial plane, its two experiential vectors—objective linearity and volitional directedness—attain a degree of complementarity, or, better, of harmony, that is denied us in the ordinary course of events. To exist simultaneously as an external observer of, and internal observer in, the perspectival image is to transcend the normal conditions of time, through being returned to it in a more *integrated* way. It is to possess the Moment in a way that no other form of symbolic expression can, and in a way, indeed, that actual experience itself cannot.

Conclusion

In this chapter, I have shown how art communicates the Moment in different ways on the basis of the different media involved. All of them have their distinctive slants, but it is the perspectival image of pictorial representation which engages with the Moment most profoundly in terms of its experiential significance. Art—and perspectival works—communicate and eternalize the Moment not only in terms of preserving it, but also by enabling it to clarify broader cognitive relations.

This is one of the reasons why artists who produce major refinements or innovations in the treatment of perspective have a significant canonic significance. For what they are working with is technical device which not only articulates the unity of space as a system of spatial relations, but also unifies it temporally as well. Through expanding the scope of visual art, it expands the possibilities of our aesthetic engagement with the world.

Near the end of Goethe's *Faust*, Faust recalls the fleeing Moment: 'Ah, still delay—thou art so fair.'

It could be said that the Moment's embodiment in art is the only realization of this desire that is available to a finite being. Through such embodiment we intuitively comprehend some metaphysical truths. The Moment cannot qua Moment be frozen, and if it were it would lose the very character which prompts the desire for its preservation. But through art, we can eternalize it in a form that is aesthetically renewable, and which can, in principle, outlast all the moments which constitute an individual's life. This is a glimpse of redemption, however slight.

Conclusion: The Status and Future of Art

In conclusion, I will first reiterate this book's central line of argument as set out in the Introduction.

I argue that Institutional definitions of art, and anti-foundational theories, distort the nature of art's claim to high cultural status. My normative alternative holds that images, qua sensible or imaginatively intended objects, are aesthetic configurations. When their *style* of making is original (or, at the very least, individual) it characterizes the subject matter from the creator's viewpoint and creates, thereby, a distinctive kind of aesthetic unity which cannot be derived from other sources. This is art. The creation and appreciation of such unity involves two broader factors. The first is an enhanced interaction of capacities which are basic to cognition. (Which capacities and interactions are involved is a function of the work's individual expression of features distinctive both to the aesthetic and to the image per se, and also to the character of the specific medium of imaging involved.) The second dimension consists of the way in which creative differences in individual styles and works, develop the medium of expression. This is the basis of canonic value.

These claims were justified in the following way. I began by analysing formalism, recent Designation theories, and various kinds of relativism, in relation to artistic meaning and value. It was shown that the formalists do little to explain why 'significant form' becomes significant, that the Designation theorists reduce art to the presentation of theoretical intentions (an act which makes art's intelligibility dependent, primarily, on external contexts), and that the relativist viewpoints are largely self-contradictory. It was also shown that in addition to their conceptual flaws, these approaches were all unconsciously racist.

During these discussions, I also provisionally introduced an alternative approach to artistic value based on the intrinsic significance of image-making. This involved first showing that the aesthetic in all its aspects involves a heightened interaction of basic cognitive competences achieved through the perception of structural aspects of appearance. Art, however, goes beyond the beauty of nature by virtue of its image-character (a character which was shown to encompass even abstract art). Qua image, the artwork is a stylistic interpretation of that which it is an image of.

'Style' in this context does not mean mere chic or fashion, but rather the artist's way of applying his or her sensible medium in relation to some subject matter. Through this formative aesthetic activity art not only enhances the interaction of imagination and understanding, but also allows experience to enjoy various 'increases of being', and to be the source of a unique form of aesthetic empathy. Art's formative power exemplifies structures which are fundamental to cognition, at the level of sensibility itself. It does so in a distinctive way which cannot be derived from other forms of activity.

It was also shown how each of the major art forms makes its own unique contribution to this general distinctiveness. Pictorial representation, for example, has a privileged relation to the transcendental imagination, and literary metaphor to the perceptual foundations of predication. Music was shown to disclose key features of emotion and its narrative settings, and through this, aspects of our basic mode of inherence in the auditory world. It was shown further how each of these media has its own distinctive relation to the aesthetic cognition of time.

All these factors in concert, give the making and appreciation of images an intrinsic aesthetic fascination, which precedes, and in part enables, the extraordinary range of practical applications which images enjoy. This is what I called the first axis of art's normative significance.

There is also a second one, which I discussed in most of my chapters (albeit with different emphases). It arises from the fact that not all images exemplify their intrinsic fascination. In the vast majority of cases, indeed, the image's intrinsic significance is absorbed within its informational, persuasive, or decorative functions.

If, however, the work is original, and achieves recognizable individuality of style, then we attend to *how* this is achieved, and thence to its intrinsic significance. To be original or individual in this sense entails that the work referred to a comparative horizon of other works in the tradition of the medium concerned.

Its position in relation to this horizon is the basis of a work's (or body of work's) canonic significance. Some works are merely original; others are so in an *exemplary* way, i.e. they negotiate factors which are fundamental to the medium concerned and refine or innovate in relation to some aspect(s) of them, and become, thereby, stylistic models for other artists.

This comparative canonic dimension is the second axis of art's normative significance. Through it we can make a distinction between mere art based on imagery per se, and Art with a capital 'A', where, through its mediation by originality of style, a work's intrinsic aesthetic significance is fully developed.

As a result of these complex strategies, it is hoped that art has been defined; the basis of its value has been explained; and criteria for making distinctions of merit between works have been clarified. However, it is worth concluding the study by considering a couple of questions arising from all these factors.

The first is that of why the intrinsic significance of the original image should be assigned any special 'high' cultural status. The aesthetic and the artistic are, in literal terms, just about *useless*.

My overall arguments have already shown the importance of art over and above its practical functions. However, I can now offer a summary and development of their most relevant aspects which answer the question more directly.

First, whilst human beings need to achieve biological gratification and secure the means of subsistence and shelter, they also need much more. The evolution of self-consciousness may be geared towards the realization of the aforementioned needs, but its achievement has brought about new needs in addition to them. We have evolved to a stage where we need to understand and develop ourselves through interacting with other persons and the sensible world per se, and through achieving recognition from, and bestowing it upon, others.

Central to this is the fact that, as self-conscious beings, our awareness is not fixed in the *present* field of sensory stimuli exclusively. Our sense of who and what we are, and what we might become, and our emotional involvement with the world, all draw explicitly on our position vis-à-vis places, times, and states of affairs other than those given in the present. But our personal states and the spatio-temporal horizon in which they occur are in constant flux. There is an inherent instability in our engagement with the world and the causal horizon.

Without such instability, of course, we would not be free, but freedom and the contingency of happenstances and the instability of the experiential flux, bring about a corresponding need for security.

Art answers this psychological/ontological need. It is a mode of making which qua image acts upon experience in all the complex ways described earlier. In particular, through the complex and ubiquitous ways in which it engages the imagination, it is especially powerful in making many aspects of the not-present or merely possible exist in a quasi-sensory form in the present.

The aesthetic and art, however, do not *just* secure the experiential flow through stabilizing it in accessible, enduring images. The fact that originality is intrinsic to art means that this securing is, *at the same time*, the opening-up of new experiential possibilities. Our taste in the aesthetic and artistic, indeed, is *educable*, and through being educable, it can show new possibilities for self-understanding, the understanding of others, and the comprehension of more general features of our relation to the world.

This is why canonic values involve much more than mere difference of styles in some dry academic sense. Each individual contribution to a medium offers a new way—however slight—of experiencing the world. And when artistic refinement or innovation is of a fundamental kind, then one has the excitement of seeing highly significant new ways of configuring the medium and world flowing out of these. The artwork is always to some degree an inert material object; but in its style of imagery and originality it exemplifies the power and potential of freedom also.

But a vital point must be emphasized. In order to appreciate aesthetic and artistic value, one does not have to believe that such appreciation will have the desirable outcomes just described. These factors operate, rather, at an *intuitive* level (on lines described in the Introduction to this book). To have aesthetic experience is to be *at home* with the world through sensibility and understanding being brought into a distinctive, reciprocally enhancing relation. This and the possibility of change and new understanding are integral to the experience of art, even though their involvement is rarely noticed or remarked upon, in explicit terms.

Of course, there are many people who would simply dismiss these arguments, and prefer instead, the pleasures of popular entertainment and mass culture. A person might affirm, for example, that he or she prefers horse racing to painting. Indeed, popular pleasures of this sort transcend the level of our mere animal being, and by watching horse races or TV soaps, or playing push-pin, all sorts of things can be learned about oneself and the world. One may even change as a result of this.

But if one has not also embraced the possibilities of art, then one has not fully engaged with the world's more complex experiential possibilities. And if the effort has been made and a person still prefers push-pin to poetry, or whatever, then another point must be pressed.

Everyone changes to some degree (however small) by virtue of being finite. The leisure and mass culture pursuits just described can help change one, or bring about self-understanding in relation to change, but these possibilities are not built into such practices in conceptual terms. Indeed, there is a strong momentum to become a passive consumer of such pleasures and to follow mere herd instincts in relation to them. The possibility of self-development is at best an accidental by-product of this.

The possibility of self-development and change, in contrast, is what art ultimately answers to. One may make or appreciate art just to 'show-off' but this is at odds, manifestly, with what art offers by virtue of its very nature. As a person's life changes, it is art that has the greater potential to engage with and clarify this, in all the positive terms which I have described throughout this book. It is a form of life based on individuality of style, and all the possibilities which it opens up. Hence if a person refuses to at least try art again, it is a self-defeating strategy.

What I am arguing, then, is that whilst there are indeed individuals who prefer push-pin to poetry, that is by no means the end of the matter. Art exemplifies and develops our trans-animal evolutionary needs and development to an inordinate degree. It is thus entitled to a level of cultural prestige which the easier options of leisure and mass culture pursuits are not.

One final key issue must be addressed. Since the last decades of the twentieth century it has become a commonplace in some western quarters, to talk about art having—in various senses—come to an end. Hence, whilst this book's central argument has explained and justified artistic value and its cultural status, perhaps this is a ratification of what has already been historically superseded.

There are two broad 'end of art' arguments which I shall consider in turn. The first is proposed by Arthur Danto. In Chapter 1, I refuted his claims concerning the primacy of theory in securing the distinction between artworks and real things. However, he has a back-up argument based on a historical narrative concerning the ultimate triumph of American Pop Art.

It centres around the claim that the invention of photography brought about a radical historical transformation of the visual arts. In order to retain their distinctive creativity these arts were driven into a search for perfect congruence with those features essential to art per se. As Danto observes,

There have been more projected definitions of art, each identified with a different movement in art, in the six or seven decades of the modern era, than in the six or seven centuries which preceded it. Each definition was accompanied by a severe condemnation of everything else, as *not* art.[1]

For Danto, modernism in the visual arts goes through a great 'philosophical' process of self-questioning during much of the twentieth century. The 'feed out' point of this process turns out to be an exhibition held at the Stables Gallery in New York in April 1964. Here Andy Warhol exhibited *Brillo Boxes*—a work that is perceptually indistinguishable from real Brillo Boxes. According to Danto, at this point art achieves a self-congruence with its own essence. The *Brillo Boxes* exemplify the fact that the only factor which separates art from real things is theory.

By virtue of this self-congruence between artwork and essence, art is supposed to have logically exhausted its real creative possibilities. It will continue to be produced, but the continuing possibilities of great innovation which shaped previous eras of artistic creativity are gone for ever.

Danto's theory is extremely problematic. Consider, for example, his description of the progression from one artistic movement to another. According to him, each new avant-garde movement offers a new definition of art which dismisses its predecessors as 'not art'.

---

[1] Arthur Danto, *The State of the Art* (New York: Prentice Hall, 1987), 217.

This is false, historically speaking. The dynamics between such movements are extremely complex and there is a massive amount of cross-fertilization—especially through the influence of Cubism and Futurism—on other tendencies. Indeed, the real preoccupation of such tendencies is not to search for new definitions of art, but to extend art's formal and expressive means so as to represent aspects of reality which traditional idioms are unable to negotiate.[2]

Danto, however, focuses his narrative on Duchamp's legacy and its development by American Pop artists, to the exclusion of the vast bulk of twentieth-century modernism—including its most important movements (notably Cubism, Futurism, and Surrealism). Actually, it could be argued that his reading of American Pop Art itself is very misleading, in so far as it omits consideration of their championing of consumer society. However, rather than follow up art historical questions, I turn now to the conceptual failings of Danto's theory.

The decisive one arises from my critical points in Chapter 1. There I argued that the links which Danto makes between art and theory cannot be used to define art. If this is true, then it follows that Danto's reading of Warhol is false, and that art has not, in fact, achieved some kind of self-congruence with its essence. In which case, no restrictions on the nature of artistic innovation can follow from this.

We must also question why the achievement of art's supposed self-congruence with its essence should necessarily restrict continuing large-scale innovation. It is true that western practices have gradually explored the boundaries of what counts as innovative art, especially in the modern era. However, these explorations do not, in themselves, involve a conceptual link to any search for the true essence of art, or new ways of defining it. Original art of the highest quality often involves new ways of using factors which have already been well established as basic to the medium involved. New definitions of art do not have to come into it at all.

On these terms, then, Danto's theory fails on both historical and conceptual grounds. There is, however, a second 'end of art' argument based on very different criteria.

---

[2] For more on this see John Golding's *Paths to the Absolute* (London: Thames & Hudson, 2002); and my book *The Language of Twentieth-Century Art: A Conceptual History* (New Haven and London: Yale University Press, 1997).

It is closely allied with (but not necessarily connected to) relativist cultural theory of the kind criticized in Chapter 2. The argument holds that in the age of global consumerism, the boundaries between high art and mass culture have been erased. Since the 1950s pop culture has heavily influenced artistic practice. The development of installation, assemblage, and Conceptual art, indeed, involves creative strategies which have no relation to those of the traditional idioms of high art.

Questions of skill, and the idea of art having some kind of distinctive value are outmoded, accordingly. Art is now no more than a mix of information, entertainment, biography, fashion, social commentary, and theory. And this is all to the good. For it 'demystifies' art and its elitist pretensions.

Now the empirical facts summarized here are true. But not their positive interpretation. As I argued in Chapter 2, art has orientated itself towards works which do not have to be made by the artist in person, and, in so doing, has been colonized by the world of managerial and consumer interests. Far from being anti-elitist, it has secured art for a new, largely western elite. The whole ethos involved here, is a passive consumer mentality—an acceptance of resurrected late nineteenth-century primitive free market ideology as if it were some kind of 'modernization'.

However, whilst this mentality is an empirical fact, it has no logical implications for artistic value. Art has its ontological character, whether or not people in a culture care to develop it. Indeed, no matter how dominant an ideology may be, it cannot last for ever. It is easily conceivable, for example, that the presently fashionable practices may be superseded by new forms of overtly high art which privilege art's made status and aesthetic dimensions.

No matter how art is colonized by the consumerist world, it remains a distinctive intrinsically significant mode of artifice. Indeed, by virtue of the normative structures described throughout this book, it has a kind of ethical significance—as a negation of prevailing shallowness (i.e. style reduced to mere fashion and sensationalism, etc.) and the passive acceptance of consumerism and instrumental reason.

Ironically enough, installation, assemblage, and Conceptual works only emerge as items of cultural interest through their dependence on visual expectations and display formats derived from traditional idioms (most notably the 'presumption of virtuality' which I discussed at length in earlier chapters). Even though such idioms appear to negate or be indifferent to traditional art, they draw upon its values in order to be distinguished from mere real things.

This dependence also extends to issues of artistic merit. Modes of image-making have well-defined criteria of artistic merit based on the kind of originality of style which they exemplify, and the subsidiary role of formal and expressive values within it. Critical verdicts can, therefore, be justified by using comparisons and contrasts based on the history of the relevant medium. If installation and assemblage art, etc. can be approached in terms derived from this, then all is well and good. In the absence of such criteria, the idioms in question are mainly dependent for their evaluation on the whims and vested interests of curators, critics, and galleries.

I am arguing then, that artistic value will persist, and that even the new marginal practices are dependent upon traditional criteria. However, whilst art *per se* has by no means reached its end, some clear limits have arisen *within specific media*, and these may have implications for issues of value and creativity. This is especially the case with pictorial representation.

For example, given that a picture is, by definition, an image of a three-dimensional item (or cognate state of affairs) generated in a two-dimensional plane, then there are, in logical terms, a finite number of possibilities in terms of the general types of reference and syntactic connections which pictorial representation can develop as a communicative code. The exact iconographic meanings of a picture and the uses to which it is put are culturally and historically relative. But such diversity of contexts and uses are functions of a more basic logical structure.

The progression of this structure to its most fully developed form is dependent upon historical transformations, but it does not give rise to the possibility of endless development. In this respect, it is notable that the logical structure of pictorial representation was completely in place by the end of the Renaissance. What has happened since then are systematic stylistic variations which extend or illuminate different aspects of this structure.

With the emergence of Cubism the limits of the structure were, in effect, acknowledged, and a search was inaugurated for new kinds of semantic and syntactic codes upon which art could be based. Despite the plethora of conflicting artistic manifestos and radically different visual content, the great abstract and abstracting tendencies are inscribed within a code based on aspects of what in Chapter 4 I called contextual space.

The advent of minimal idioms such as works by Agnes Martin and Ad Reinhardt's 'black' paintings, seems to suggest again that this code has been taken to its logical limits. Similar considerations apply in those cases where conceptual work attains a marginal artistic status.

Where do we go next, then? The answer has already, in effect, been given. For I have argued that artistic merit is at its highest when an artist articulates or refines factors which are fundamental to the logical structure of an artistic code. Of course, the sheer quantity of art which is now produced makes it harder to produce highly original work, but this remains possible, in principle. And whilst traditional codes have been logically developed as far as they can in logical terms, there is always the possibility that artists will create new ones.

One exciting prospect here is the creation of non-naturalistic codes, which are based on invention rather than notions of resemblance or visual consistency between the artwork and that which it represents. Such non-naturalistic codes stipulate basic visual axioms or a vocabulary, which can then be transformed on the basis of invented rules—drawing on conventional or abstract or even conceptual idioms.

The challenge would be to find such codes which—despite their artificial basis—were relatively easy to learn, and which could generate interesting and original variations within the respective codes.[3] If this challenge is not met, then the scope and structure of art will continue to be defined exclusively in the dead-end terms of western managerial classes.

Music and literature present similar problems and possibilities. The logical structure of music is highly accessible, in that the tonal system is easily learned and is bound up with fundamental aspects of bodily expression and auditory reality. A similar developmental problem has arisen, however. In Chapter 7 we saw the canonic effects of music's creative appropriation of techniques for mechanically reproducing sound. It is not likely that this admits of much further development. And whilst serialism and aleatory developments per se have established themselves as alternative musical codes, they have not attained anything like the authority of the tonal system.

---

[3] For an example of this see my discussion of Mojca Oblak's 'Transcendental Mannerism' in *Language of Twentieth-Century Art*, ch. 11.

It may be therefore, that music's way forward will be akin to that of visual art, and will involve the formulation of artificial expressive auditory codes which might 'take' in a way that existing alternatives to tonalism have not. (One possibility is that third-world idioms could be of decisive significance in leading the way here.)

In terms of literature and film, the fundamental categories which form the structure and scope of these media and their idioms are not as manifest (at least to the present writer). This may indicate that their continuing radical development is not as restricted by inherent characteristics of the respective medium. But whether it is or not, new possibilities may be opened up anyway through the role of new electronic media.

I am arguing, then, that by virtue of the normatively significant structures described throughout this book, art will continue to meet—as Hegel would put it—our 'highest needs'. Individuality of vision and good art will always be possible. In order to achieve more revolutionary transformations, non-naturalistic codes (of the sort described earlier) and the invention of new media with their own distinctive structures and scope may be required.

Indeed, perhaps the most exciting possibility of all is the use of electronic, digital, and traditional formats which enable creativity which crosses established boundaries between, say, literature and the visual arts, and even between art and other forms of knowledge, including the sciences.

Art, then, is of continuing normative significance. It may even be on the verge of radical and dynamic new transformations.

Acknowledgements

The majority of chapters in this book were written as separate essays over a twelve-year period. However, all have been revised and linked so as to form a continuous structure of argument. This involves some repetition, but never just that. Well over a third of the book consists of entirely new material written specifically for this volume.

The major part of Chapter 1 was published as 'Cultural Exclusion, Normativity, and the Definition of Art' in the *Journal of Aesthetics and Art Criticism*, 61/2 (2003), 121–31. Chapter 2 was first published under the same title in the *British Journal of Aesthetics*, 44/4 (2004), 361–77. Chapter 3 is a revised and heavily extended version of 'The Significance of Kant's Pure Aesthetic Judgement' which first appeared in the *British Journal of Aesthetics*, 36/2 (1996), 9–21. Part of Chapter 4 appeared in the paper 'Art, Knowledge and Historicity', *Nordisk Estetisk Tidskrift*, 10 (1993), 33–70. Chapter 5 was published as 'Twofoldness; From Transcendental Imagination to Pictorial Art', in Rob van Gerwen (ed.), *Richard Wollheim on the Art of Painting: Art as Representation and Expression* (Cambridge: Cambridge University Press, 2002), 85–100. Chapter 6 appeared as 'Literary Metaphor and Philosophical Insight: The Significance of Archilochus', in G. Boys-Stone (ed.), *Metaphor and Allegory in the Ancient World*, (Oxford: Clarendon Press, 2003), 87–100.

My thanks are due to Miruna Cuzman for formatting the manuscript and preparing the Index.

Bibliography

Allison, Henry, *Kant's Transcendental Idealism: An Interpretation and Defense* (New Haven: Yale University Press, 2004).

Barthes, Roland, *Camera Lucida*, trans. R. Howard (London: Jonathan Cape, 1982).

Battersby, Christine, *Gender and Genius: Towards a Feminist Aesthetics* (London: The Women's Press, 1989).

Beardsley, Monroe, *The Aesthetic Point of View* (Ithaca and London: Cornell University Press, 1982).

Bell, Clive, *Art* (London: Chatto & Windus, 1914).

_____ 'The Metaphysical Hypothesis', in *Art*.

Benjamin, Walter, 'The Work of Art in the Age of Mechanical Reproduction', trans. Harry Zohn, in *Illuminations* (London: Fontana, 1970).

Bergson, Henri, *Matter and Memory*, trans. N. M. Paul and W. S. Palmer (London: Harvester, 1978).

Bernstein, J. M. (ed.), *German Classic and Romantic Aesthetics* (Cambridge: Cambridge University Press, 2002).

Black, Max, *Models and Metaphors* (Ithaca: Cornell University Press, 1962).

Bourdieu, Pierre, *Distinction: A Social Critique of the Judgement of Taste*, trans. R. Nice (London: Routledge & Kegan-Paul, 1984).

_____ *The Field of Cultural Production* (Oxford: Polity Press, 1993).

Budd, Malcolm, *Music and the Emotions: The Philosophical Theories* (London: Routledge, 1985).

Burgin, Victor, *The End of Art Theory: Criticism and Postmodernity* (London: Macmillan, 1986).

Carroll, Noel, *The Philosophy of Mass Art* (Oxford: Clarendon Press, 1998).

Cassirer, Ernst, *The Philosophy of Symbolic Forms*, 3 vols., trans. R. Manheim (New Haven and London: Yale University Press, 1966).

Crowther, Paul, *Art and Embodiment: From Aesthetics to Self-Consciousness* (Oxford: Clarendon Press, 1993).

_____ 'Sociological Imperialism and the Field of Cultural Production: The Case of Bourdieu', *Theory Culture, and Society*, 2/1 (1994), 155–69.

_____ *The Language of Twentieth-Century Art: A Conceptual History* (New Haven and London: Yale University Press, 1997).

_____ *The Transhistorical Image: Philosophizing Art and its History* (Cambridge: Cambridge University Press, 2002).

Crowther, Paul, *Philosophy After Postmodernism: Civilized Values and the Scope of Knowledge* (London: Routledge, 2003).

Danto, Arthur, C., 'The Transfiguration of the Commonplace', *Journal of Aesthetics and Art Criticism*, 33 (1974), 139–48.

_____ *The Transfiguration of the Commonplace: A Philosophy of Art* (Cambridge, Mass.: Harvard University Press, 1981).

_____ *The State of the Art* (New York: Prentice Hall, 1987).

_____ *After the End of Art: Contemporary Art and the Pale of History* (Princeton: Princeton University Press, 1997).

Davey, Nicholas, 'Hermeneutics and Art Theory', in P. Smith and C. Wilde (eds.), *A Companion to Art Theory* (Oxford: Blackwell's, 2002).

_____ 'Sitting Uncomfortably: Gadamer's Approach to Portraiture', *Journal of the British Society for Phenomenology*, 34/3 (2003), 231–46.

Davidson, Donald, 'What Metaphors Mean', in *Inquiries into Truth and Interpretation* (Oxford: Clarendon Press, 1984).

Davies, Stephen, *Definitions of Art* (Ithaca and London: Cornell University Press, 1991).

_____ *Musical Meaning and Expression* (Ithaca and London: Cornell University Press, 1994).

_____ *Kant After Duchamp* (Cambridge, Mass. and London: MIT Press, 1997).

Dickie, George, *Art and the Aesthetic* (Ithaca and London: Cornell University Press, 1974).

_____ 'Art and Value', *British Journal of Aesthetics*, 40/2 (2000), 228–41.

Dissanayake, Ellen, *What Art is For* (Washington: Washington University Press, 1988).

Dodd, Julian, 'Musical Works as Eternal Types', *British Journal of Aesthetics*, 40 (2000), 424–40.

de Duve, Thierry, *Kant After Duchamp* (Cambridge, Mass. and London: MIT Press, 1997).

Evans, Gareth, *Varieties of Reference* (Oxford: Clarendon Press, 1982).

Gadamer, Hans-Georg, *Truth and Method*, trans. William Glen-Doepel (London: Sheed and Ward, 1979).

Gibbons, Sarah, *Kant's Theory of Imagination: Bridging Gaps between Judgement and Experience* (Oxford: Clarendon Press, 1994).

Gilmore, Jonathan, *The Life of a Style* (Ithaca and London: Cornell University Press, 2000).

Ginsborg, Hannah, *The Role of Taste in Kant's Theory of Cognition* (Cambridge, Mass. and London: Harvard University Press, 1988).

Goldie, Peter, *The Emotions: A Philosophical Explanation* (Oxford: Clarendon Press, 2000).

—— 'One's Remembered Past: Narrative Thinking, Emotion, and the External Perspective', *Philosophical Papers*, 32/3 (2003), 301–19.

Golding, John, *Paths to the Absolute: Malevich, Kandinsky, Pollock, Newman, Rothko, and Still* (London: Thames & Hudson, 2004).

Gombrich, Ernst, *Art and Illusion* (London: Phaidon, 1978).

Goodman, Nelson, *Languages of Art* (Indianapolis: Hackett and Co., 1976).

Greek Lyric Poetry, trans. M. L. West (Oxford: Oxford University Press, 1994).

Greenberg, Clement, *Homemade Esthetics: Observations on Art and Taste* (New York and Oxford: Oxford University Press, 1999).

Guyer, Paul, *Kant and the Claims of Taste* (Cambridge, Mass. and London: Harvard University Press, 1979).

Hanslick, Edward, *On the Musically Beautiful*, trans. Geoffrey Payzant (Indianapolis: Hackett, 1986).

Harrison, Andrew, *Philosophy and the Arts: Seeing and Believing* (Bristol: Thoemmes, 1997).

Heal, Jane, *Mind, Reason, and Imagination* (Cambridge: Cambridge University Press, 2003).

Heine, H., and Korsmeyer, C. (eds.), *Aesthetics in Feminist Perspective* (Bloomington: Indiana University Press, 1993).

Henrich, Dieter, *Aesthetic Judgement and the Moral Image of the World* (Stanford: Stanford University Press, 1992).

Hopkins, Robert, *Picture, Image and Experience: A Philosophical Inquiry* (Cambridge: Cambridge University Press, 1998).

Johnson, Mark, *The Body in Mind: The Bodily Basis of Meaning* (Chicago: University of Chicago Press, 1990).

Kant, Immanuel, 'The Deduction of the Pure Concepts of Understanding', in *Critique of Pure Reason.*

—— *Critique of Pure Reason*, trans. N. Kemp-Smith (London: Macmillan and Co., 1973).

—— *Critique of Judgement*, trans. J. C. Meredith (Oxford: Clarendon Press, 1973).

—— *Critique of Judgement*, trans. W. Pluhar (Indianapolis: Hackett and Co., 1987).

Kieran, M., and Lopes, D. M. (eds.), *Imagination, Philosophy, and the Arts* (London: Routledge, 2003).

Kitcher, Patricia, *Kant's Transcendental Psychology* (New York: Oxford University Press, 1994).

Kivy, Peter, *Philosophies of Arts: An Essay in Differences* (Cambridge: Cambridge University Press, 1997).

_____ *New Essays on Musical Understanding* (Oxford: Clarendon Press, 2001).

Langer, Suzanne K., *Feeling and Form* (London: Routledge & Kegan Paul, 1953).

Levinson, Jerrold, 'Defining Art Historically', *British Journal of Aesthetics*, 19/3 (1979), 233–50.

_____ 'Music and the Negative Emotions', in his *Music, Art, and Metaphysics: Essays in Philosophical Aesthetics* (Ithaca: Cornell University Press, 1990).

_____ 'Musical Expressiveness', in *The Pleasures of Aesthetics*.

_____ *The Pleasures of Aesthetics: Philosophical Essays* (Ithaca and London: Cornell University Press, 1996).

_____ *Music in the Moment* (Ithaca and London: Cornell University Press, 1997).

Lopes, Dominic M., *Understanding Pictures* (Oxford: Clarendon Press, 1996).

Lyons, William, *Emotion* (Cambridge: Cambridge University Press, 1980).

MacIntyre, Alasdair, *After Virtue: A Study in Moral Theory* (London: Duckworth, 1980).

McGinn, Colin, *Mindsight: Image, Dream, Meaning* (Cambridge, Mass.: Harvard University Press, 2005).

Makkreel, Rudolf, *Imagination and Interpretation in Kant: The Hermeneutical Import of the Critique of Judgment* (Chicago: University of Chicago Press, 1990).

Marra, Michele (ed.), *Modern Japanese Aesthetics: A Reader* (Honolulu: University of Hawaii Press, 2003).

Matravers, Derek, *Art and Emotion* (Oxford: Clarendon Press, 1998).

Merleau-Ponty, Maurice, *Signs*, trans. Richard C. McCleary (Evanston: Northwestern University Press, 1964).

_____ 'Eye and Mind', in James Edie (ed.), *The Primacy of Perception* (Evanston: Northwestern University Press, 1964).

_____ *The Visible and the Invisible,* trans. Alphonse Lingis (Evanston: Northwestern University Press, 1968).

_____ 'Eye and Mind', in Harold Osborne (ed.), *Aesthetics* (Oxford: Oxford University Press, 1970).

_____ *Phenomenology of Perception*, trans. Colin Smith; rev. Forrest Williams (London: Routledge & Kegan Paul, 1974).

Moxey, Keith, *The Practice of Persuasion: Paradox and Power in Art History* (Ithaca and London: Cornell University Press, 2001).

Mukherji, Parul Dave, 'Visual Politics and the Binary Logic of Art History : From Maillard's "Western Misunderstandings" to Bryson's "Gaze and the Glance" ', paper (Slovene Society of Aesthetics, 2002).

Novitz, David, *Pictures and their Use in Communication: A Philosophical Essay* (The Hague: Martinus Nijhoff, 1976).

Nussbaum, Martha, *Love's Knowledge: Essays on Philosophy and Literature* (Oxford: Clarendon Press, 1990).

Pitt, David, 'Peter Kivy, *Introduction to a Philosophy of Music, New Essays on Musical Understanding*', *The Sunday Times of London Literary Supplement* (2003), 23.

Pollock, Griselda, *Vision and Difference: Feminity, Feminism, and the Histories of Art* (London: Routledge, 1988).

——*Differencing the Canon: Feminism and the Writing of Art's Histories* (London: Routledge, 1999).

Ricoeur, Paul, *The Rule of Metaphor*, trans. Robert Czerny, John Costello, Kathleen McLaughlin (London: Routledge, 1994).

Schapiro, Meyer, 'Style', in *Theory and Philosophy of Art: Style, Artist, and Society* (New York: George Braziller, Inc., 1994).

Schier, Flint, *Deeper into Pictures* (Cambridge: Cambridge University Press, 1986).

Schopenhauer, Arthur, *The World as Will and Representation*, trans. E. Payne (New York: Dover, 1980).

Scruton, Roger, *Art and Imagination* (London: Methuen, 1974).

Shusterman, Richard, *Pragmatist Aesthetics: Living Beauty, Rethinking Art* (Oxford: Blackwell, 1992).

——*Performing Live: Aesthetic Alternatives for the End of Art* (Ithaca and London: Cornell University Press, 2000).

Solomon, Robert, *The Passions: Emotion and the Meaning of Life* (Indianapolis: Hackett, 1993).

de Sousa, Ronald, 'The Rationality of Emotions', in Amelie O. Rorty (ed.), *Explaining the Emotions* (Berkeley and Los Angeles: University of California Press, 1980).

Strawson, Peter, *Individuals* (London: Methuen & Co., 1959).

Virilio, Paul, *The Vision Machine*, trans. Julie Rose (Bloomington and Indianapolis: Indiana University Press, 1994).

Vogel, Susan M., *Baule: African Art/Western Eyes* (New Haven and London: Yale University Press, 1997).

Walton, Kendall, 'Categories of Art', in Joseph Margolis (ed.), *Philosophy Looks at the Arts* (Philadelphia: Temple University Press, 1978).

——*Mimesis as Make-Believe: On the Foundations of the Representational Arts* (Cambridge, Mass. and London: Harvard University Press, 1990).

Waxman, Wayne, *Kant's Model of the Mind: A New Interpretation of Transcendental Idealism* (New York: Oxford University Press, 1991).

Wilde, Carolyn, 'Style and Value in the Art of Painting', in Rob van Gerwen (ed.), *Richard Wollheim on the Art of Painting* (Cambridge: Cambridge University Press, 2001).

Wollheim, Richard, *Art and its Objects* (Cambridge: Cambridge University Press, 1980).

_____ *The Thread of Life* (Cambridge: Cambridge University Press, 1980).

_____ *Painting as an Art* (London: Thames & Hudson, 1990).

_____ *The Mind and its Depths* (Cambridge, Mass. and London: Harvard University Press, 1993).

Young, James O., *Art and Knowledge* (London: Routledge, 2001).

Index

abstract 10, 28, 48, 52, 57, 83, 89–93,
    95–97, 102, 105–107, 113, 114, 170,
    187, 212, 236, 244; aspect of 96;
  body of 102; case of 36; excess of the
    113;
  explanation of 94; realms of 36
actuality 133, 175, 189, 229, 230
aesthetic 1–5, 8–10, 16, 17, 19, 22, 27–29,
    34–38, 40, 43, 50–53, 55, 57–60, 63,
    67–70, 72, 74–81, 83, 84, 100, 107,
    110, 114, 115, 118, 120–23, 136, 162,
    163, 170, 180, 184, 186, 188, 196, 197,
    200, 210, 211, 214, 223, 234–38;
    activity of the 76;
  art and the 15, 42–45, 50, 51, 55, 89;
  artwork and 153; aspect of 69; being and
    115;
  case of 78; character of 67; characteristics
    of 89;
  cognitive and 40; constitution of the 27;
  criterion of 18, 36; disinterestedness of
    187;
  embodiment of 83; enjoyment of 19;
  example of the 123; experience of 19;
  features of the 82; form of 214, 236;
  formalist 81; freedom of 74; historical
    and 63;
  judgment 121; making and 8, 53, 98,
    123;
  metaphysical and 164; moment of 76;
  normative and 46; notion of the 19, 45;
  objectivity of 42; possibilities of 56;
  power of 52;question of 16, 136;
  readings of 136; status and 242;
  transformations and 87; understanding of
    45;
  varieties of 52, 53, 114
aesthetics 10, 15, 17, 35, 42, 67, 87;
  dimension of 42; normative 1, 2, 42, 64
alienation 82, 83
allographic 226, 227
analogy 151, 158, 178, 179, 181, 208;
  associational 155;

analysis 48, 52, 59, 68, 70, 79, 89, 98, 116,
    119, 142, 165, 171, 173, 192, 204, 211;
    basis of 58;
  cultural 46; phenomenological 206;
  philosophical 142, 153, 155, 159, 161,
    228
analytic 87, 89, 143, 164, 172
anthropology 35, 48
anti-foundationalism 61–63, 201;
  western 64
appearance 68, 93, 95, 106, 109, 115, 172,
    220; aspects of 236;
  formal 122; interpretation of 106;
  order and 75; projection of 74;
  sensory 175; spatial 95; visible 96
arabesque 73, 74
Archilochus 11, 146, 155–61
architecture 36;
  sculpture and 192, 208
art 1–5, 8–10, , 15–18, 20–25, 27–29, 34,
    35, 37, 38, 40–48, 50, 51, 53–57,
    59–63, 67, 68, 79–85, 87, 89, 93, 95,
    97, 99–102, 105, 107–122, 127,
    135–38, 146, 163, 166, 180, 186, 190,
    194, 197, 204–208, 213–15, 217, 222,
    223, 234–43, 245; abstract 28, 36,
    89–96;
  achievement of 241; aesthetic 84, 238;
  appreciation of 4; aspect of 180;
  axis of 8, 29, 34, 38, 110, 236, 237;
  basis of 2, 3, 20, 28, 118; beauty and 67,
    68;
  boundaries of 4; canon of 63;
  centre of 17; claims of 87;
  class of 29; codes of 87;
  concept of 1, 9, 17, 20, 25, 28, 41, 46,
    51, 53, 54; conception of 2, 16, 44;
  conceptual 36, 37, 242; content and 25;
  creation of 16, 21; criterion of 41;
  critique of 50; definition of 2–4, 9, 10,
    15–17, 20, 21, 29, 35, 40–43, 45, 55,
    60, 67, 240, 241;
  determination of 102; dimension of 21;
  element of 54; end of 11, 240, 241;

art   (*cont.*)
    enjoyment of 80; essence of 27, 54, 98,
        241;
    evaluation of 117;
    experience and 89; experience of 9, 98,
        100, 107, 115, 233, 239; fields of 110;
        history of 23, 59;
    idea of 242; idiom of 23; image and 117,
        205;
    importance of 237; interpreters of 85;
    literary 145; making of 28, 62;
    mechanical 84, 135; member of the 20;
    musical 180, 194, 196–98, 200, 201, 204;
    nature of 8, 9; normativity of 20;
    notion of 17; ontology of 98;
        ornamental 77;
    phenomenon of 20; philosophy of 5 n.7;
        pictorial 127, 128, 135, 137, 143, 144,
        155, 199, 204;
    possibilities of 239; qualities of 1;
    quantity of 244; realms of 89, 118;
    reception of 100, 108, 110; scope of 43,
        58;
    significance of the 2, 47, 110; sphere of
        9;
    status of 16, 21, 64, 98; structure of 101,
        244;
    theory of 10, 20, 28, 43, 54, 64, 67;
    tradition of 38; treatment of 43, 67;
    understanding of 61; visual 1, 10, 188,
        234, 245;
    western 45, 119; work of 21, 22, 45, 53,
        82, 209
artifice 36, 48, 49, 59, 110, 136, 140, 177,
        223; case of 110; formulaic 4, 109;
    functional 117; instance of 3; knowledge
        and 4;
    mode of 110, 242; model of 48;
    products of 80, 113; spheres of 116
artist 16, 20, 21, 23, 25–28, 34, 37–40, 45,
        51, 56–59, 82, 83, 85, 87, 93, 95–100,
        103, 106–109, 112, 115, 116, 137–40,
        154, 160, 180, 186, 188, 206, 207,
        209–213, 221, 227, 228, 236, 242, 244;
    honorific 37; identity of the 26;
    imagination and the 81; knowledge of
        the 114;
    perception of the 80; relation of 23; role
        of the 95;
    skill of the 37; style of the 39
artwork 46, 89, 99, 100, 102, 103,
        105–109, 112, 113, 115, 119, 120, 136,

        180, 189, 202, 212, 232, 236, 238, 240,
        244; identities of the 113;
    literary 153, 161; musical 197; pictorial
        137, 138
artworld 21, 23, 28
assemblage 218, 242;
    installation and 243
association 152, 154, 181;
    imaginative 151, 152; patterns of 179
atonalism 193, 199;
    cases of 193
axis 40, 84, 110, 236, 237;
    normative 29, 34, 37, 38, 40, 84, 110

Beardsley, Monroe 17–19, 69
beauty 67–69, 74, 80, 81, 114, 121, 182,
        196, 200, 236; artistic 80, 180;
    aspect of 70; characteristics of 70;
    decorative 80; definition of 68;
    enjoyment of 69, 76; experience of 69,
        78, 80, 83;
    phenomenology of 68; significance of
        67; variety of 80
behaviour 75, 98, 129, 172, 173, 189, 225;
    appearances and 71; states and 172
belief 51, 52, 135, 136;
    association and 55; religious 51, 161
Bell, Clive 17–19, 53, 69
Black, Max 146–48

Cage, John 199, 200, 213
canon 7, 8, 17, 18, 39, 40, 42, 56, 58, 63,
        86, 87; account of the 120;
    development of the 58; idea of a 43;
    musical 203; notion of a 87; theory of
        the 117
canonic 2, 11, 39, 60, 86, 87, 118, 123, 146,
        160, 161, 197, 199, 200, 201, 234, 237,
        238, 244; aesthetic and 42; art and 2;
    basis of 10, 235; consideration of 166;
    criterion of 39;
    distinctions of 84; exemplariness and 10;
    experience and 89; idea of 10;
    margins of the 17; possibilities of 11
capacity 30–32, 70, 71, 74, 78, 81, 81, 100,
        101, 105, 116, 127–30, 132, 133, 136,
        143, 145, 148, 153, 159, 161, 163, 164,
        167–69, 191, 204, 205, 225; cognitive
        33, 71, 81;
    perceptual 127; projective 33, 141;
    trans-ostensive 32

Cassirer, Ernst 131, 226
character 90, 104, 105, 107, 108, 122, 123,
    130–32, 134, 135, 141, 147, 152, 159,
    164, 165, 168, 174, 176–79, 183, 186,
    189, 190, 200, 207, 208, 210, 212, 214,
    224–26, 230, 234–36; aesthetic 223;
    emotional 184, 185; event- 100; image-
    90, 91, 109, 187, 188, 206, 236; logical
    109; metaphorical 154;
    metaphysical 166; musical 195, 197;
    ontological 242;
    phenomenal 93; sentential 146; spiritual
    191
    tensional 153; visceral 163; visual 93
class 44–46, 48, 57, 58, 62, 67, 79, 116,
    130, 201
code 59, 60, 90, 96, 244;
    artistic 244; communicative 59, 243;
    iconography of the 59; medium and 212;
    reference and 243; representational 59;
    semantic and 243; syntactic 55
cognition 8, 9, 16, 70, 74, 75, 84, 100, 101,
    131, 133, 153, 161, 201, 204, 235, 236;
    act of 122, 159; aesthetic 236;
    aspects of 81; awareness and 100;
    bases of 68; intellectual 116; rule of 72
colour 95, 149, 217, 224;
    bands of 139; dab of 93; light and 136,
    139, 140
composition 7, 132, 186, 200, 201, 204;
    narratives and 34; production and 136
concept 4, 5, 9, 16–17, 20, 25, 28, 32, 37,
    39, 41, 46, 53, 54, 70–72, 74, 112, 116,
    130–32, 139, 141, 143, 180; analytic 3;
    application of the 71; powers of 130;
    unity of the 70; western 4
configuration 97, 153, 218, 222, 228;
    aesthetic 184; narrative 184;
    spatial 220; visible 95
consciousness 104, 133, 141, 142, 167, 169;
    modes of 167;
    object of 104; states of 101
consistency 219, 230;
    isomorphic 29, 101; visual 97, 244;
construct 17;
    western 53
consumerism 242;
    global 60–64, 242; western 50
consumerist 43, 46, 49, 55, 58, 61, 63, 163,
    242; fanatical 57;
    global 64

content 23, 25, 30, 40, 83, 99, 105, 179,
    186, 193, 212, 213, 227, 229, 230;
    associational 97; cognitive 122;
    conceptual 72, 83, 101; elements of 180;
    emergence of 140; emotional 176, 182,
    188; factual 178;
    interpretation of 100; issues of 17;
    metaphorical 159;
    narrative 18; referential 105;
    representational 138–42, 180;
    spatial 190; structure and the 160;
    symbolic 97, 102, 105; visual 243
context 11, 16, 18, 22, 23, 27, 28, 35, 40,
    44, 46, 49, 56, 69, 71, 92, 94, 96, 118,
    119, 122, 123, 133, 138, 140, 141, 146,
    148, 153–55, 163, 165, 172, 179, 180,
    183, 184, 188, 189, 193, 194, 198, 211,
    214, 231, 233, 236; artistic 162; basis of
    46; comparative 120;
    contemporary 10; cultural 56, 86, 154;
    existential 152;
    expression of 1; historical 7, 8;
    knowledge of a 156;
    literary 146, 155; musical 170; narrative
    171, 183, 203;
    perceptual 77; ritual 79; visual 77
continuity 100, 105, 207, 218;
    cognitive 78; factual 30; structural 150
creation 9, 16, 21, 80, 81, 160, 180, 227,
    235, 244; artistic 53, 54;
    modes of 87; psychology of 85
creativity 7, 41, 106, 111, 112, 240, 245;
    artistic 240; mode of 116; musical 198;
    value and 243
creator 6, 9, 34, 35, 43, 51, 80, 96, 105,
    106, 109, 112–114, 116, 121, 161, 197,
    209, 235; complexity of 47;
    distinctiveness of the 80; horizons of
    100;
    identity of the 112; personality of the
    113, 160;
    significance of the 210; standpoint of the
    7
criterion 18, 35, 36, 39, 62, 85, 87, 122,
    142, 148, 172, 196; formalist 35
critique 54, 79, 137;
    genealogical 44
Cubism 241;
    emergence of 243; influence of 241
culture 15, 40–42, 60, 110, 111, 115, 117,
    118, 182, 195, 201, 239, 242; aesthetic
    57;

culture (*cont.*)
  contemporary 62; dimensions of 42;
  musical 198; non-western 17;
  western 17, 28, 40, 43, 44, 46, 62, 181

Danto, Arthur 16, 21–28, 53, 54, 92, 240,
    241
definition 2, 4, 5, 9, 10, 42, 43, 45, 48, 55,
    60, 68, 80, 85, 103, 109, 122, 151, 179,
    189, 193, 212, 240, 243; functional 4;
  mimetic 3; nominal 146; normative 67
density 95, 97
depth 76, 78, 85, 206, 211, 213, 215;
  illusions of 93; metaphysical 163–66,
    169, 170, 189, 192, 194, 204; notion of
    76; physical 77, 78;
  realization of 77; virtual 77, 78
designation 54, 84, 92, 96, 235;
  acts of 53; artistic 85
diachronic 16, 43, 58, 59, 87, 208;
  synchronic and 160
dialectic 52, 79
Dickie, George 16, 21, 28, 69;
difference 7, 22, 38, 40, 51, 168, 197, 208,
    225, 228, 238; basis of a 84;
  creative 10, 56, 195; dimension of 191;
  historical 85, 166, 197–201; perspective
    and 50;
  sameness and 100, 154, 222
digital 175, 245
dimension 109, 116, 122, 150, 159, 166,
    167, 172–76, 181, 183, 189–191, 200,
    211, 213, 225, 231, 235; abstract
    113; auditory 203;
  canonic 237; comparative 123;
  iconographic 221; metaphysical 192
Dionysian 35, 36
discourse 50;
  consumerist 49; critical 85; literary 161
discrimination 70, 71;
  cognitive 130; mental 76
disinterestedness 68, 187;
  critics of 69; notion of 68, 83
diversity 119, 139, 243;
  unity and 73, 118, 119
doctrine 188;
  Christian 154
Donatello, Donato di Niccolò di Betto
    Bardi 220, 221
  Feast of Herod (Siena Baptistery) 220,
    221

drama 111;
  rhythms and 36
Duchamp, Marcel 20, 21, 29, 37, 120, 241
van Dyck, Anthonis 220, 221, 227
  Portrait of Charles I (London, National
    Gallery) 220

elite 29;
  curatorial 41; social 45;
  western 18, 19, 34, 37, 40, 242
embodiment 27, 82, 83, 110, 136, 150,
    170, 172, 173, 175, 185, 204, 212, 220,
    234; aesthetic 52, 184;
  perception and 145; sensuous 34, 102;
  time and 219; virtual 165, 178, 182, 183,
    185, 193
emotion 11, 152, 165, 170–77, 184–87,
    203;
  aesthetic 187; ascription of 172;
  aspect of 173, 174, 184, 191;
    characterization of 185;
  development of 188; dimension of 176;
  embodiment of 173, 176, 182, 183;
    features of 236;
  gestures of 172; life of 171;
    manifestations of 172;
  organ of 174; presentation of 164; states
    of 176;
  structure of 177, 183; virtual 175, 176,
    184
empathy 197, 203;
  aesthetic 115, 188, 236; description and
    222;
  form of 115, 197; mode of 114; sense of
    197
empirical 4, 22, 31, 45, 46, 53, 61, 73, 74,
    114, 242
enigma 168, 169, 191;
  qualitative 167, 169, 185, 190
epistemology 24, 72;
  anti-foundationalist 49; foundational 44;
  general 71; western 61
equality 61;
  narrative of 62
essence 27, 54, 69, 98–100, 102, 240, 241;
  artwork and 240;
  presentation of 99; revelation of 100,
    102
ethical 53, 54, 242;
  epistemological and 62;
ethnic 25, 29

evaluation 117, 243
exclusionism 15, 16
  modes of 15; unconscious 16–18, 20,
    28, 35, 37, 41
exclusionist 15–17, 20, 28, 29, 35, 36
exemplification 26, 27, 97, 116, 146, 153,
    168, 184, 191;
  artefactual 41
existence 23, 34, 68, 69, 105, 114, 116,
    145, 155, 172, 176, 179, 191, 227, 228;
  physical 114;
  practical 40; travails of 158
experience 15, 19, 30–32, 44, 46, 55, 56,
    63, 69, 71, 77, 78, 80, 81, 83, 90, 91,
    100, 102–109, 113, 114, 118, 129, 133,
    136, 141–45, 150–53, 159–61, 165,
    167, 168, 171, 179, 181, 184, 190, 194,
    201, 202, 204, 206, 207, 213, 214, 218,
    223, 225, 226, 230–33, 236, 238, 239;
  acoustic 167; actuality of 82;
  aesthetic 8, 52, 69, 77, 89, 98, 107, 114,
    123, 200, 211, 238; areas of 48, 53, 55;
    aspects of 89, 105;
  auditory 11, 165–170, 173, 185, 186,
    189, 191, 192, 195; chains of 230;
    condition of 128;
  continuity of 105; core of 137;
    dimension of 48, 161;
  disinterested 19; embodiments of 108;
    essence of 100, 102;
  fabric of 137; intentional 225; levels of
    195; limits of 81;
  making and 115; moments of 159, 206,
    207, 225, 226, 230;
  musical 204; narrative of 137; object of
    165, 189, 194, 195, 203; olfactory 169;
    ontogenesis of 75;
  ontology of 104; origins of 142;
    perception and 143;
  possibilities of 132, 229; range of 106;
    representation and 42;
  richness of the 116; stages of 76;
    structure of 89, 152;
  subject of 32; subjective 206, 208; unity
    of 170;
  visual 223; zone of 55
expression 1, 6, 7, 11, 25, 28, 34, 37, 51,
    81, 83, 101, 143, 146, 155, 165, 168,
    169, 174, 176, 181, 183, 193, 195, 228,
    235, 244; abstract 106; audible 187;
  embodiment of 193, 195; gesture and
    201;

medium of 10, 237; metaphorical 155;
  possibility of 188, 192; projection of 204;
  symbolic 212, 233; virtual 90, 165,
    178–186, 188, 191, 192, 198–200,
    203, 204

fantasy 94, 223;
  cognate 95; desire and 101;
figure 77, 93, 135, 139, 179;
  relation of 179; temporal 179;
film 11, 118, 205, 208–211, 223, 227, 232;
  literature and 209, 211, 223–26, 245;
  reel of 227; writing and 209
foreshortening 217;
  colour and 224
form 9, 19, 22, 35–38, 40, 48, 50, 61, 72,
    75, 77, 80, 83, 90, 91, 95, 98, 99, 102,
    105–107, 109, 120, 131, 140, 147, 152,
    154, 156, 157, 161, 166, 170, 174, 176,
    179, 180, 183, 184, 186, 190, 194, 197,
    198, 206, 207, 209, 212, 214, 215, 217,
    222, 228, 230, 231, 233, 234, 236, 239,
    243, 245; aesthetic 19, 76, 80, 115,
    123, 136;
  analytic 143; articulation of 138; artistic
    180;
  experience of 19; linguistic 151; literary
    153;
  musical 165, 181, 182; natural 80;
    objective 74;
  phenomenal 73, 74, 80; poetic 155, 160,
    161;
  questions of 166; sensible 52; sensory
    238; shape and 139;
  significant 17, 19, 52, 235; stylized 30;
    symbolic 102, 161;
  unconscious 15, 109; ur- 79; visual 222
formalism 17–19, 34, 52, 53, 181, 182,
    235; weight of 20
formalist 1, 10, 16–20, 35, 41, 68, 89, 107,
    122, 181, 182
formalization 165, 175–77, 182, 185, 193;
  musical 193; style of the 176
Fra Angelico 217, 218
  Madonna and Child with Saints (Florence,
    San Marco Convent) 217
Friedrich, Caspar David 154, 231
  Arctic Shipwreck (Hamburg,
    Kunsthalle) 154
function 19, 21, 28, 31, 33, 36, 37, 40, 45,
    55, 68, 71, 74, 84, 90, 98, 100, 102,

function (*cont.*)
    109, 112, 113, 115–118, 128, 130, 131,
    135, 137–41, 148, 150–53, 161, 164,
    170, 179, 192, 194, 196, 210, 225, 228,
    229, 231, 235; form and 36;
    ostensive 149; referential 25, 90;
    trans-ostensive 31

Gadamer, Hans-Georg 10, 52, 89, 98–103,
    105
gender 58, 79, 85,
    class and 46, 62; issues of 84; race and
    201
genealogical 43–45;
genesis 182;
genius 84, 85;
    notion of 85; product of 84;
    property of 84; question of 84;
    romantic 28; taste and 67
gestalt 73, 97, 138;
    figure of 135
globalism 62;
    western 63
Gombrich, Ernst 135, 137, 138
Goodman, Nelson 45 n.7, 147, 153
Greenberg, Clement 121 n.15
ground 77, 78, 93, 102, 139, 157, 179;
    figure and 179

harmony 17, 70, 83, 95, 152; degree of 233;
    expressive 119; form of 83;
    formal 18; relations of 211
Hegel, Georg Wilhelm Friedrich 52, 102,
    245
history 5, 6, 11, 28, 30, 31, 48, 58, 67, 82,
    87, 104, 105, 107, 122, 129, 150, 171,
    186, 222, 225, 226, 243; of art 23;
    comparative 58, 89; cultural 58;
    diachronic 43, 59;
    empirical 53; excess of 225; experiential
    33;
    knowledge of 123; origins and 193

iconic 128, 134, 137
iconography 54, 216; cultural 59;
    patterns of 222
idea 24, 43, 45, 61, 69, 111, 112, 172, 183,
    200, 242; aesthetic 37, 81–83, 100
Ideal 82, 200;
    notion of the 82

identity 15, 24, 26, 30–33, 35, 58, 61, 83,
    104, 105, 108, 110, 112, 113, 121, 131,
    187, 189, 222; cultural 18, 29, 35;
    notion of 24
idiom 23, 138, 161, 170, 198; creative 34;
    musical 199; poetic 161; western 28
illusion 77;
    optical 77, 92, 93, 131; reality and 139
image 2, 5–10, 16, 29, 30, 34–37, 40, 41,
    89–91, 97, 98, 101, 102, 105, 106,
    109, 110, 116–118, 123, 130, 133, 134,
    136–38, 141, 142, 159, 186–88,
    205–207, 209, 210, 212, 213, 216, 217,
    219–221, 224–32, 235–38, 243;
    allusive 97;
    artefactual 35, 90; artistic 4, 10, 89, 114,
    117, 128, 143;
    exemplificational 37; experiential 76;
    feature of the 133;
    interpretation of the 231; - making 4,
    36, 38, 41, 143;
    mental 33, 138; mode of 116; notion of
    89;
    perspectival 219–224, 226–33;
    photographic 231;
    physical 34; pictorial 10; recognition of
    the 35;
    richness of the 221; role of the 207;
    scope of 10, 91; sense of 110;
    significance of the 3, 38;
    structure of the 32; style of the 227;
    three-dimensional 86; variety of 37
imagery 130, 131, 134, 237;
    aspect of 35; centrality of 34;
    generation of 137, 138; heart of the 30;
    interaction of 236; mental 29, 30, 31, 33,
    34;
    musical 35; realm of 101; style of 161;
    zone of 102
imagination 30–33, 70, 71, 73–75, 81–83,
    97, 101, 127–34, 137, 141, 152, 189,
    208, 211, 215, 218, 222–24, 231, 232;
    aspect of 133, 134;
    case of 133; exercise of 132; faculties of
    67;
    function of 131, 138; habit-memory and
    129;
    images and 16; memory and 101, 179;
    power of 129, 142; presentation of the
    81;
    productive 71, 72, 74; role of 68, 230;

self-consciousness and 10; senses and 113;
significance of 128, 137; style of 238; terms of 91;
theory of 148; transcendental 142, 143, 236;
understanding and 71, 75, 78, 83, 133; use of the 134
imitation 84, 99;
object of 51
indexicality 167, 169, 185, 190, 191
individuality 7, 8, 38–40, 56, 87, 113, 117–119, 198, 237, 239, 245;
achievement of 89;
awareness of 4; stylistic 40
innovation 57, 60, 87, 148, 164, 200, 238, 240, 241; artistic 241; evidence of 200; musical 199; refinement and 112, 204
installation 157, 242, 243;
development of 242
intention 25, 27, 61, 106, 137;
concept of 3; object and 25; theoretical 27
interpretation 46, 82, 92, 100, 103, 105–107, 109, 122, 134, 231; individual 9; patterns of 150;
stylistic 3, 10, 82, 89, 93, 107, 163, 187, 188, 191, 236, 242; subjects of 206; visual 137
intonation 176, 177;
accent and 175; fixing of 191; range of 174; vocal 175, 177, 185
intrinsic 2, 7, 8, 18, 19, 27, 29, 30, 33, 34, 36, 38, 40, 42, 52, 55, 56, 60, 78, 82, 92, 119, 150, 164, 168–70, 174, 177, 181, 190, 221, 224, 231, 236–38
intuition 122, 128;
empirical 73; manifold of 70; sensible 74

judgement 149, 159, 171;
categories of 3

Kant, Immanuel 10, 52, 64, 67–76, 79–85, 87, 88, 110, 111, 128, 135, 136, 148, 180, 208, 214
    Critique of Judgment 68 n. 1, 70 n. 3; 72 n. 5, 74 n. 8, 81 n. 14, 85 n.19, 135 n.10, 148 n. 9, 214 n.3
    Critique of Pure Reason 70 n. 4, 73 n. 7, 74 n.8, 81 n. 16, 84 n. 17, 128 n.3, n.4, 208

kitsch 110, 111, 115
Kivy, Peter 164, 187, 188
knowledge 23, 29, 31, 33, 34, 44, 48, 50, 51, 70, 80, 108, 111, 114, 115, 122, 123, 128, 152, 156, 179, 227, 229, 230; body of 111;
comparative 122, 123; conditions of 50; empirical 114;
factual 69, 114, 123; forms of 4, 102, 110, 111, 113, 245;
formulation of 116; historical 122; intuitive 143;
latent 101; mode of 102;objective 30–32, 150;
perceptual 8; status of 102; stock of 152

Langer, Suzanne 90, 164, 170, 175–77
language 11, 32, 33, 71, 81, 90, 101, 131, 145, 147, 149, 151, 155, 170, 175, 182, 185, 193, 222; acquisition of 82, 131, 132, 174, 175; articulations of 155; conventions of 147;
feature of 147; form of 152; formalization of 160;
levels of 90; literary 155; possession of 32;
precondition of 162; rules of 149; style of 91; thought and 31
Levinson, Jerrold 187, 188
literature 1, 11, 82, 83, 89, 144, 170, 188, 192, 204, 205, 208, 209, 211, 223, 224, 245; arts of 225; case of 209;
example of 226; image-character of 90, 91;
interpretative 5, 74; language and 155; music and 90, 244; narrative 91; order of 210;
pictures and 163; unity of 210
logic 69, 90

manipulation 51, 227;
elements of 209; perception and 74
marginalization 51, 63
Martin, Agnes 92, 244
masterpiece 28, 118, 202;
history of the 28
meaning 23, 24, 26, 27, 29, 35, 44, 46, 48, 49, 55, 57, 58, 85, 86, 89, 91, 92, 95, 98, 108, 109, 120, 156, 175, 177, 178, 182–85, 190–92, 204; allegorical 156; artifice and 49;

meaning   (*cont.*)

artistic 1, 5, 26, 28, 53, 96, 118, 119, 128, 206, 209, 212, 235; avenues of 52; basis of 96;

burden of 3; canonic 10; connotational 27;

construction of 46; dimensions of 46. 181; emotional 174, 175;

factor of 192; focus 118; forms of 164, 222; fullness of 116;

literary 147, 188; mode of 49; musical 11, 161–65, 167, 170, 171, 178, 179, 189, 190, 192–94, 201, 203, 204; narrative 58;

nature of 46; openness of 96; part of the 227;

penumbra of 192; production of 47, 48;

self-congruence of 109; sensuous 90; significance and 206;

space 161; theory of 193; virtualization of 192

medium 4, 6, 7, 10, 33, 39, 55–58, 60, 81, 82, 85–87, 89, 99, 105, 106, 112, 120, 122, 127, 135, 136, 192, 207, 208, 212, 229, 235–38, 241, 243, 245; artistic 29; awareness of the 136;

choice of a 6; constraints of the 7; demands of the 82;

development of a 59; excellence in the 7; handling of 34; knowledge of the 122, 123; making and 79;

nature of the 40; particularity of the 52; perspective and the 220;

possibilities of a 56; power of the 87;

scope of the 39, 56, 57, 59, 63, 85–87; tradition of the 237; visual 218

melody 175, 176, 178; rhythm and 176, 177, 191, 195

memory 101, 133, 138, 179, 191, 225; basis of 134; context and 133; core of 134; experiential 144; habit- 129

merit 40, 117, 122, 140, 200, 237; artistic 40, 87, 117, 120–23, 243, 244; canonic 84; criteria of 118; distinction of 38, 197; expressive 118; judgments of 89, 118; musical 183; questions of 121

Merleau-Ponty, Maurice 52, 91, 106, 145, 149, 150, 192, 223

metaphor 10, 11, 25, 26, 48, 49, 97, 145–48, 150–55, 158–62; achievement of 161;

articulation of 161; character of 153; characteristics of 146; criterion of a 148; definition of 146; deployment of 155; effect of the 151; feature of 148; form of 161;

function of 148, 153, 161; literary 145, 160, 236;

martial 158; mode of 154; phenomenon of 152;

power of 151, 159; role of 145; sacrament 156;

significance of 153, 155; structure of 145; style of 160; theory of 159; treatment of 146, 160;

usage of 146

metaphysical 47, 50–53, 56, 103, 163–67, 169, 170, 174, 189, 192–94, 196, 198, 200, 201, 203, 234; account of the 181; basis of 165; embodiment of 204; possibility of 163; sense of the 82

metaphysics 11, 173, 185; form and 165; idea of 200

mimesis 3, 51; image- 101, 102; importance of 3; processes of 51; scope of 4; significance of 3; vividness 51

modernism 240, 241; Romanticism and 198; western 4, 54

mosaic 217, 218

Moxey, Keith 44, 45, 50

multiculturalism 28, 29, 37

music 1, 11, 90, 112, 164–66, 168, 170, 173–205, 236, 244, 245; analysis of 165;

appreciation of 180, 181; arts and 90;

canonic 166; case of 183;

character of the 179, 185; characterization of 187;

dances and 48; depth and 166; dimension of 200;

effects of 244; film and 208–210; forms of 196, 201;

function of 170; functional 194, 196;

image-character of the 187; instrumental 176, 191;

literature and 89; otherness of the 189; piece of 188;

postmodern 202; scope of 200; significance and 197;

situation of 204; structure of 244; substance of 178;

tonal 202; ubiquity of 182; vocal 176, 194

narrative 18, 46, 58, 62, 63, 83, 90, 91, 134, 137, 138, 156, 165, 171, 173, 178, 180, 182–85, 188, 190, 191, 203, 209, 210, 212, 216, 217, 220, 221, 224, 225, 236, 241; appraisal and 184; case of 91; character of 177; cognitive and 172; development of a 215; embodiments of 182; emotional and 200; gestural and 188; gestures and 185; historical 240; meaning and 190; point of 209; psychological 104; realizations of the 83; sensory 101; subjective 160, 161; symbolic 100, 217; tonal 179; transformation of the 183; vocal 202; volitional 169
nature 30, 46, 63, 77, 81, 89, 93, 96, 116, 118, 119, 135, 153, 157, 174, 179, 183, 184, 189, 203, 205, 219, 225, 228, 229, 233, 235, 239, 241; beauty of 236; style and the 40
necessity 133, 173, 190, 191, 220; temporal 166, 168, 169, 185, 190
negation 70, 75, 78, 132, 139, 242; logic of 69
nexus 143 causal 108, 109; experiential 138
normative 1–3, 8, 9, 15, 16, 19–22, 27, 29, 34, 35, 37, 38, 40–46, 55, 60, 63, 64, 67, 68, 84, 87, 89, 110, 115, 117, 118, 235–37, 242, 245; aesthetic 16; multicultural 15; transcultural 17
normativity 16, 42, 43; aesthetic 16; axes of 16, 40, 164; deep 19, 20; understanding of 16

object 2, 9, 17, 25–27, 32, 47, 48, 51, 52, 57, 68, 70, 74, 83, 84, 86, 87, 92, 93, 100, 104, 107, 113, 116, 121, 127, 128, 138, 147, 156, 158, 159, 162, 163, 167, 171, 179, 183, 189, 211, 223, 238; aesthetic 27, 110, 153; control of the 51; correlation of 32, 34; existence of the 68; intentional 179; kind of 45; material 24; perceptual 150; physical 114; predicate of the 150;

spatial 208, 232, 233; stylization of the 229; subject and 165, 189, 194, 195, 203; theory and 25; unity of the 73, 74
objectivity 42, 44, 59
occupancy 6, 81; space- 93, 189
oeuvre 39, 120, 160, 166
ontogenesis 78, 79; repetition of the 75
ontological 22–24, 26, 52, 70, 98, 101, 103, 107, 109, 113, 142, 160, 166, 168, 176, 185, 205, 238, 242
ontology 10, 24, 35, 98, 104, 163, 168, 169
optical 78, 92, 93, 95, 97, 139, 219; pictorial and 77
originality 9, 38, 39, 84, 85, 112, 113, 115, 116, 118–121, 136, 237, 238, 243; artistic 85, 112, 114, 180; characteristic of 136; dimension of 116, 122; imagery and 238; importance of 10, 136, 201; individuality and 4; issues of 121; level of 39; modes of 86; notion of 110; secondary 86; stylistic 8, 85
otherness 189; listener and the 192; self and 113; world of 116

painterly 86; articulation of the 87; linear and 86
painting 23, 25, 26, 95, 97, 119, 180, 186, 192, 208, 218, 221, 227, 230, 239; abstract 95; aspects of a 23; European 87; limits of 205; phenomenon of the 223; profundity of 26
paradigm 28, 53, 79, 116
paradox 57, 58, 64; visual 221
patriarchy 45, 57
pattern 158, 209, 232; content and 230; narrative 210
perception 32, 52, 55, 80, 81, 94, 101, 127, 128, 132, 134, 136–42, 145, 149, 150, 166, 172, 179, 212, 225, 228, 233, 236; act of 150; articulation and 145, 150, 151, 162; characterization of 150;

perception   (*cont.*)
depths of 143; empirical 74;
spatial 179
perspective 39, 47, 50, 76, 107, 161, 217,
219, 220; convention of 220;
development of 217; existential 166;
experiential 179; mathematical 58;
periphery of 221; philosophical 184;
question of 219; structure of 221;
treatment of 234; unity of 221
phenomenal 18, 20, 23, 29, 30, 37, 40, 73,
74, 80 82, 92, 93, 101, 108, 116, 117,
119, 133, 141, 142, 214
phenomenology 205;
analysis of the 68
phenomenon 11, 20, 92, 98, 131, 142, 152,
172, 173, 181, 191, 223; auditory 190,
203; western 60
philosophical 2, 5, 17, 20, 41, 53, 72, 142,
152, 153, 155, 160, 162, 170, 184, 212,
215, 216, 228, 240
philosophy 63, 83, 111, 165, 171;
analytic 164
photography 205, 228, 229;
fascination of 231; function of 228;
images of 230; invention of 240
pictorial 57–59, 77, 78, 86, 90, 92, 93, 96
127, 128, 135–40, 143, 144, 206,
217–22, 224, 228–30, 232, 233, 236,
243
picture 39, 77, 82, 103, 136, 137, 140,
153–55, 216–218, 224, 228–31, 243;
character of 154; conventions of 154;
edge of the 218; limit of the 77;
photograph and the 230;
sense of the 77; structures of 155;
subject of the 103
plurality 75, 78, 132
poem 156, 159, 160, 162, 186, 211, 227;
climax of the 157;
verses of a 210
poetry 91, 205, 239;
development of 161; example of 90;
origins of 160
Pollock, Jackson 119, 139
postmodern 11, 44, 49, 119, 166, 200–202
postmodernism 44 n.12; 49 n.12;
potency 191;
linguistic 146; ritual 35, 52
power 35, 36, 46, 52, 70, 72, 79, 87, 97,
110, 129, 134, 142, 151, 158, 159, 195,
206, 229, 230, 238; aesthetic 35, 52;

affective 143; formative 52, 236;
gender 62; generative 130 ;
metaphysical 200; money and 70;
transformative 24; western 60; will- 28
predicate 147, 150;
analogical 151;
predication 146, 148–50, 152, 153; acts of
151; foundations of 236;
perceptual 149, 150
production 18, 44, 46, 48, 55, 58, 99,
110–113, 169, 216; bulk of 110;
circumstances of 15; contexts of 50;
cultural 48; forms of 115;
formulae of 56; metaphor 49;
practices of 136; process and 115;
social 46, 47; technique of 112, 116;
tradition of 40
projection 147, 204, 220, 224; association
and 151;
perspectival 223; visual 233
proposition 149;
immediate 76; language and 145;
level of 83, 107, 145; making and 43;
object of 113; possibilities of 132;
predication and 146; process of 135;
self-consciousness and 162; simultaneous
135;
terms of 6; visual 140
psychology 85, 135;
empirical 31

quality 16, 30, 118, 120, 122, 151, 210,
212, 241; aesthetic 122;
artistic 196, 197; judgments of 120

racism 43, 53, 54, 60–62, 64
ready-made 27, 28, 54, 182, 183
reality 35, 54, 76, 78, 82, 132, 139, 190,
192, 231, 244; ambiguity of 139;
aspects of 241; characterization of 75;
construction of 24; dimensions of 95;
historical 186; nature of 63;
sense of 75, 200; totality and 75
reason 74, 81, 94, 99, 109, 117, 118, 121,
151, 152, 187, 191, 194, 220, 228;
example of 81;
instrumental 47, 49, 62, 242
reception 58, 221;
aesthetic 100; critical 87; making and
108;

performance and 189; production and
110, 216
recipient 174, 215;
creator and 100
recognition 95, 102, 116, 122, 137, 139,
172, 237; act of 130, 149;
dependence of the 152; intellectual
113;
process of 99
reference 91–93, 95, 97, 99, 120–122, 142,
153, 161, 171, 172, 175, 189, 193, 197,
202, 216; content and 190; mimetic
102;
mode of 216; pictorial 154;
types of 243
refinement 57, 60, 87, 101, 112, 136, 164,
200, 204; artistic 238;
innovation and 199; stylistic 200
relativism 43, 45, 46, 48–51, 53, 55–57,
63, 64, 23 ; academic 49;
anti-foundationalist 61; cultural 42,
44;
normativity and 42; version of 43;
worth and 63
Renaissance 39, 86, 243
representation 40, 43, 47–53, 55, 56, 59,
60, 74, 103, 127, 135–38, 142, 143,
154, 205, 207, 216; artifice and 49;
artistic 99, 137, 141–43;
form and 136; forms of 42, 44;
idioms of 42, 56; imaginative 55;
medium of 135; mode of 60, 97, 135;
notion of 50; perspectival 223;
pictorial 57, 92, 93, 135, 139, 140, 154,
206, 219, 222, 224, 228, 230, 233, 236,
243; ritual 5, 7, 18, 38;
sculptural 59, 153; self- 98;
significance 60; status of 50; symbolic
100
resemblance 96, 140;
notions of 244; visual 92
revelation 54, 100, 102
rhythm 175, 176, 178, 191, 195;
formalization of 177;
instrumentation and 195
Ricoeur, Paul 146–49
ritual 18, 38, 52, 55, 79, 115, 161, 194;
context of 44;
functional and 35; level of 40, 51;
range of 195; religious 56
Romanticism 67, 198
Rubens, Peter Paul 87, 112, 113

Sartre, Jean-Paul 82, 83
Nausea 82
schematization 137;
element of 134
Schoenberg, Arnold 199, 200
Schopenhauer, Arthur 52, 165, 177
scope 1, 6, 10, 32, 33, 38–40, 46, 56, 61,
68, 76, 82, 83, 87, 89, 91, 96, 114, 115,
123, 155, 167, 174, 182, 191, 194, 200,
202, 204, 207, 234, 244; explanatory 4;
extensional 32; functional 6; general 24;
logical 43, 55–60, 63, 85, 87;
musical 198; nature and 89; perceptual
135;
structure and 164, 245; syntactic 85, 86;
understanding of the 83
sculptural 59;
pictorial and 90, 96, 153
sculpture 47, 186, 192, 208
self-consciousness 101, 102, 105, 107, 110,
116, 162, 167, 207; aspect of 34;
development of 123; evolution of 237;
exemplification of 107; fabric of 79;
individual 76; life of 101; ontogenesis of
78, 79;
origins of 78; perception and 212
semantic 48, 55, 60, 85–87, 212, 221, 243;
syntactic and 87
sense 2, 4, 6, 7, 8, 24, 27, 30, 32, 36, 37,
39, 41, 48, 51, 54, 55, 59, 71, 75, 77,
79–82, 87, 96, 98, 100, 103–105, 107,
109, 110, 113, 114, 116–119, 122, 123,
129, 133, 135, 137, 139–42, 145,
148–50, 154, 155, 159, 160, 163, 164,
166–68, 170, 172, 173, 174, 178–82,
185, 189, 191, 193, 194, 197, 200, 201,
203, 204, 211–213, 215, 216, 222–26,
229–31, 233, 237, 238; artistic 23, 26,
39;
classificatory 21; definiteness of 24, 71,
73, 75;
descriptive 136; existential 103; formal
181;
iconographical 217; Imperialistic 54;
interests and 171; lack of 2; metaphorical
114;
mimetic 98; modalities of 142; notional
105;
objective 146; ontological 6; perceptual
138, 143, 149, 150;
practical 132; qualitative 107; radical 23,
39; subjective 148;

sense   (*cont.*)
traditional 119; volitional 152
serialism 193, 244;
atonalism and 193; possibilities of 199
shape 95, 133, 139, 231
Shostakovich, Dmitri 194, 199
sign 167;
indexical 167, 168, 174, 191
significance 2, 9, 17, 29, 33, 36–38, 40, 41,
43, 47, 53, 55, 56, 61, 63, 69, 75, 76,
80, 85–87, 97, 100, 105–107, 116,
121, 127, 137, 142, 144, 147, 148, 153,
160, 163, 165, 167, 171, 174, 178,
181–83, 185, 197–99, 202, 203, 206,
208, 215, 217, 218, 224, 228, 230, 232,
233, 245; aesthetic 3, 4, 8, 16, 36, 40,
60, 118, 120, 164, 211, 237; canonic
39, 60, 146, 160, 161, 234, 237;
cognitive 40, 67, 97; conceptual 106,
214;
connotative 37; dimension of 109, 190;
ethical 242;
experiential 68, 233; expressive 119, 120,
169, 170, 181, 190; formal 180;
historical 202;
interpretative 24; intrinsic 2, 33, 34, 38,
84, 236, 237; level of 188; logical 69;
magical 79;
metaphysical 53, 181; multicultural 15;
narrative 210; normative 3, 8, 15, 22, 27,
35, 68, 110, 236, 237, 245;
philosophical 152, 153, 155, 216;
reflective 110; religious 51; scope and 68;
theoretical 27; transcendental 128, 137;
transcultural 17, 18, 51, 63;
transhistorical 198;
transindividual 194;
universal 18, 57; value and 45
signification 49, 57, 167;
basis of 152; field of 62; forms of 43;
layers of 48; modes of 49, 191;
origins of 167; variety of 48
space 26, 31, 61, 77, 78, 93, 95, 97, 141,
142, 150–52, 156, 160, 161, 166, 179,
189, 193, 217–222, 224–26, 231, 244;
contextual 94–97;
existential 101; occupancy of 6, 81;
optical 139; part of 6; perspectival
218–221;
pictorial 39, 58, 136, 218;
three-dimensional 76, 216; time and
206, 223;

unity of 234; virtual 73, 95, 141,
218–220, 226, 231; visual 37, 94
specificity 109;
imaginative 51
standard 18, 84, 148, 176;
aesthetic 210; narrative 210
status 2, 9–11, 43, 47–50, 54, 72, 77, 81,
83, 98, 99, 102, 117, 163, 171, 187,
193, 214, 215, 233, 235, 242; artistic
244;
cultural 64, 235, 237, 240; image- 136,
137;
metaphorical 154
stereotype 52 n.14;
avoidance of 119
structure 19, 31, 32, 57, 68, 70, 73, 76–79,
87, 89, 91, 97, 99, 102, 107–109, 114,
118, 121, 133, 134, 137, 139, 145, 152,
153, 155, 162, 164, 179, 183, 191,
206–208, 210, 212, 214, 217, 219, 221,
226, 228, 233, 243–45; aesthetic 120,
163;
awareness and the 162; canonic 17;
cognitive 114, 144, 145, 165, 179;
compositional 77, 201; formal 140, 196;
geometrical 95; limits of the 243;
metaphorical 155; metaphysical 167, 197;
narrative 165, 171, 178, 184, 188, 190,
209;
ontological 70, 98, 101, 160, 166, 205;
optical 97;
origins and 101; perspectival 207, 218,
226, 231, 232;
phenomenal 18, 23, 37, 60, 92, 101;
possibilities of 214; predicative 148;
scope and 244; sensory 30; spatial 209;
temporal 190;
understanding of the 150; visual 232
style 5–7, 9–11, 77, 80–82, 86, 87, 91, 98,
99, 106, 112, 113, 119, 120, 137, 153,
154, 160, 161, 175, 176, 196–99, 202,
205, 207, 210, 211, 223, 225–27, 235,
236, 238, 242; achievement of a 85;
aspect of 7, 8 ; beauty of 114; concept of
5;
expression of 6; format and 121;
individual 118, 119;
individuality of 119, 237, 239;
interpretative 10; literary 11;
originality of 9, 85, 114, 115, 121, 237,
243; pictorial 86; poetic 161;
role of 89; sense of 6; significance of 208

subject 3, 6, 7, 9, 34, 35, 59, 72, 76, 78, 82,
    83, 89, 91–94, 96, 103, 104, 106, 107,
    113, 114, 119, 133, 135–37, 142, 147,
    148, 150–54, 159, 161, 162, 165, 169,
    172, 173, 180, 183, 186, 189, 194, 195,
    201, 203, 205–207, 209, 211, 212, 218,
    219, 223, 225, 232, 235, 236;
  demands of the 82; embodied 113;
  experience and 165, 195; experiential
    105;
  features of 6; object and 32; observer and
    183;
  subject and 165, 189, 195, 197, 203;
  totality of the 104; unity of the 208
subsumption 70;
  acts of 71
superstition 35, 51
Surrealist 25, 154
syntactic 39, 87;
  reference and 243; semantic and 85–87,
    243
system 234;
  scale- 178: tonal 193, 198, 199, 244

taste 67, 68, 167, 168, 181, 197, 238
technology 115, 215
text 156, 215, 216;
  resources of the 155
texture 95, 139, 217, 224, 231
theory 2, 10, 11, 17, 22–26, 28, 33, 34, 44,
    49, 50, 53, 54, 60, 67, 68, 72, 79, 81,
    85, 102, 110, 111, 117, 120, 128, 148,
    159, 185, 193, 194, 201, 202, 240–42;
    aesthetic 79;
  aesthetics and 10, 43; art and 241;
  artistic 23; artwork and 24; cultural 242;
  Designation 22, 27, 28, 54, 92;
    embodiment of 27;
  exemplar of 27, 120; formulation of 111;
  general 46; meta- 50;
  musical 199; normative 64; practice and
    22;
  primacy of 240; production and 113;
  relativist 10; systematic 97;
  vehicles of 27; western 53
time 83, 104, 117, 130, 131, 133, 134, 141,
    142, 148, 151, 153, 155, 157, 166, 169,
    186, 190, 194, 197, 199, 203, 209–211,
    213–217, 219–226, 228, 231–33, 238;
    cognition of 204, 236;
  conditions of 233; dependence of 233;

experience of 133, 206; image of 210;
  moments of 129, 205, 216, 232;
  objective 210, 232; orders of 232;
  pace and 78, 179, 217, 219; passage of
    142;
  period of 228; projections of 205, 233;
  quasi-mythic 209; rearrangements of
    210;
    rendering of 228; virtual sub 232;
    volitional 233
totality 104, 105, 107, 113, 132, 152;
  awareness of 105;
  plurality and 75, 78;
  sense of the 105
tradition 28, 29, 37, 38, 53, 69, 115, 207,
    212, 237; analysis and the 116;
  analytic 52; continuity of 207;
  critical 38; Designation 37;
  Duchampian 53; future of the 207;
  horizon of 207; interpretative 69;
  musical 199, 200
transcendence 195, 233
transcendental 128, 133–35, 137, 138,
    141–43, 236
transcultural 17, 43, 181, 182, 198, 203;
  transhistorical and 28, 40, 51, 56, 60,
    63, 86
transformation 99, 183;
  avenues of 185; creative 53;
  historical 240; ideality and 99; qualitative
    168
truth 50, 53, 54, 62, 63, 98, 107, 142, 159,
    203, 212; evaluative 117;
  phenomenological 31
twofoldness 127, 128, 136–38, 140;
  character of 153; elements of 135, 136,
    154, 155;
  imagination and 143; notion of 128, 135,
    139, 143; perception of 138;
  relation of 139; significance of 142;
  version of 141

ubiquity 201;
  transcultural 182
understanding 45, 48, 49, 54, 61, 70, 71,
    83, 102, 109, 114, 116, 119, 128, 133,
    150, 163, 166, 182, 188, 195, 200, 238,
    239; abstract 83; calibration of 75;
  concepts of the 74; cooperation of 133;
  imagination and 67, 68, 73, 75, 236;
  interaction of 78; intuition and 70;

understanding   (*cont.*)
  objective 133; perception and 225;
  philosophical 162; play of 83; powers of
    52;
  sensibility and 238; unconscious 96
unity 7, 20, 30, 31, 70, 73, 75, 76, 78, 106,
    107, 118, 119, 132, 133, 141, 142, 166,
    183, 193, 208, 210, 212, 220, 221, 226,
    232, 234; aesthetic 9, 36, 74, 77, 121,
    235;
  criteria of 31; expressive 120; form of
    120;
  formal 118, 196; objective 74, 208, 210,
    211, 213, 214, 232;
  organic 107; possibilities of 74, 214;
    qualities and 17;
  relations of 73, 139; self-consciousness
    and the 34;
  subjective 170; temporal 78, 141, 211

validity 21, 58, 63;
  transcultural 60; universal 43
value 2, 8, 9, 15, 16, 19, 22, 36, 115, 163,
    196, 204, 237, 242; aesthetic 60, 121;
  art and 1; artistic 1, 11, 84, 123, 146, 1
    60, 236, 238, 240, 243; canonic 2, 10,
    11, 89, 235;
  categories of 166; criteria of 121, 196;
  degree of 21; distinctions of 117, 195;
  existential 205; experiential 166;
    explanatory 119;
  expressive 10; forms of 22; intrinsic 82;
  issues of 22, 243; judgments of 203;
  levels of 204; meaning and 1, 11, 163,
    164, 203, 235; musical 166, 192, 197,
    200, 204;
  normative 15; objective 56; questions of
    21; scope and 89, 123;
  transhistorical 40; truth- 50;
  use- 36; vision and 197
virtuality 92;
  direction of 177; level of 177;

presumption of 92, 93, 96, 180–82, 185,
    193, 242
volition 47;
  role of 168
volume 95, 139, 231;
  auditory 174; intensity of 167

Wagner, Richard 198, 199
Warhol, Andy 54, 240, 241
Wollheim, Richard 127, 128, 135–40, 143
work 3, 6, 8, 9, 11, 16, 18, 19, 21, 22, 23,
    26–28, 34, 37–40, 45, 47, 51–54, 56,
    58–60, 62, 63, 77, 80–84, 86, 91–93,
    95–97, 100, 105–110, 112–122,
    136–40, 155, 160, 161, 163, 166, 178,
    180, 183, 186, 188–91, 193, 195–99,
    201, 202, 205, 207, 209–218, 220, 221,
    223–28, 231, 235, 237, 240, 244;
  abstract 92, 93, 96, 97;
  appearance of the 95; awareness of the
    77;
  body of 87; burden of the 212;
    circumstances of a 216;
  concreteness of the 100; distinctiveness
    of the 197;
  element of the 190; end of a 212, 224;
  enjoyment of the 114; field of the 224;
  function of the 9; identity of the 108;
  level of the 96; literary 223; making of
    the 137;
  medium and 82; musical 177, 182–84,
    189, 203, 210;
  particularity of the 121; perception of
    the 136;
  perspectival 219, 226; philosophical 72;
  presumption and the 93; property of the
    120;
  resources of the 154; richness of the
    188;
  sense of the 215; style of the 91;
    temporal 214;
  twofoldness of the 136;
  unity of the 210, 211